Reviving Catalan at School

MIX
Paper from
responsible sources
FSC® C010693
FSC
www.fsc.org

Full details of all our publications can be found on http://www.multilingual-matters.com, or by writing to Multilingual Matters, St Nicholas House, 31–34 High Street, Bristol BS1 2AW, UK.

Reviving Catalan at School

Challenges and Instructional Approaches

Edited by
Joaquim Arnau

MULTILINGUAL MATTERS
Bristol • Buffalo • Toronto

Institut
d'Estudis
Catalans

Library of Congress Cataloging in Publication Data
Reviving Catalan at School: Challenges and Instructional Approaches/Edited by
Joaquim Arnau.
Includes bibliographical references.
1. Catalan language--Study and teaching. 2. Catalan language--Social aspects.
3. Language policy. 4. Language planning. 5. Sociolinguistics. I. Arnau i Querol,
Joaquim, editor of compilation.
PC3811.R48 2013
306.44'9467–dc23 2013022825

British Library Cataloguing in Publication Data
A catalogue entry for this book is available from the British Library.

ISBN-13: 978-1-78309-025-9 (hbk)
ISBN-13: 978-1-78309-024-2 (pbk)

Multilingual Matters
UK: St Nicholas House, 31–34 High Street, Bristol BS1 2AW, UK.
USA: UTP, 2250 Military Road, Tonawanda, NY 14150, USA.
Canada: UTP, 5201 Dufferin Street, North York, Ontario M3H 5T8, Canada.

The policy of Multilingual Matters/Channel View Publications is to use papers that are
natural, renewable and recyclable products, made from wood grown in sustainable for-
ests. In the manufacturing process of our books, and to further support our policy, preference is given to printers that have FSC and PEFC Chain of Custody certification. The FSC
and/or PEFC logos will appear on those books where full certification has been granted
to the printer concerned.

Typeset by Techset Composition India (P) Ltd., Bangalore and Chennai, India.
Printed and bound in Great Britain by the Lavenham Press Ltd.

Contents

Contributors   vii

Introduction   xiii

1   Language-in-education Policies in the Catalan Language Area   1
Joaquim Arnau and F. Xavier Vila

2   The Acquisition of Catalan by Immigrant Children. The Effect
of Length of Stay and Family Language   29
Àngel Huguet, Jose-Luis Navarro, Silvia-Maria Chireac and Clara Sansó

3   Language Attitudes of Latin-American Newcomers in Three
Secondary School Reception Classes in Catalonia   49
Mireia Trenchs-Parera and Adriana Patiño-Santos

4   Training a Primary Education Teacher to Teach Expository Text
Comprehension Strategies   72
*Núria Castells, Isabel Solé, Cristina Luna, Eva Lordán, Esther Nadal,
Mariana Miras and Sandra Espino*

5   Teacher Training in Literacy Instruction and Academic
Achievement in a Multilingual Classroom   96
Joaquim Arnau, Haridian M de Aysa and Sonia Jarque

6   Production of Texts with Multimodal Resources by Two Groups of
Primary Education Students   120
Aneska Ortega, Júlia Coromina and Ana Teberosky

7   Interlinguistic Reflection on Teaching and Learning Languages   136
Oriol Guasch Boyé

8   Affording Students Opportunities for the Integrated Learning of
       Content and Language: A Contrastive Study on Classroom
       Interactional Strategies Deployed by Two CLIL Teachers   158
     Cristina Escobar Urmeneta and Natalia Evnitskaya

9   Integrated Languages Project   183
     Rosa Maria Ramírez and Teresa Serra

Contributors

Joaquim Arnau is an Emeritus Professor in the Department of Developmental and Educational Psychology at the University of Barcelona. His research interests include second language teaching and learning, immersion and migrant. education. He has published in the *Journal of Multilingual and Multicultural Development,* the *International Journal of Bilingual Education and Bilingualism* and in the Spanish journal *Infancia & Aprendizaje.* He has been working in the field for 40 years.

Núria Castells is an Associate Professor in the department of Developmental and Educational Psychology at the University of Barcelona. Her research interests include teaching and learning to read and to write – from childhood through university. She has published in the *Written Communication Journal, Electronic Journal of Reasearch in Educational Psychology; Studies in Writing,* and the Spanish journal *Infancia & Aprendizaje.* She has been working in the field of learning to read and to write for 15 years.

Silvia-Maria Chireac is a Lecturer in the Department of Romance Languages at Alexandru Ioan Cuza University (Iaşi, Romania). Her research interests include topics such as second language acquisition, speech and written discourse in L2 and L3, as well as bilingual education and multicultural communication. She has published academic papers in refereed journals as *Language and Intercultural Communication* or *Journal of Psychodidactics.* She has been working in the field for 12 years.

Júlia Coromina is an Associate Professor at the University of Barcelona. Her research interests include visual literacy and the design and creation of digital education materials. She has been working in the field for over two years.

Haridian M de Aysa is Psychologist and Elementary School Teacher in Barcelona. Her research interests include the teaching and learning of language and informal learning in social networks. She has been working in the field for over two years.

Cristina Escobar is a Professor in the Department of Language Education at the Autonomous University of Barcelona. She has published in the *International Journal of Bilingual Education and Bilingualism* and *Sociolinguistica* and researches in the areas of interaction and foreign language learning; foreign teacher education; CLIL and portfolio assessment. She has been working in the field for over 20 years.

Sandra Espino is a Research Fellow and Professor at the University of Barcelona. Her research interests are related to understanding how the reading and writing processes are used as learning instruments in educational contexts. More specifically, she is interested in studying the use of note-taking and how the variables involved in its conditions of use are related to the students' learning approach. She has published in the *Written Communication Journal* and *Revista Mexicana de Investigación Educativa*. She has been working in the field for 10 years.

Natalia Evnitskaya is a Postdoctoral Researcher in the Department of English Studies at the Autonomous University of Madrid. Her research interests include classroom interaction and foreign language learning; foreign teacher Education and CLIL. She has been working in the field for over three years.

Oriol Guasch is an Associate Professor in the Faculty of Education at the Autonomous University of Barcelona. He is interested in the areas of second language writing, grammar teaching and multilingual education. He has pubished in the Spanish journals *Textos de Didáctica de la Lengua y Literatura, Cultura y Educación and Lectura y Vida*. He has been working in the field for over 25 years.

Àngel Huguet is a Professor in the Department of Pedagogy and Psychology at the University of Lleida. His research interest include bilingual education, second language acquisition, psycholinguistics and sociolinguistics. He has published the book *Multilingualism in European Bilingual Contexts: Language Use and Attitudes* (with David Lasagabaster, Multilingual Matters, 2007), and more recently in different refereed journals as *Language and Intercultural Communication, International Journal of Intercultural Relations, International Journal of Multilingualism* and *VIAL-International Journal of Applied Linguistics*. He has been working in the field for more than 20 years.

Sonia Jarque is an Associate Professor in the Departament of Developmental and Educational Psychology at the University of Barcelona. Among her research interests are teacher training, special Education, learning disabilities and Attention Deficit Hyperactivity Disorder (ADHD). She has published in *The 21st Annual World Congress on Learning Disabilities* (2012) and in the

Spanish review *Anuario de Psicologia*. She has been working in the field for more than three years.

Eva Lordán is a Research Fellow in the Department of Developmental and Educational Psychology at the University of Barcelona. Her research is focused on reading, writing and epistemological beliefs and their impact on reading comprehension and writing composition and reading and writing processes and results in different educational levels. She has published in the *Proceedings of the 17th European Conference on Reading: Literacy & Diversity*. She has been working in the field for five years.

Cristina Luna is an Educational Psychologist in the Department of Developmental and Educational Psychology at the University of Barcelona. Her research interests include epistemic reading and writing and reading comprehension and writing strategies. She has published in the *Proceedings of the 17th European Conference on Reading: Literacy & Diversity*. She has been working in the field for five years.

Mariana Miras is an Emeritus Professor of the Department of Developmental and Educational Psychology at the University of Barcelona. Her research interests include reading comprehension and writing strategies and epistemic reading and writing. She has published in the *Written Communication Journal, Electronic Journal of Reasearch in Educational Psychology; Studies in Writing: Writing as a Learning Activity* and the Spanish journal *Infancia & Aprendizaje*. She has been working in the field for 40 years.

Esther Nadal is a Research Fellow in the Department of Developmental and Educational Psychology at the University of Barcelona. Her research interests include reading comprehension and writing strategies and epistemic reading and writing. She has published in the *Proceedings of the 17*th *European Conference on Reading: Literacy & Diversit* and *Articles de Didàctica de la Llengua i la Literatura*. She has been working in the field for five years.

José Luis Navarro is an Associate Professor in the Department of Pedagogy and Psychology at the University of Lleida. His research interest is focused on the development of linguistic competence, as well as the conditions of schooling for students of immigrant origin. He has recently published in *VIAL-International Journal of Applied Linguistics* and *Annals of Psychology*. He has been working in the field for 12 years.

Aneska Ortega has a PhD from the University of Barcelona and is interested in research in the areas of visual literacy, the display of information in digital format and the design and creation of educational materials. She has been working in the field for over three years.

Adriana Patiño-Santos is a Lecturer in the Department of Department of Modern Languages at the University of Southampton. Her research interests include ethnographic sociolinguistics, interactional sociolinguistics, intercultural education and intercultural communication. She has published in the *International Journal of Bilingual Education and Bilingualism, Spanish in Context* and the *Journal of Language, Identity and Education.* She has been working in the field for 13 years.

Maria Rosa Ramírez spent 15 years as the head teacher of Vila Olímpica School of Barcelona (1996–2011) and is now a teacher advisor. Her research interests include language learning and teaching languages across curricular areas. She has been working in the field for 20 years.

Clara Sansó is a Lecturer in the Department of Pedagogy and Psychology at the University of Lleida. Her research interests include bilingual and multilingual education, particularly analyzing the development of the immigrant students' linguistic knowledge. She has recently published in *VIAL-International Journal of Applied Linguistics* and *Annals of Psychology.* She has been working in the field for six years.

Teresa Serra is the headteacher of Vila Olímpica School of Barcelona. She started the Integrated Language Project in 1996 as a Deputy of studies and she has been working in the development of this project for 16 years. Her research interest includes language as tool of math learning. She published a book *Parlant de matemàtiques per apredre'n* (2011). She got an especial award 'Rosa Sensat' of Pedagogy in 2010, related to Math and language learning in Primary School. She has been working in the field for 20 years.

Isabel Solé is a Professor in the Department of Developmental and Educational Psychology at the University of Barcelona. She has published in the *Written Communication Journal, Electronic Journal of Reasearch in Educational Psychology; Studies in Writing: Writing as a Learning Activity* and the Spanish journal *Infancia & Aprendizaje.* She has been working in the field of reading comprehension for 30 years and includes reading acquisition, reading comprehension and writing strategies among her research interests.

Ana Teberosky is a Professor in the Department of Developmental and Educational Psychology at the University of Barcelona. Her research interests include academic performance and oral and written language. She is the co-author with Emilia Ferreiro of the book *Literacy before Schooling* (1982). She has published in the journals *Theory and Practice, Infancia y Aprendizaje, Lectura y Vida* and *Comunicacion y Lenguaje.* She has been working in the field for more than 40 years.

Mireia Trenchs-Parera is a Professor in the Department of Humanities at University Pompeu Fabra in Barcelona. Her research interests include language attitudes, ideology and practices in multilingual and multicultural contexts as well as processes of foreign language learning and teaching. She has published in *Journal of Multilingual and Multicultural Development, Journal of Sociolinguistics, Canadian Modern Language Review* and *International Journal of Bilingual Education and Bilingualism* among other publications. She has been working in the field for 20 years.

Francesc Xavier Vila is an Associate Professor at the University of Barcelona. He was the first director of the CRUSCAT Research Network on sociolinguistics of the Institut d'Estudis Catalans, the Catalan National Academy of Sciences, and is the current Director of the University Centre for Sociolinguistics and Communication at the Universitat de Barcelona (CUSC-UB). He has published a wide range of books and specialist articles in the areas of sociolinguistics, demolinguistics and language policy, including *Survival and Development of Language Communities* (2013). He has been working in the field for 20 years.

Introduction

The territories where Catalan is spoken have developed quite different language-in-education policies and models. In Spain, where the bulk of Catalan speakers live, this language has become official in almost all historical territories (Catalonia, Valencia and the Balearic Islands), while Spanish remains the State's sole official language. All schoolchildren, including non-Catalan L1s, living in these territories are expected to learn both official languages. Today, after a decade of unexpected, massive foreign immigration, these very systems have to adapt to a new multilingual, multicultural environment.

The purpose of this book is to present a broad overview of studies carried out in Catalonia and centred on a type of school that has been, and is, an instrument for recovering Catalan, a school in which Catalan is the language in which the majority of curricular subjects are taught. A school that has the objective of educating citizens to be competent in three languages (Catalan and Spanish, official languages, and a foreign language).

The first chapter by Arnau and Vila (Language-in-education Policies in the Catalan Language Area) describes the policies and models in all of the regions, both within Spain (Catalonia, Valencia, the Balearic Islands, La Franja) and abroad (Andorra, Northern Catalonia in France and the Sardinian city of Alghero in Italy). In all of them, although using different policies and having different effects, significant efforts have been made to include Catalan in education since the last decades of the 20th century. The results of these policies (linguistic competences and uses) and the challenges they face are analysed, particularly in Catalonia, where the majority of the research has been carried out.

Two studies analyse the new and very complex situation in which immigrants should learn Catalan in a context in which this language is often barely spoken in some places, because those living there do not speak it as their first language. Huguet *et al.* (The Acquisition of Catalan by Immigrant Children. The Effect of Length of Stay and Family Language) present a classic study that has also been carried out in other contexts with the presence of immigrants. They determine the effect that length of stay, family language and closeness of their language to Catalan has on competences in Catalan, among a sample of students in their final year of compulsory secondary education. Trenchs-Parera and Patiño-Santos (Language Attitudes of Latin-American Newcomers in Three Secondary School Reception Classes in Catalonia) analyse the challenges that migrant education situations present to teachers, as well as the factors that determine positive attitudes towards Catalan among students in these classrooms.

Three studies discuss teacher training in literacy instruction and its effects on the academic performance of students. The researches have been carried out 'with' teachers and their students rather than 'on' the teachers and their students. Castells *et al.* (Training a Primary Education Teacher to Teach Expository Text Comprehension Strategies) present a training project for a primary education teacher, with the objective of helping her teach reading comprehension strategies. They propose a training model based on a guided participation process that assumes that teachers have a broad theoretical, practical and tacit knowledge that constitutes the basis for their future learning. The results of the teacher's intervention show improvements among the students in reading comprehension. Arnau *et al.* (Teacher Training in Literacy Instruction and Academic Achievement in a Multilingual Classroom) analyse the effects of a teacher-training-in-literacy-instruction programme (secondary education, social science). The comparison of academic results before and after training confirms that teaching vocabulary, and reading and writing strategies, related with academic language are valuable practices. Ortega *et al.* (Production of Texts with Multimodal Resources in Two Groups of Primary Students) compare the quality of texts with multimedia resources produced by two groups of students (natives and immigrants) in year four of primary education, also produced in a teacher-training process. The results show larger differences in linguistic aspects than in multimodal aspects between the groups (immigrants and natives) and suggest the current importance of including these resources in education.

In Catalonia and in other Catalan-speaking regions of Spain, another third language, English, is gaining ground as a language of instruction. Schools that are structured in this way are trilingual, with Catalan as the first and base language for teaching and with Spanish and English also as vehicular languages for teaching academic contents. Three chapters refer to aspects within this type of scenario. In a still incipient research study, Guasch Boyé (Interlinguistic Reflection on Teaching and Learning Languages) presents an experience, based on the joint reflection made by a Catalan language teacher and an English language teacher in secondary education, on teaching and learning tenses in both languages, an example of collaboration that could and should be encouraged in our context. Escobar Urmeneta and Evnitskaia are members of a research group working with CLIL teachers (content and language integrated learning). Their chapter (Affording Students Opportunities for the Integrated Learning of Content and Language: A Contrastive Study on Classroom Interaction Strategies Deployed by Two CLIL Teachers) shows how a teacher's instructional choices in the form of conversational adjustments afford students greater or lesser opportunities in the integrated learning of English and content. Ramírez and Serra (Integrated Languages Project), members of the Vila Olímpica School governing board, present the principles and organisational aspects on which the integrated teaching model of the three languages of the curriculum are based. It is a model that could be implemented in many schools within our context.

1 Language-in-education Policies in the Catalan Language Area

Joaquim Arnau and F. Xavier Vila

The territories where Catalan is traditionally spoken as a native language are: Catalonia, Valencia, the Balearic Islands and la Franja, in Spain; Northern Catalonia, in France; Andorra; and the Sardinian city of Alghero (Italy). In the past, all these societies developed quite different language-in-education policies and models, ranging from monolingualism in the State language to many different bilingual and even plurilingual programmes. Today, after a decade of unexpected and massive recent foreign immigration, these very systems have to adapt to a new multilingual, multicultural environment, where immigrant languages combine with globalisation, turning them into an attractive sociolinguistic laboratory for comparative language-in-education policies. This chapter provides a summary of available research results in connection with language learning, language practices, the impact on social integration and cohesion, and on academic achievement.

Introduction

Catalan is a Romance language closely related to Occitan, French, Italian and Spanish, native to a geographical area divided among four states, namely Spain, France, Andorra and Italy. In Spain, the historical Catalan language area covers Catalonia (7,512,381 inhabitants); most of Valencia (also called the Valencian Community)[1] (4,327,320); the Balearic Islands (1,106,049); a stretch of land in Aragon on the border with Catalonia, known as la Franja (48,888); and a handful of hamlets in the Murcia Region known as Carxe/ Carche (769). In France, Catalan is the historical language of the Department of the Eastern Pyrenees (445,737). Catalan is the sole official language of

Andorra, the small independent state in the Pyrenees (85,015). Finally, Catalan has also been the traditional language of the Sardinian city of Alghero (l'Alguer in Catalan: 40,803), in Italy, since the 14th century (Sorolla, 2011).

A fully standardised language during the late middle ages, when it was the main official language of the Crown of Aragon, the position of Catalan weakened at the turn of the 15th to 16th centuries, when this Crown became part of the Habsburgs' multinational empire, soon associated with Castilian, also known as Spanish. After the Spanish War of Succession (1700–1714),[2] which put an end to the wide autonomy of the kingdoms of the Crown of Aragon, the successive central authorities pursued the linguistic homogenisation of Spain by spreading the knowledge and use of Spanish (Ferrer, 1986). Leaving aside the small parenthesis of the 2nd Spanish Republic (1931–1939), Catalan was repeatedly banned from schools even before the beginning of compulsory education in Spain. The military dictatorships of Miguel Primo de Rivera (1923–1929) and especially Francisco Franco (1936/39–1975) were particularly severe in their anti-Catalan practices (Vila-i-Moreno, 2008).

In this context, the Catalan-speaking population started to learn the state language and to internalise its hegemonic position vis-à-vis Catalan. Both processes were sped up by the massive immigration of native speakers of the official languages (Spanish, French or Italian, according to the territory) during the 20th century, and by the ever-increasing presence of mass media (Pueyo, 1996). Thus, between 1900 and 1950 monolingual Catalan speakers gradually disappeared, replaced by bilingual and monolingual speakers of the official languages, basically *internal* immigrants.

Contemporary Language-in-education Policies and Models

The last decades of the 20th century and the beginning of the 21st century witnessed remarkable changes in language policies (Strubell & Boix-Fuster, 2011; Vila-i-Moreno, 2008). On the one hand, the nation–state structures changed. Spain evolved into a constitutional, parliamentary monarchy with a semi-federal structure known as the 'State of autonomies', which allowed the three largest Catalan-speaking societies (i.e. Catalonia, Valencia and the Balearic Islands) to start to develop their own language-in-education policies. France and Italy also introduced some degree of regionalisation into their state structures. On the other hand, the general ideological context evolved, with new discourses and practices slowly emerging that were more respectful of individuals' linguistic preferences and of linguistic diversity in general (Spolsky, 2004).

In Spain, where the bulk of Catalan speakers live, contemporary language policies have become much more pluralistic than they used to be, and, while Spanish remains the state's sole official language, Catalan has become official in almost all its historical territories, namely Catalonia, Valencia and the Balearic Islands. All schoolchildren (i.e. including those with a non-Catalan L1) living in these territories are expected to learn both official languages. Since the late 1980s, language policies have been distributed among the central and the autonomous authorities, and each autonomous government has developed its own (educational) language policy, causing great disparity.

Language-in-education policies in the 1980s and 1990s were mainly concerned with introducing Catalan as a subject and/or as a means of instruction into a society formed basically by the descendants of locals (usually Catalan speakers except in some spots where language shift had effectively taken place) and the children and grandchildren of basically Spanish-speaking immigrants who had arrived in the territories particularly between 1950 and 1975. However, in the early 2000s, two ingredients had to be taken into account: more than 2 million foreign immigrants arrived in these territories from all over the world in less than a decade, basically attracted by the construction industry, jumping from less than 1% to more than 16% of the total population. On the other hand, globalisation was taking its toll in the form of increased pressure to significantly improve the mastery of English. Owing to the population movements of the last decade, successive surveys (even the most recent ones) only coincide partially regarding the demolinguistic composition of the territories analysed (Sorolla, 2011, *op. cit.*). In Catalonia, for example, during 2008–2009, Catalan L1 speakers represented a third of the total inhabitants, while the number of speakers with Spanish as their first language (including the hundreds of thousands of Latin Americans that had recently arrived) represented a little over half of the total population. Catalan–Spanish bilingual L1 speakers only accounted for 5%, while 10% of the population, mainly newly arrived immigrants, spoke other languages and language combinations as their L1. However, it is important to remember that the situation is fluctuating because there are no clear barriers between linguistic groups; so at any given time and place, 40% of inhabitants state Catalan to be their language of identification and usual language, and a third of individuals with Spanish as their first language pass Catalan on to their children, especially in mixed couples. Regarding those individuals that speak languages other than those of the country, they tend to adopt Spanish as their vehicular language, even in the family environment. Nonetheless, major economic recession has overturned the migratory flux. The *Instituto Nacional de Estadística* (the Spanish National Institute of Statistics) (2011) calculates that around 80,000 immigrants, especially Latin Americans, will have left Spain by the end of 2011, a trend that looks to continue for several years, although this has not been shown by the surveys available. In any case, in less than a century, the virtually monolingual Catalan-speaking society has become first bilingual and later multilingual.

In the next sections, we will look at the language-in-education models applied in each territory. We will provide more in-depth information on

Catalonia owing to the weight it represents as a whole as opposed to the other territories and to the number of studies carried out there. Only after the models have been clarified will we turn to the results of such models, in the next chapter, also with the focus mainly being on Catalonia.

The language-in-education model in Catalonia

The establishment of a linguistic conjunction model

The 1979 Statute of Autonomy established the official status of Catalan and Spanish and stipulated that both languages would be taught to the school-going population. Initially, each centre is allowed to choose the means of instruction, and hence a linguistic continuum is formed between schools where Catalan is the vehicular language, centres where both languages are used in equal amounts and centres where Spanish is the vehicular language. Although initially there is a strong correlation between the language of the student body and the vehicular language, an important aspect of this policy that is maintained today is that it attempts to avoid creating separate schools for Catalan speakers and Spanish speakers.

The redefining of the language-in-education model in Catalonia towards introducing and extending the position of Catalan was initially based in Catalonia's 1983 Linguistic Normalisation Act. The new *model de conjunció en català* ('Catalan conjunction model') made Catalan the normal (but not necessarily exclusive) medium of instruction in Catalonia. Catalan and Spanish should have a proper presence in curricula so that all students become bilingual and biliterate by the end of compulsory education. Initial instruction in Spanish is granted to children whose parents apply for it, although this only happens on very rare occasions. At the same time, schools with at least 70% of non-Catalan L1 speakers may take advantage of language immersion programmes.

The education system in Catalonia progressively adopted Catalan as its language of teaching, especially in primary education: while only 3% of primary schools used Catalan as the main vehicular language in 1978, by 1990, 90% of primary schools and practically 50% of secondary schools declared that they use Catalan as the prevalent means of instruction.

There are no recent official figures regarding linguistic use in teaching. In theory, Catalan is the normal vehicular language in all primary schools, although often some subjects have been introduced in Spanish and, even more so, in English, with these languages being taught as subjects, three hours per week.

In 1994, a ruling by Spain's Constitutional Court declared that the conjunction model was constitutional.[3] The 1998 Language Policy Act consolidated this model in Catalonia. In 2006, Catalonia approved by referendum a new Statute of Autonomy, which considers the essential elements of this linguistic model, including the right of newly arrived students to receive special help with the language. However, in 2010, after four years of heated and hugely politicised debate, the Spanish Constitutional Court ruled that Spanish had to be reintroduced as a language of instruction on par with Catalan, and similar rulings by the Supreme Court (September 2010) and Catalonia's High Court (2011, 2013) have confirmed this decision. In the midst of great media turmoil, the Government of Catalonia has answered that nothing should (or would) be changed in the model. Applying this new law would force Catalonia to change its current linguistic model.

Immersion programmes

The first Catalan immersion programme was created in 1983 in Santa Coloma de Gramenet, a town in Barcelona's industrial belt, where Spanish is the first language of more than 90% of the population (Vila-i-Moreno, 1996). It was believed that the benefits of a programme based on additive bilingualism provided maximum competence in L2 without losing competence in L1. In contrast to immersion programmes implemented in other locations, such as Canada, the immersion programme in Catalonia was not an enrichment programme designed as an option among others. The model, promoted by the education administration, was based on the belief (and later confirmed by evidence) that other school models aimed at Spanish speakers would not be as effective as the immersion model. As was soon proved, in the same way as in Canada or the Basque Country, in contexts with little presence of the school language, only maximum exposure to Catalan ensured learning: without immersion, the Spanish-speaking student body only achieved a very precarious competence in the L2 (Alsina et al., 1983). Thanks to stimulus given by the administration, teaching staff and families, the experience was extended throughout the territory, so that ten years later, in 1993, more than 200,000 students had enrolled in the programme (Artigal, 1995). In this sense, the Catalan immersion programme has been a very important educational experience, considering the number of students involved and the goals set to ensure that the entire Spanish-speaking school population masters both official languages, Catalan and Spanish, in a school system rooted in the Catalan cultural reality (Arenas & Muset, 2007).

The results obtained met expectations, as two assessments performed on a wide range of students illustrated (Ribes, 1993; Serra, 1997). The Spanish-speaking students in the immersion programme, when compared with other children in their same linguistic group that followed a mainly Spanish-dominated syllabus, had better oral and written competence in Catalan at all school levels (from second to fifth year in primary education). As regards Spanish, the students of the immersion programme achieved a level of understanding and expression similar to their Spanish-speaking counterparts who did not follow the programme. Furthermore, Ribes showed that students who were less competent cognitively were those that took best advantage of the immersion programme. In addition, the Spanish-speaking students had a favourable attitude towards Catalan and Spanish, whatever programme was followed.

Four factors explain these positive results. The first are psychological: students that learn a L2 transfer these skills easily to L1, which is also taught at school (Arnau, 1985a). The second is pedagogical: a L2 is learnt more effectively when contents of the syllabus are taught through it and when teachers monitor understanding and adapt to students' emerging L2 skills (Arnau, 1994). There are also social factors: the students' L1 is a dominant language in society; therefore students have greater opportunity to use it. Finally, the favourable attitude to learning Catalan was also an important factor.

Owing to its success, the Catalan immersion programmes have been an observation ground for European psychopedagogy experts and psycholinguists (Arnau & Artigal, 1998). More specifically, 'Catalan-style' Swedish immersion programmes were created in Finland after a number of collaboration sessions between teachers and the Finnish education administrations (Laurén, 1994).

Teaching for immigrant students (a 'new immersion')

Catalonia has received a considerable amount of foreign immigrants of different cultural and linguistic origins in a short period. The arrival of new immigration flows has had a clear reflection in classrooms: while foreign students represented 0.58% in Catalan classrooms in 1999, by the 2007–2008 academic year they represented 12.9%. More than 90% are children of economic immigrants. Most come from South and Central America (43.8%) and the Maghreb (25.8%), although there are also significant percentages from Eastern Europe (EU and non-EU), Asia and Oceania, and from other parts of Africa (Querol & Strubell, 2009). These students are present in similar numbers at all educational levels, and between 2000 and 2010, they were able to enter schools at any point during the academic year, which caused major teaching problems.

As opposed to the Spanish immigrations of the 20th century, the new immigration flows have been very heterogeneous. In 2006, in primary education reception classrooms, there were students speaking 57 different languages, from 96 countries of origin (Vila Mendiburu et al., 2009a), many of which could not express themselves in their mother tongue in the classroom because the teachers did not understand them. All had to learn Catalan, Spanish and English as a necessary requirement for their academic progress. In this sense, during the first decade of 2000, a new immersion model needed to be developed in Catalonia.

The Generalitat de Catalunya (2004) drafted and implemented the *Pla per a la Llengua, la Interculturalitat i la Cohesió Social* (Plan for Language, Interculturality and Social Cohesion) in order to deal with this population. The plan defines the objectives, purpose, areas of action and expected resources. Each centre must draft its own *pla d'acollida* (reception plan), an action protocol for newly arrived immigrant students that includes organisational strategies and methodologies, procedures for encouraging the participation of families and actions to create awareness of cultural diversity among the whole student body. According to this plan, *aules d'acollida* (reception classrooms) are set up: these are spaces where late arrivals to the educational system (from third year in primary education) spend a number of hours and a flexible period essentially learning Catalan. These children spend the rest of the school time in the mainstream class, according to a transition programme, which starts with them taking subjects with a more understandable input (PE, music, art, workshops), and then going on to other subjects that require more complex linguistic input (social science, natural science, etc.). For the 2008–2009 academic year there were a total of 1236 reception classrooms throughout the compulsory education system, which addressed the needs of 24,505 students (Departament d'Educació, Catalan Department of Education, 2008).

An evaluation of the principles and actions proposed by the *Pla per a la Llengua, la Interculturalitat i la Cohesió Social* (Arnau, 2005) indicates that it includes many quality indexes, in accordance with the standards proposed for an authentically inclusive education (Coelho, 2005). It is a comprehensive integration plan in which students are not segregated and can interact in the normal classroom scenario with native classmates from day one.

Another important resource of the immigrant education programme is its *Plans d'Entorn* (Environment Plans), support networks for the educational community (municipal services, cultural, social and sports entities) that create spaces with different objectives: recreational, language use and learning, awareness about the country, support for academic tasks, etc. Here, students and their families can socialise with others in a different way to that of the school. It is an initiative that is particularly necessary in areas where Catalan has a lower presence.

For some time now, the Catalan Department of Education has been carrying out a pilot programme to teach languages of origin after school hours.

The Plan for Language, Interculturality and Social Cohesion does not include bilingual teachers as yet (competent in Catalan and the students' language) who can perform support and tutorial tasks, one of the requirements that would contribute to increasing quality according to the quality standards proposed.

Languages of instruction in the public universities of Catalonia

Catalonia has seven public universities. A total of 60% of the classes are taught in Catalan, and 40% in Spanish (Generalitat de Catalunya, 2010). The University of Girona is the one with the highest use of Catalan (85.2%), and the Polytechnical University is the one with the lowest index (60%). Professors can choose the language in which they will teach their classes, and the students can choose the language in which they express themselves orally and in writing. In the same class, the professor can speak in Catalan and the students in Spanish, and vice versa. The language in which the professor will conduct lessons is public information that appears in the course catalogues. There are not Catalan and Spanish curriculums separated by language, and this does not cause any problems among the native students, who reach the university with a mastery of both languages. For students from the rest of Spain and for foreign students, a multimedia system exists to give them the opportunity to become familiar with Catalan before their arrival and to inform them of linguistic reception programmes.

In Masters courses, the professors tend to adapt to the language needs of their students in a flexible way. Learning Catalan is easy for students who have prior knowledge of another Romance language.

Language-in-education models in Valencia

Historically divided into two linguistic areas (Valencian on the coast, Spanish in the inner-most areas) and having experienced a deeper process of language shift towards Spanish, the Valencian language-in-education policy has followed a path that is quite different from that in Catalonia. In practice, bilingual education is only available in the Catalan-speaking areas, and the school system is organised along linguistic lines or programmes.

- The *Progressive Incorporation [into Valencian]*[4] Programme (PIP), in which Spanish is the means of instruction and Valencian is a compulsory subject and is used for teaching in some areas of knowledge.
- The *Teaching in Valencian Programme* (PEV), in which Valencian is the means of instruction and Spanish is a compulsory subject and the language in which some areas of knowledge are taught;
- The *Linguistic Immersion in Valencian Programme* (PIL), aimed at students whose first language is not Valencian and in which teaching is carried out in Valencian, with Spanish being introduced progressively from the third year of primary school as a language of instruction.

In secondary education, only the first two models (i.e. PIP and PEV) are applied. For their part, in the Spanish-speaking areas, there is only one school language mode, called the *Basic Programme*, in which the means of instruction is Spanish and the teaching of Valencian is declared compulsory. In practice, however, the teaching of Catalan in this area has become optional and is carried out only if the school community is interested.

Assessing the importance of PEV and PIL in the overall Valencian education system is a difficult task, since the region's Department of Education provides no direct information on the matter. In 2010–2011, around 29% of all pupils studied in Catalan-medium schools (STEPV, 2011). According to the same source, these figures show a sharp drop from primary (33.3% in

Catalan) to secondary education (23.3% in compulsory secondary education), and even 4.6% in non-compulsory vocational training, owing to the lack of availability in both the public and private sectors rather than to any lack of demand. Furthermore, teaching in Valencian is much more common in public than in private schools.

Early education in foreign languages has been introduced by means of the Enriched Bilingual Education Programme (PEBE), which is combined with one of the existing ones (PIL, PEV or PIP). The 1998–1999 academic year saw 53 schools implementing it, a figure that had risen to 278 by 2006–2007. It is worth noting that, according to the *Servei d'Ensenyament del Valencià* (Valencian Teaching Service) (now extinct), in 2010, the majority of schools applying the PEBE (160) were public centres included in the programmes in Valencian (PEV/PIL).

Shortly after the autonomous elections in May 2011, again won by the conservative *Partido Popular (PP)*, the Valencian Government announced that the educational system would be globally restructured: linguistic streams would be suppressed, schools would theoretically teach in the language chosen by parents, and English would be widely used as a means of instruction, all of which aroused strong protests.

Language-in-education models in the Balearic Islands

The defining of the language-in-education model in the Balearic Islands occurred much more recently than in Catalonia and has proved to be much more unstable. The Islands' Language Normalisation Act of 1986 requires that schoolchildren be able to use Catalan and Spanish correctly by the end of their compulsory education, but the government of the Balearic Islands did not take over powers over education until 1998. Only in 1997, after large-scale popular mobilisations, the autonomous government, in the hands of the conservative *Partido Popular*, passed the so-called 'Decree of Minimums',[5] requiring that at least half of the subjects be taught in Catalan.

However, it was not until the next centre-leftist *Pacto de Progreso* Government (1999–2003) that the measures to ensure effective compliance with this decree were implemented, including a provision that all teachers should demonstrate knowledge of Catalan. By the 2010–2011 academic year, a majority of primary schools (62%) declared that they used Catalan as the only medium of instruction, 4% did so with less than 50% in Catalan and the remainder (34%) declared that they used Catalan and Spanish in more or less the same proportion. As far as secondary education was concerned, 54.7% of schools taught 80% or more of their subjects in Catalan (Colom, 2011).

In 2003, the conservatives returned to government in the Balearic Islands thanks, among other things, to the vote of the thousands of Spanish speakers from the mainland attracted by the property and tourism boom. The new government passed a decree designed, in principle, to encourage the use of foreign languages in teaching, but which by doing so allowed for a reduction in the use of Catalan to only one third of teaching hours. These and other initiatives encountered strong opposition from the education community, and very few centres took their provisions on board.

The Islands' parliamentary elections of 27 May 2007 led to another change in government. The new centre–leftist government put an end to the pressure to reduce the use of Catalan as medium of instruction, announced measures to spread trilingual education and put an eye on measures to integrate the large number of foreign immigrants who had arrived during the 2000s. However, in May 2011, the rightist *Partido Popular* came back into power and announced radical changes in education: both the Normalisation Bill and the Decree of Minimums would be repealed, and schools would be required to teach local dialects rather than the standard language. At the time of writing, the conservative government was changing the current system into a trilingual system with all children being taught in Catalan, Spanish and English, amid of protests.

Language-in-education models in la Franja (Aragon)

Catalan in la Franja is not an official language. Aragon's reformed Statute of 2007 still does not give the language any official status and leaves provisions for its use in education to a Language Law that was only passed in late 2009. As a consequence, the presence of the language in schools is very weak. In 1985, within the framework of the collaboration agreement with Spain's Ministry of Education and Science, schools in la Franja began to teach Catalan on a voluntary and optional basis. The agreement, which was extended automatically until the full entry-into-force of the powers over education contained in Article 36 of the Statute (adopted from 1 January 1999 on), allows for a progressive expansion of Catalan teaching, with the result that, today, almost all primary school students and half of secondary students take Catalan classes. Catalan classes began in the 1984–1985 academic year with 700 students, and by 2004–2005, they were being taken by around 3500. Additionally, a number of primary and secondary schools have some experience of 'bilingual' programmes, where Catalan is used for one subject matter (Mayans & Tort, 2011; Pons & Sorolla, 2009).

Although they are followed by a majority of the school population, the fact is that few hours of Catalan classes are given (2–4 hours a week). Bearing in mind that Catalan is not an official language and has little written or formal presence, these few hours of teaching do not even guarantee that native Catalan speakers will be able to properly read or write their own language. It goes without saying that non-native pupils do not acquire productive competence with these classes.

Language-in-education models in Andorra

Andorra is a small independent state in the Pyrenees, which has managed to remain independent from both Spain and France, and Catalan is its only official language. Once a poor, rural country, Andorra became a centre of tourist and financial attraction during the second half of the 20th century. In 1940, 17% of Andorra's population was foreign, basically Catalans (Planelles, 1999). But in the following decades, the ethnolinguistic landscape of Andorra changed dramatically, with the arrival of Spanish-speaking Spaniards, French, Portuguese and eventually people from a wide variety of origins. Thus, in 2004 only 28.2% of Andorrans older than 14 years of age had an Andorran passport (Torres *et al.*, 2006).

The educational landscape in Andorra is quite complex, as, in practical terms, several educational systems coexist in its territory: the Andorran system, the French system, and the Spanish system. The reason for this complexity goes back in history: during a good part of the 20th century, Andorrans were content to be served basically by foreign educational systems (the French and the Spanish), which granted them free education and access to universities. Massive immigration of non-Catalan speakers in the 1960s and 1970s changed the status quo, and Andorra changed its educational policy to develop a national educational system: on the one hand, the authorities required the teaching of Catalan and Andorran history and culture in all systems; on the other, a new Andorran educational system was created in 1983–1984. This new system was from inception a bilingual school, with Catalan as the main language of instruction and an important role attributed to French. This design was rooted in Andorra's sociolinguistic situation: for decades, most Andorrans (with Catalan as their L1) used to attend the French system to acquire French, while Spanish was much easier to pick up owing to the large amount of Spanish residents in the country. The design proved to be wise. In 2010, 38.9% attended the Andorran schools, 31% were in the French system, and 30% were in the Spanish one, with 60% of the latter in mostly Catalan-medium schools. Today, the Andorran model is evolving into a plurilingual one, with English and Spanish also being used to some extent (Mayans & Tort, 2011, *op. cit.*).

Language-in-education models in Northern Catalonia (France) and l'Alguer/Alghero (Italy)

Official language policies, demographic movements and massive language shifts have put Catalan in Northern Catalonia and in l'Alguer/Alghero in a very delicate position (Querol *et al.*, 2007). In both territories, the intergenerational language transmission within families was massively interrupted during the 20th century; therefore, the education system has become the most important social institution where Catalan can be acquired. The position of Catalan in the education systems of both territories has improved during the last decades. Nevertheless, it remains peripheral and fragile: only 17% of all pupils have some teaching of Catalan (Mayans & Tort 2011, *op. cit.*).

Like the rest of the regional and minority languages in France, in mainstream schools in Northern Catalonia, French and Catalan courses are optional. Although they are on the increase, only a minority of pupils receive any effective teaching of Catalan at all. In fact, demand is always greater than supply (Becat, 2000; Secretaria de Política Lingüística, 2004), and the teaching of Catalan is possible along three different paths. In the first place, Catalan lessons are offered in a number of mainstream schools. A second option of Catalan language learning is provided by *bilingual* schools, which in 2010–2011 served 2668 pupils from elementary to *lycée* level. The linguistic model of these schools is quite heterogeneous and ranges from a very weak use of Catalan to parity use of French and Catalan. These are public schools that aspire to making the children bilingual in terms of language competence and attitudes, but do not work actively to encourage the reintroduction of Catalan in interpersonal communication.

Finally, there exists a private, partly subsidised network of Catalan-medium schools called La Bressola, i.e. 'the cradle' (La Bressola, 2007). In 2010–2011, this network served more than 1144 children from pre-school (2 years old) to secondary education in seven schools and one *collège*. La Bressola schools use Catalan as their main language of instruction and encourage the interpersonal use of Catalan among the children, while preserving the highest levels of French and making significant efforts to teach English.

The social situation of Catalan in the Sardinian city of l'Alguer/Alghero is fragile, with an almost total interruption of intergenerational transmission (Querol *et al.*, 2007, *op. cit.*). Nevertheless, a number of initiatives have been launched in order to reverse the process. In the school context, two major initiatives are worth a mention. First, since 1998, the Palomba Project has taught Alguerese Catalan to primary education children in almost all local schools. Second, in 2004–2005 'La Costura', a trilingual (Catalan/Italian/English) branch of a private school, was introduced. La Costura has the support of the local city council as well as Catalonia's Department of Education. In several aspects, these schools are based upon the experience of La Bressola, where Catalan is the main language of instruction and the interpersonal use of this language is encouraged.

The Results of Language-in-education Policies: Competences and Usage in Catalonia

Competences

Several assessments performed at primary-education level in Catalonia when the different school linguistic models were in place have consistently confirmed that, as the presence of Catalan increased in the curriculum, the competence of Spanish-speaking students in Catalan improved. Conversely, the greater or lesser presence of Spanish was not a determining factor in the competence in this language, in either native Catalan speakers or Spanish speakers (Alsina *et al.,* 1983, *op. cit.;* Arnau, 1985b; Arnau *et al.,* 1994). In other words, schools with Catalan as the means of instruction provided the closest competences in both languages. As we have already mentioned, the competences of the Spanish speakers in the immersion programmes were much better in Catalan and at the same level in Spanish, in comparison to those of their Spanish-speaking classmates who did not participate in the programme.

In Catalonia, the *Consell Superior d'Avaluació del Sistema Educatiu* (Evaluation Council of the Educational System) has, for many years, carried out a written test assessment of students' linguistic competences in Catalan and Spanish (reading comprehension and written expression). The 2011 exam was given to all sixth-year students in primary education, except those with special educational needs (5.5%) and newcomers (2.7%) (CSASE, 2011).

Although the authors do not explain the differences, the difference between competences in one language or another seems to be insignificant and the students are also distributed in an equal proportion in the different pass levels (Tables 1.1 and 1.2).

Analysing the influence of specific variables on the linguistic competences marked by family language is not decisive, generally speaking, in explaining the differences. The reason for the different performances is owing to a number of factors: socio-economic level, quality of education at the different centres, gender, sociolinguistic context, etc.

Table 1.1 Global mean

	Catalan	Spanish
Global mean	77.2	73.6

Range of marks: 0–100

Table 1.2 Pass levels (% students)

	Catalan	Spanish
Low	22.6%	22.2%
Average	44.2%	42.0%
High	33.2%	35.8%

Range of marks: 0–100
Pass level: low (less than 70 points: failed the basic competence level), average (between 70 and 90 points) and high (90 points or higher)

Regarding skills in Spanish, a recent assessment at state level indicated that students in Catalonia have a basic competence (written) average in Spanish comparable with that of students in the rest of the State (Ministerio de Educación y Ciencia, 2010).

The opinion of the speakers themselves confirms the achievement of the objectives proposed in schools throughout these years: to provide the entire native population with bilingual competences.

In fact, in Catalonia in 2006, students in the last year of compulsory secondary education proved to be slightly more competent in Spanish than in Catalan, especially when speaking and writing (CSASE, 2008a). This is not just owing to the newcomers, rather because there are notable segments of the young native population (descendents of immigrants from the 1960s and 1970s) that, despite the official status of Catalan in schools, never use Catalan (Vila-i-Moreno & Sorolla, 2011).

As can be seen in Tables 1.3 and 1.4, most adolescents appear to be highly competent in both languages, with a slight tendency towards Spanish (3.5% of the population sampled state that they speak other languages and the majority are immigrants).

The conjunction model with Catalan as the predominant vehicular language has achieved its objective of making the native population bilingual. Contextual factors, such as Spanish's position as a majority language, favour competence in this language. However, it is clear that without this

Table 1.3 Evaluate your skills in Catalan (%)

	Understand	Speak	Read	Write
Very low	2.4	2.9	2.7	2.9
Low	0.1	1.1	0.4	0.9
Intermediate	1.5	5.7	2.7	9.8
High	5.0	15.9	10.7	25.8
Very high	91.0	74.4	83.5	60.6

Source: CSASE, 2008a

Table 1.4 Evaluate your skills in Spanish (%)

	Understand	Speak	Read	Write
Very low	2.2	2.5	2.9	3.1
Low	0.1	0.4	0.1	0.2
Intermediate	1.1	3.1	1.3	5.2
High	4.2	10.1	7.5	21.6
Very high	92.4	83.9	88.2	69.9

Source: CSASE, 2008a

model, based on a significant presence of Catalan in the curriculum, the Spanish-speaking and immigrant population would not achieve acceptable levels of competence. In this regard, Catalonia is one of the few countries in the world that has a socially cohesioned education model that largely provides bilingual competences to the entire native population. Other language-in-education models applied in other Catalan-speaking territories do not provide these competences. In the Balearic Islands, only 50% of students in the fourth year of primary school have a consolidated competence in Catalan (Colom, 2011, *op. cit.*). In Valencia, less than half of adolescents state that they have mastered Catalan (understanding, speaking, reading and writing) (Generalitat Valenciana, 2010).

The impact on linguistic use

A number of observational studies or experiments have analysed the linguistic behaviour of students in order to directly measure the impact of the conjunction model on linguistic usage.

Vila-i-Moreno (1998) analysed the degree to which an immersion programme located in Santa Coloma de Gramenet (predominantly Spanish speaking) promoted the spontaneous use of Catalan. In this context, Spanish-speaking and Catalan-speaking students systematically addressed teachers in Catalan both inside and outside the classroom. However, the use of Catalan by Spanish speakers with their classmates (Catalan-speaking and Spanish-speaking) was extremely scarce and only appeared in highly ritualised activities, such as in-class debates. Catalan-speaking students appeared to maintain this language not only when speaking with the teacher but also with a certain number of classmates, essentially Catalan speakers or bilingual students. The study concluded that, with regard to predominate usage in the community, the programme gave students the opportunity to practise Catalan with teachers and sometimes with classmates. If this had not happened in the school, students from these contexts would have lost all practical opportunity to use the language spontaneously at school.

These results were qualified by the study carried out by de Rosselló (2003) in Sant Andreu del Palomar, a district of Barcelona that is on the threshold of Santa Coloma but with a higher native and Catalan-speaking population than in the latter. Here Catalan gained in presence as the language of exchange and was not considered as only an in-group language.

From another angle, Morera and Teberosky (1998) illustrated the language that is spontaneously chosen for writing by third-year secondary students from a working class sector, who had followed an immersion programme at the primary education level and who attended a secondary school in a district of the Barcelona belt in which education was predominately carried out through Catalan. The investigator asked students to write two essays based on their reading experience. The heading of the tasks was given in Catalan and the investigator always addressed students in that language, without giving explicit instructions to write in Catalan. A total of 52% of the students wrote in Spanish and 48% in Catalan. The dominating presence of Spanish in communication with classmates and in the extracurricular context favoured the use of this language in a formal class situation in which restrictions operated in favour of Catalan.

The study *Llengua i ús* (Galindo, 2006; Vila-i-Moreno & Vial, 2000; Vila-i-Moreno *et al.*, 2005) registered the spontaneous linguistic use of sixth-year primary education students in the playgrounds of Catalan schools during the latter half of the 1990s. It can be deduced from the analysis that, although the conjunction model gives priority to Catalan as the vehicular language, the Catalan-speaking student body tended to adopt Spanish to address their Spanish-speaking interlocutors and not the opposite. Apart from school, only in contexts with a clearly predominant demographic of Catalan speakers were Spanish speakers to adopt Catalan with these people. However, Catalan speakers and Spanish speakers continued to use their L1 in conversations with speakers of the same language. These norms of linguistic selection reproduce the *etiquette* imposed especially in the 20th century that required speakers to change to Spanish in the presence of non-Catalan speaking individuals.

With his research on three-year-old preschool children, de Rosselló (2010, 2012) illustrated that the norm is not applicable among children of this age, who have less obstacles in adopting Catalan as the common language. All this leads us to think that we are dealing with a phenomenon strongly rooted in Catalan society.

As shown by Bretxa and Parera (in press), Spanish-speakers living in areas with a high immigration density during the 20th century only adopted Catalan when they left their social surroundings and closest networks. The same was corroborated later by Pujolar *et al.* (2010), indicating that moments of transition, such as the change to secondary school or university, were moments in which the redefinition of linguistic usage was possible.

L'estudi sociodemogràfic i lingüístic de l'alumnat de quart de Secundària de Catalunya (The sociodemographic and linguistic study of the student body in fourth year of secondary education in Catalonia), to which reference is made (CSASE, 2008a, *op. cit.*) analysed the uses that students state that they make of Catalan and Spanish inside and outside the classroom (sample of 1393 students distributed according to first language: 42.8% Spanish, 39.9% Catalan, 14.1% bilingual and 3.2% other languages). In this context, Catalan is the language that predominates (used always and frequently) when teachers address the class (73.9%) and on exams (85.7%). The use of Catalan is slightly lower when students address teachers (64.6%). The usage in social relations, however, is even lower: 49.2% and 50.1% of students declare that they never speak Catalan with friends in school and outside school, respectively, and 32.9% and 30.9% say they always use it. Spanish is also the predominate language of the cultural consumption of these adolescents: television (70.4%), internet (70.5%) and cinema (93.9%). These students perceived the usefulness of languages for finding work, on a scale of 0 to 9, in this order: Spanish (9.2), English (8.9), Catalan (8.2) and French (6). It is probable that the young people had realistic expectations on this issue. The differences, however, do not seem to be significant and provide positive data for Catalan, showing that it has a significant instrumental value.

The data on usage analysed up to this point shows the gap between competences and usage with a clear conclusion: schools can help language learning, but they cannot change the sociolinguistic dynamics by themselves as they cannot change society. 'School is not enough' (Fishman, 1991) and the operation of languages and the dynamics established in the social environment only partly depend on education systems.

The results of the new immersion

Immigrant students have had to adapt to a new country and new education system. Those who have joined the system late have had to develop the necessary linguistic competences in a short time in order to follow the normal academic curriculum. In this situation, the problems that are shown in our context are not far from those that appear in similar contexts.

Studies performed with Moroccan primary education students indicate that only after three years do they have basic conversational competences in Catalan and more time would have to pass for them to develop an acceptable reading comprehension and written expression (Maruny & Molina, 2001) because, in many cases, the locations where they live offer few opportunities to hear Catalan spoken and to use it. In fact, while Spanish learning among immigrants seems to be relatively uniform across the Catalan territory, regarding the level of Catalan of those who learn it, the sociolinguistic environment in which they develop (Comajoan et al., in press) and more specifically, the immediate social network in which they develop (Oller & Vila Mendiburu, 2011), are fundamental. Furthermore, some authors (Lapresta et al., 2008; Trenchs-Parera & Newman, 2009) have suggested that some groups, especially Latin Americans, may have a less favourable attitude towards Catalan, although other studies do not confirm this (Gomàriz, 2008). The attitude can also depend on the integration process carried out by the school (Trenchs-Parera & Patiño-Santos, in this volume).

Regarding the academic results, the percentage of failure is much higher than in the normal population (Fullana et al., 2003; Siguan, 1998) and few of them obtain a diploma on finishing compulsory secondary education (Alegre et al., 2008). The level of education of their parents, the quality of schooling beforehand, age on arrival, family stability, the opportunities offered to the families by the receiving society, the quality of the school and student body concentration in certain schools are all factors that influence the progress of these students.

With regard to the immigrants that join the educational system late, and except for differences marked by the original languages and the social level, overall data indicates that these students need six years or more to develop competences in Catalan similar to those of native students (Huguet *et al.*, this volume). In this regard, Querol (2011) found that after six years, the student body obtained an equal level of Catalan and Spanish.

To explain the level of Spanish obtained and the predominance of Catalan as a vehicular language, we need to remember that in most of Catalonia, the immigrants settle in districts where the Spanish immigration of the 1960s had settled, without forgetting that a vast part of foreign immigration is already monolingual Spanish-speakers. Among the newcomer adults, Spanish operates as the default lingua franca (Alarcón & Alcalde, 2010; Vila-i-Moreno *et al.*, 2010). Even a wide majority of immigrant students, both Latin Americans and students with other languages, used Spanish as the main means of relation with their classmates and with non-teacher adults (Comajoan *et al.*, in press, *op. cit.*; Vila Mendiburu *et al.*, 2009b).

A Model Towards an Optimum Multilingualism?

The academic results

In general terms, the conjunction model being applied in Catalonia, and to a certain extent in the Balearic Islands, is directed towards plurilingualism: guaranteeing competence in both official languages and encouraging the acquisition of a foreign language. Whether it is optimum or not will depend on, among other factors, whether the linguistic model provides good academic results or not. To answer this question, the PISA (Programme for International Student Assessment) assessments are taken into account, which compare the results of students in Catalonia with the results of students in other contexts (the Spanish State and abroad). Catalonia has participated in successive PISA assessments, with the last one analysing results in terms of reading, mathematical and scientific literacy of 15-year-old students in secondary education. The comparison was carried out across 35 countries in the Organisation for Economic Co-operation and Development (OECD) (CSASE, 2010).

These are the results of the exams carried out in Catalonia in Catalan and in Spain in Spanish (Table 1.5).

Reading, as assessed by PISA, is an important element of academic performance, as it involves understanding, using and reflecting on written texts in order to achieve objectives, develop learning and personal potential and participate in society. It is not just a dimension of linguistic competence, but rather a necessary skill for learning all academic contents, as they

Table 1.5 Position of Catalonia and Spain in the ranking of countries according to the 2009 PISA results

	Position in reading	Position in mathematical competence	Position in scientific competence
Catalonia	15	19	23
OECD mean	23	26	18
Spain	28	30	31

are all based on written texts that need to be interpreted. In reading, Catalonia is located in an intermediate position, significantly above the OECD average and the average for Spain, although in Catalonia there is a significant number of students that do not have Catalan as a first language (59% of the students assessed declared that they speak mainly Spanish at home, 37% declared the language spoken to be Catalan and 4% said they speak other languages; 9% of students indicated that they were born in another country). On the other hand, Spain as a whole, with a vast majority of the population living in a monolingual Spanish-speaking environment and attending programmes in their first language, obtain results lower than those of Catalonia.

We need not say that the data of the PISA report should be taken with a certain level of caution. In absolute terms, the results are not satisfactory, as Catalonia (and Spain) is far from the leading positions, and this leaves much room for improvement. Nonetheless, the comparison between the data for Spain attests that the conjunction system with Catalan as a predominant vehicular language does not determine lower results than education in the first language.

In another sense, education in Catalonia also aims as a primary objective to provide good competence in at least one foreign language. Parents, teachers and society in general consider that this language must be English, a language that has displaced French as the top foreign language studied in schools in the course of a few decades. However, there are also proposals to include French as an option, given that it is geographically closer and also a Romance language (Teixidó, 2009).

Nonetheless, the results in English throughout the Catalan-speaking territory continue to be low. In 2006, under the compulsory secondary education evaluation framework, the English results of fourth-year secondary students in Catalonia were analysed (CSASE, 2008b). The overall results of the study are as follows: 5 out of every 10 students understand simple oral information about daily life topics; 5 out of every 10 understand specific information in simple texts, and only 1 out of every 4 is capable of interacting effectively in short conversations in structured situations. The report qualifies the results as low performance and does not present comparative data for other countries, as there are different contextual factors that may influence competences more so than the schools.

English is being incorporated in many schools at an increasingly early age. According to a study carried out in 2003 at the end of primary education (sixth year) (CSASE, 2006), the initial moments for incorporating English learning were: 24% before six years of age, 24% at the age of six, 15% at seven years of age, 24.5% at the age of eight and 11.4% later than eight years of age. What is more, 34.1% of students declared having studied or to be studying English as an extracurricular activity. The study showed that the earlier students started learning English, the better their competences.

However, early learning does not guarantee the best learning. The BAF project (Barcelona Age Factor), undertaken in Catalonia, assessed the English learning of students that had started learning this language at 8, 11, 14 and later than 18 years of age. The result was that the older students (adolescents and adults) learnt quicker owing to their higher cognitive development and to the advantage of learning using explicit procedures such as reflecting on language (Muñoz, 2006).

Low performance in English, when compared with other countries, can be attributed to various factors. One such factor is that students are more exposed to English (TV and cinema) in many European countries, as English-language productions are subtitled and there is no dubbing into their own language. This is not the case in Spain. Another factor is the training of teachers. Primary school teachers have didactic training, but, although there are no studies in this area, it seems that not all have good competence in English. The study performed at primary level (CSASE, 2006, *op. cit.*) showed that only 22.7% had lived for at least three months in an English-speaking country and 37.1% declared that they had never participated in on-going training seminars. Secondary school teachers may have better linguistic competence owing to the nature of their studies, but in general they have received less didactical and psychological training. Furthermore, the teaching methodology is, without a doubt, an influential factor. In secondary education, the information that students have given on teaching practices indicates that 'traditional or not very innovative methodologies are often, normally or always used in the classrooms' (CSASE, 2008b: 110, *op. cit.*).

The Challenges for Language-in-education Policies in Catalonia

All the evidence presented shows that the current language-in-education model in Catalonia is one that favours generalised bilingualisation of the student body without harming their academic level. This is made evident by the models in other territories, such as Valencia and the Balearic Islands, where Catalan does not have as much of a presence in the curriculum. If the current model were changed in the direction indicated by the Constitutional Tribunal, those who would most likely lose out would be the students that do not have Catalan as their L1 (Spanish speakers and immigrants), given the few opportunities that they have to use it in a social context outside school. All in all, the possibilities for improving this model are still considerable in many senses.

First, the procedures for teaching Catalan as a base language and a learning bridge need to be optimised and improved in such a way that good skills acquired in this stage are transferred to other areas and especially to Spanish, a language closely related to Catalan and to which students are greatly exposed in our social context. The skills that students can learn in languages are not closed compartments. Good bases for speaking, reading and writing in Catalan are also good bases for speaking, reading and writing in other languages. In this sense, it is also fundamental to continue along the line of associating school learning with the option of using the language in a wider social environment and with peers, and along the line of environment plans, as only in relationships with equal counterparts does the language become more colloquial.

A second aspect is the ability to adapt the school to the environment. According to the sociolinguistic context, each school needs to decide the weighting of Spanish and foreign languages within a flexible legal framework. For example, Spanish and/or foreign languages could have a larger role in teaching in certain aspects of the curriculum, which would enable a more integrated teaching of languages. This would imply a change in the role of language teachers and a closer collaboration between them and the teachers of other subjects.

Third, Catalonia has made a major effort in receiving and integrating immigrant students in an exceptional situation, given the massive arrival of newcomers in a short period of time. When these students enter at the initial levels of the school system, the conditions for their integration are easier. When they join the system later on, academic performance is poor, as shown by the results for linguistic competences in ours and other contexts. The perceptions and needs displayed by secondary education immigrant students (Alegre *et al.*, 2006) indicate that they require quality teaching in the reception classroom adapted to their linguistic competences and academic level, well-structured transition to the ordinary classroom, teaching of subjects that takes into account their limited linguistic competences (Arnau, 2009) and a personalised support system (Esomba, 2008). In these schools, especially in secondary education, where there are a high number of immigrant students, a change in the school's structure is required (Castro & Montoya, 2008). We also need to be aware that immigration languages are not only an element of identity, but also a resource that can be beneficial for Catalan society. It is absurd to waste the linguistic and cultural knowledge that newcomer immigrants bring with them, especially when Catalan society needs to open up to fronts as important as the Maghreb and Asian markets. Therefore, academic strategies need to be developed that effectively value the knowledge of immigration languages as a tool, so that children speaking them retain their knowledge.

All of these challenges are of prime importance in training teachers preservice and in-service (Castells *et al.*, this volume; Guasch Boyé, this volume; Ortega *et al.*, this volume). Resources and a comprehensive, coordinated plan are also required.

Summary and Conclusions

Catalan has been progressively banned from schools since the 18th century, and between 1900 and 1950 monolingual Catalan speakers gradually disappeared, replaced by bilinguals and, in some areas, by monolingual speakers of the official languages of the states. In the 2000s, moreover, more than 2 million foreign immigrants, speakers of more than 50 languages, arrived to these territories from all over the world in less than a decade. The arrival of the new wave of immigration has made Catalan lose importance within its own territory.

The last decades of the 20th century and early years of the 21st century have witnessed remarkable changes in language policies in Catalan territories. In Spain, where the bulk of Catalan speakers live, while Spanish remains the state's sole official language, Catalan has also become official in almost all its historical territories, namely Catalonia, Valencia and the Balearic Islands. Language-in-education policies in the 1980s and 1990s were mainly concerned with introducing Catalan as a subject and/or as a means of instruction into a society formed basically by the descendants of locals (Catalan and Spanish speakers). All schoolchildren living in these territories are expected to learn both official languages, and there is now increased pressure to significantly improve their mastery of English.

This chapter has analysed the different language-in-education policies that each autonomous territory has been putting into practice since the late 1980s. The differences among them are owing to factors such as different sociolinguistic contexts that determine the values given to the two official languages, which probably also influence the decisions made by politicians regarding educational planning.

Special emphasis has been given to Catalonia owing to the weight it represents as a whole as opposed to the other territories and to the number of studies that have been carried out there. Catalonia has followed a policy to progressively include Catalan in the curriculum. A fundamental pillar of this policy has been to create immersion programmes, aimed at the

Spanish-speaking population, programmes that have had very positive effects on the development of competences in Catalan without any loss in competences in Spanish. The arrival of recent immigration has created new challenges just when the language-in-education model was being consolidated. Over these years, Catalan has progressively acquired a more important presence in the curriculum. Although it has never managed to become the absolute vehicular language, it has a predominant presence, especially at the primary-education level. This policy ensures that the majority of the student body obtain a competence in both official languages, a result that the other Catalan-speaking territories, with all their differences, cannot guarantee.

The objective of providing a bilingual competence to the entire population has not been accompanied by a significant extension in the use of the language among students, although it has possibly slowed down the minoritising effect that the State language and successive migration have generated. The data on usage analysed up to this point shows the gap between competences and usage, with a clear conclusion: schools can help language learning, but cannot change the sociolinguistic dynamics by themselves as they cannot change society.

The current, trilingual model will be the most optimum if schools progressively assume a set of challenges: to provide optimum competence in Catalan, the bridge language for learning other languages; to plan the teaching of the three languages of the curriculum in as integrated a manner as possible; to ensure better quality teaching in foreign language learning as well as to provide better support for integration and learning processes in the immigrant population. An indispensable condition for this improvement is teacher training.

These challenges must be faced in a context where Catalan is often barely present in some places (where those living there do not speak it as their first language), does not possess the instruments of a State and coexists with major international languages, not to mention in a context where the importance given to it in the curriculum in the different territories depends greatly on the ups and downs of political ruling.

Notes

(1) In 2010, the Valencian population, including its Spanish-speaking regions was 5,111,706 inhabitants.
(2) In 1659, and as a result of the Treaty of the Pyrenees, the Catalan regions of Roussillon and Cerdagne were annexed by France and became subject to France's language policies.
(3) Constitutional Court Ruling 337/1994, of 23 December.
(4) Valencian is the name most commonly used in the Autonomous Community of Valencia when referring to Catalan.
(5) Decree 92/1997, of 4 July, confirmed by a ruling of the Spanish Supreme Court of 4 October 2002.

References

Alarcón, A. and Alcalde, R. (2010) *Joves d'origen immigrant a Catalunya. Necessitats i demandes. Una aproximació sociològica.* Barcelona: Generalitat de Catalunya, Departament d'Acció Social i Ciutadania, Secretaria de Joventut.

Alegre, M.A., Benito, R. and González, S. (2006) *Immigrants als instituts. L'acollida vista pels seus protagonistes.* Col·lecció Polítiques 55. Barcelona: Fundació Bofill/Editorial Mediterrània.

Alegre, M.A., Benito, R. and González, S. (2008) *De l'aula d'acollida a l'aula ordinària: Processos d'escolarització de l'alumnat estranger.* Barcelona: Universitat Autònoma de Barcelona/Institut de Govern i Polítiques Públiques.

Alsina, A., Arnau, J., Bel, A., Garolera, N., Grijalbo, S., Perera, J. and Vila, I. (1983) *Quatre anys de català a l'escola.* Barcelona: Generalitat de Catalunya, Departament d'Ensenyament.

Arenas, J. and Muset, M. (2007) *La immersió lingüística a Catalunya. Un projecte compartit.* Vic: Eumo Editorial.

Arnau, J. (1985a) Educación en la L2 y rendimiento escolar: Una revisión de la problemática general. In M. Siguan (coord.) *Enseñanza en Dos Lenguas y Resultados Escolares, IX Seminario sobre Lenguas y Educación* (pp. 9–20). Barcelona: ICE/Publicacions Universitat de Barcelona.

Arnau, J. (1985b) Catalunya: Influencia del contexto sociolingüístico y del modelo de escuela en el dominio y uso de las lenguas. *Actas del segundo Congreso Nacional de Lingüística Aplicada. Las Lenguas en España: Adquisición, Aprendizaje, Uso.* (pp. 369–382). Murcia: Universidad de Murcia.

Arnau, J. (1994) Teacher-pupil communication when commencing Catalan immersion programs. In C. Laurén (ed.) *Evaluating European Immersion Programs. From Catalonia to Finland,* Vaasa, 1993, The First Conference on Immersion, Research Papers, University of Vaasa 185, 27, 47–76.

Arnau, J. (2005) El modelo catalán de atención educativa a los escolares inmigrantes. *Cultura y Educación* 17 (3), 265–282.

Arnau, J. (2009) Ensenyant història en una aula ordinària de secundària amb alumnes nouvinguts: Un projecte de formació de professors. In J. Arnau *La integració acadèmica i social dels alumnes nouvinguts: Una anàlisi de casos* (pp. 47–70). Barcelona: Institut d'Estudis Catalans.

Arnau, J. and Artigal, J.M. (1998) *Els programes d'immersió: Una perspectiva Europea. Immersion Programmes: A European Perspective.* Barcelona: Edicions de la Universitat de Barcelona.

Arnau, J., Bel, A., Serra, J.M. and Vila Mendiburu, I. (1994) A comparative study of the knowledge of Catalan and Spanish among 8th-grade schoolchildren in Catalonia. In C. Laurén (ed.) *Evaluating European Immersion Programs. From Catalonia to Finland,* Research Papers, Proceedings of the University of Vaasa, 185/27, pp. 107–127.

Artigal, J.M. (ed.) (1995) *Els programes d'immersió als territoris de parla catalana.* Barcelona: Fundació Jaume Bofill.

Becat, J. (2000) *La situació del català a França. Aspectes jurídics i docents i estudis sobre la matèria.* Barcelona: Institut d'Estudis Catalans.

Bretxa, V. and Parera, A. (in press) 'Et dóna la base': Itineraris biogràfics d'adquisició i ús del català del jovent castellanoparlant de Sabadell i Santa Coloma de Gramenet. In F.X. Vila-i-Moreno (dir.) *Posar-hi la base. Usos i aprenentatges lingüístics en el domini català.* Barcelona: Institut d'Estudis Catalans.

Castro, G. and Montoya, G. (2008) IES Joan d'Àustria. Una altra organització de l'aula d'acollida. In *Nouvinguts, fins quan? La incorporació de l'alumnat estranger nouvingut al currículum ordinari* (pp. 181–184). Girona: ICE Universitat de Girona.

Coelho, E. (2005) *Ensenyar i aprendre en escoles multiculturals. Una aproximació integrada.* Barcelona: ICE/Horsori.

Colom, A. (2011) *Descripció del sistema educatiu de les Balears: Una aproximació.* Unpublished manuscript, Institut d'Estudis Catalans, Barcelona.

Comajoan, L., Vila-i-Moreno, F.X., Bretxa, V., Sorolla N., Tenorio, X. and Melià, J. (in press) Els usos lingüístics en família i amb amics de l'alumnat autòcton i al·lòcton de sisè de primària a Catalunya, Mallorca i la Franja. In F.X. Vila (ed.) *De nouvinguts a novíssims catalans? La incorporació lingüística de les noves immigracions.* Barcelona: PPU.

CSASE (Consell Superior d'Avaluació del Sistema Educatiu) (2006) *L'avaluació de l'educació primària 2003.* Generalitat de Catalunya. Departament d'Educació.

CSASE (Consell Superior d´Avaluació del Sistema Educatiu) (2008a) *Estudi sociodemogràfic i lingüístic de l'alumnat de quart d'ESO de Catalunya. Avaluació de l'educació secundària obligatòria 2006* (població de 15 anys). Generalitat de Catalunya: Departament d'Educació http://www20.gencat.cat/docs/Educacio/Home/Consell%20superior%20d%27avalua/Pdf%20i%20altres/Static%20file/Informes11.pdf

CSASE (Consell Superior d'Avaluació del Sistema Educatiu) (2008b) *Resultats de llengua anglesa de l'alumnat de 4t d'ESO de Catalunya. Avaluació de l'educació secundària obligatòria 2006.* Generalitat de Catalunya: Departament d'Educació.

CSASE (Consell Superior d'Avaluació del Sistema Educatiu) (2010) *Resultats de l'alumnat a Catalunya. Avaluació de l'educació secundària obligatòria PISA 2009.* Generalitat de Catalunya: Departament d'Educació.

CSASE (Consell Superior d'Avaluació del Sistema Educatiu) (2011) *Prova d'avaluació de sisè curs d'educació primària 2011.* Generalitat de Catalunya: Departament d'Educació.

Departament d'Educació [Catalan Department of Education] (2008) Evolució de les aules d'acollida i del seu alumnat des del curs 2004/5 fins al curs 2008/9. Unpublished manuscript.

de Rosselló, C. (2003) Catalan or Spanish? Language choice from home to school. In L. Sayahi (ed.) *Selected Proceedings of the First Workshop on Spanish Sociolinguistics* (pp. 30–42). Somerville, MA, USA: Cascadilla Proceedings Project. http://www.lingref.com/cpp/wss/1/index.html

de Rosselló, C. (2010) Aprendre a triar. L'adquisició de les normes d'ús i alternança de codis en l'educació infantile. Doctoral dissertation, Universitat de Barcelona, Barcelona. Available from Tesis Doctorales en Red database. (http://hdl.handle.net/10803/21625)

de Rosselló, C. (2012) Estratègies comunicatives a l'aula. In F.X. Vila-i-Moreno and E. Gomàriz (eds) *Posar-hi la base. Usos i aprenentatges lingüístics en el domini català* (pp. 25–30). Barcelona: Institut d'Estudis Catalans.

Esomba, M.A. (2008) Adolescents immigrats a Catalunya i construcció de la identitat cultural. Trajectòries de vida i processos d'inclusió. *Recerca i Immigració* 1, 53–69. Generalitat de Catalunya: Departament d'Acció Social i Ciutadania, Secretaria per a la Immigració.

Ferrer, F. (1986) *La persecució política de la llengua catalana. Història de les mesures preses contra el seu ús des de la Nova Planta fins avui.* Barcelona: Ed. 62.

Fishman, J.A. (1991) *Reversing Language Shift* (pp. 368–380). Clevedon: Multilingual Matters.

Fullana, J., Besalú, X. and Vilà, M. (2003) *Alumnes d'origen africà a l'escola.* Girona: CCG Edicions.

Galindo, M. (2006) *Les llengües a l'hora del pati. Usos lingüístics en les converses dels infants de primària a Catalunya* (Doctoral dissertation, Universitat de Barcelona, Barcelona). Available from Tesis Doctorales en Red database. (http://hdl.handle.net/10803/1681)

Generalitat de Catalunya (2004) *Pla per a la Llengua, la Interculturalitat i la Cohesió Social.* http://www.xtec.es/acollida.

Generalitat de Catalunya (2010) *Informe sobre la llengua catalana 2010.*

Generalitat Valenciana, Conselleria d'Educació (2010) *Knowledge and Social Use of Valencian Language. General Survey 2010. Synthesis of results.* València: Generalitat Valenciana, Conselleria d'Educació. http://www.edu.gva.es/polin/docs/sies_docs/encuesta2010/index.html

Gomàriz, E. (2008) Competència i actituds lingüístiques de l'alumnat de sisè d'educació primària de Vic. Unpublished manuscript, Barcelona: Departament de Filologia Catalana, Universitat de Barcelona.

La Bressola (2007) *La realitat d'un somni. Trenta anys d'escoles catalanes a la Catalunya del nord.* Barcelona: Edicions de 1984.

Lapresta, C., Huguet, A., Janés, J. and Chireac, S. (2008) Anàlisi discursiva de les actituds lingüístiques de l'alumnat nouvingut a Catalunya: Una aproximació qualitativa. *Recerca i Immigració* 1, 53–69. Generalitat de Catalunya. Departament d'Acció Social i Ciutadania.

Laurén, C. (ed.) (1994) Evaluating European Immersion Programmes. From Catalonia to Finland. *Proceedings of the University of Vaasa* 192, 39.

Maruny, L. and Molina, M. (2001) Identidad cultural y aprendizaje lingüístico: El caso de la inmigración. *Textos* 26, 55–64.

Mayans, P. and Tort, T. (2011) Ensenyament. In M.À. Pradilla and N. Sorolla (coord.) *Informe sobre la situació de la llengua catalana (2010)* (pp. 60–78) Barcelona: Observatori de la Llengua Catalana. http://www.observatoridelallengua.cat -

Ministerio de Educación y Ciencia (2010) *La Evaluación General de Diagnóstico 2010.* http://www.educacion.gob.es/horizontales/prensa/notas/2011/07/evaluacion-diagnostico.html

Morera, M. and Teberosky, A. (1998) Les experiències lletrades a secundària en un context bilingüe. In J. Arnau and J.M. Artigal (eds) *Els programes d'immersió: Una perspectiva europea. (Immersion Programmes: A European Perspective)* (pp. 238–250). Barcelona: Edicions Universitat de Barcelona.

Muñoz, C. (2006) The effects of age on foreign language learning: The BAF Project. In C. Muñoz (ed.) *Age and the Rate of Foreign Language Learning* (pp. 1–40). Clevedon: Multilingual Matters.

Oller, J.A. and Vila Mendiburu, I. (2011) Variables asociadas al conocimiento del catalán y castellano escrito del alumnado extranjero. Un estudio empírico en sexto de primaria en Catalunya. *Infancia y Aprendizaje* 34 (4), 427–447.

Planelles, M. (1999) La llengua catalana avui al Principat d'Andorra. In M.À. Pradilla (ed.) *La llengua catalana al tombant del mil·lenni* (pp. 233–249). Barcelona: Empúries.

Pons, E. and Sorolla, N. (coords.) (2009) *Informe sobre la situació de la llengua catalana (2005–2007).* Barcelona: Observatori de la Llengua Catalana. http://www.observatoridelal-lengua.cat/observatori.php?llengua=ca

Pueyo, M. (1996) *Tres escoles per als catalans.* Lleida: Pagès editors.

Pujolar J., Gonzàlez, I., Font, A. and Martínez, R. (2010). *Llengua i joves. Usos i percepcions lingüístics de la joventut catalana.* Barcelona: Generalitat de Catalunya, Departament d'Acció Social i Ciutadania, Observatori de Joventut. http://www20.gencat.cat/docs/Joventut/Documents/Arxiu/Publicacions/Col_Aportacions/aportacions43.pdf

Querol, P., Chessa, E., Sorolla, N. and Torres, J. (2007) *Llengua i societat als territoris de parla catalana a l'inici del segle XXI. L'Alguer, Andorra, Catalunya, Catalunya Nord, La Franja, Illes Balears i Comunitat Valenciana.* Barcelona: Generalitat de Catalunya, Departament de Vicepresidència, Secretaria de Política Lingüística.

Querol, E. and Strubell, M. (2009) *Llengua i reivindicacions nacionals a Catalunya.* Barcelona: UOC.

Querol, M. (2011) Relacions entre actituds i competències lingüístiques al final de l'Educació Secundària Obligatòria. El cas de l'alumnat d'origen immigrant a Catalunya (Unpublished doctoral dissertation). Universitat de Lleida, Lleida.

Ribes, D. (1993) Els programes d'immersió al català: Avaluació d'alguns aspectes del rendiment escolar (Unpublished doctoral dissertation). Universitat de Barcelona, Barcelona.

Secretaria de Política Lingüística (2004) *Enquesta d'usos lingüístics a la Catalunya Nord 2004. Dades sintètiques.* Barcelona: Generalitat de Catalunya. http://www20.gencat.cat/docs/ Llengcat/Documents/Dades%20origen%20territori%20i%20poblacio/Altres/Arxius/ catnord2004.pdf

Serra, J.M. (1997) *Immersió lingüística: Rendiment acadèmic i classe social.* Barcelona: Horsori.

Siguan, M. (1998) *La escuela y los inmigrantes.* Barcelona: Paidós.

Spolsky, B. (2004) *Language Policy.* Cambridge: Cambridge University Press.

Sorolla, N. (2011) *Context demogràfic i econòmic. L'evolució de la comunitat lingüística.* In M.À. Pradilla (ed.) *Informe sobre la situació de la llengua catalana (2010)* (pp. 8–38). Barcelona: Observatori de la Llengua Catalana. http://www.observatoridelallengua.cat

STEPV (Sindicat de Treballadors i Treballadores de l'Ensenyament del País Valencià) (2011) *De l'entrebanc a la involució. Informe sobre l'ensenyament en valencià STEPV 2011/ From Hindering to Involution. Report on the Education in Valencian STEPV, 2011.* València: Sindicat de Treballadors i Treballadores de l'Ensenyament del País Valencià. http://www.intersindical.org/stepv/polival/informevalencia2011.pdf

Strubell, M. and Boix-Fuster, E. (eds.) (2011) *Democratic Policies for Language Revitalisation: The Case of Catalan.* London: Palgrave.

Teixidó, M. (2009) L'ensenyament de les llengües a Catalunya. Cap a un model català romanístic amb anglès com a llengua franca. *Revista Catalana de Pedagogia* 6, 77–91.

The Instituto Nacional de Estadística (2011) *Estudio de la población española.* Madrid: Ministerio de Trabajo y Seguridad Social.

Torres, J. (coord.) Vila, F.X., Fabà, A., Bretxa, V., Natxo, N. and Pradilla, M.À. (2006) *Enquesta sobre els usos lingüístics a Andorra 2004. Llengua i societat a Andorra en els inicis del segle XXI.* Barcelona: Generalitat de Catalunya Secretaria General de Política Lingüística.

Trenchs-Parera, M. and Newman, M. (2009) Diversity of language ideologies in Spanish-speaking youth of different origins in Catalonia. *Journal of Multilingual and Multicultural Development* 30, 509–524.

Vila Mendiburu, I., Canal, I., Mayans, P., Serra, J.M. and Siqués, C. (2009a) Las aulas de acogida de la educación primaria de Catalunya el curso 2005–2006. Sus efectos sobre el conocimiento del catalán y la adaptación escolar. *Infancia y Aprendizaje* 32 (3), 307–327.

Vila Mendiburu, I., Siqués, C. and Oller, J. (2009b) Usos lingüístics de l'alumnat d'origen estranger a l'educació primària de Catalunya. *Zeitschrift für Katalanistik / Revista d'Estudis Catalans* 22, 95–124.

Vila-i-Moreno, F.X. (1996) *When Classes Are Over. Language Choice and Language Contact in Bilingual Education in Catalonia.* Brussels: Faculteit der Letteren en Wijsbegeerte. http://fxvila.files.wordpress.com/2011/07/vila-i-moreno-1996-when-classes-are-over.pdf

Vila-i-Moreno, F.X. (1998) El model de conjunció en català: Impacte sobre les normes d'ús lingüístic. In J. Arnau and J.M. Artigal (eds) *Els programes d'immersió: Una perspectiva europea. Immersion Programmes: A European Perspective* (pp. 381–390). Barcelona: Edicions Universitat de Barcelona.

Vila-i-Moreno, F.X. (2008) Catalan in Spain. In G. Extra and D. Gorter (eds) *Multilingual Europe: Facts and Policies* (pp. 157–183). Berlin: Mouton de Gruyter.

Vila-i-Moreno, F.X., Sorolla, N. and Larrea, I. (2010) *Les trajectòries lingüístiques dels joves d'origen estranger a Catalunya.* Informe per a l'Agència Catalana de la Joventut, Barcelona.

Vila-i-Moreno, F.X. and Vial, S. (2000) *Informe 'Escola i Ús'. Les pràctiques lingüístiques de l'alumnat de 2n nivell de cicle superior d'educació primària de Catalunya en situacions quasi-espontànies.* Barcelona: Generalitat de Catalunya, Departament d'Ensenyament.

Vila-i-Moreno, F.X., Vial, S. and Galindo, M. (2005) Language practices in bilingual schools: Some observed, quantitative data from Catalonia. In X.P. Rodríguez-Yáñez, A.M. Lorenzo Suárez and F. Ramallo (eds) *Bilingualism and Education: From the Family to the School* (pp. 263–273). Munich: Lincom.

Vila-i-Moreno, F.X. and Sorolla, N. Vidal. (2011) Els grups segons els usos lingüístics. In Enquesta dels usos lingüístics de la població 2008: Anàlisi. Volum 1. *Les llengües a Catalunya: Coneixements, usos, transmissió i actituds lingüístics* (pp. 136–149). Generalitat de Catalunya: Secretaria de Política Lingüística. http://www20.gencat.cat/docs/ Llengcat/Documents/Publicacions/BTPL/arxius/8_EULP_2008.pdf

2 The Acquisition of Catalan by Immigrant Children. The Effect of Length of Stay and Family Language[1]

Àngel Huguet, Jose-Luis Navarro, Silvia-Maria Chireac and Clara Sansó

During the last decade in Catalonia, linguistic, cultural, ethnic and identity heterogeneity has grown considerably. As a consequence, our schools are a setting where ethnic, religious, cultural and linguistic plurality has become increasingly evident. However, in contrast to other territories in Spain, one of the fundamental characteristics of Catalonia's education system is that it is organised on the parameters of bilingual education. Thus, apart from promoting a high degree of competence in Catalan, which is both a vehicular language and the language of instruction, a good knowledge of Spanish is also pursued. In this context, different studies make evident the key role played by a good command of the language of the school (usually Catalan in our context). This is so both in terms of academic success and when dealing with integration and social cohesion. Within this framework, levels of competence in Catalan are analysed and compared in two samples: 185 students of immigrant origin and 341 native students, all of them attending the last academic year of compulsory secondary education. According to our data, students in the latter group show a considerably higher level of competence than immigrant students. In addition, we study the effect of factors such as the 'length of stay' in the host country and the 'family language' (L1). In relation to these variables, the results obtained indicate that the process is always very long and complex, even in the case of pupils whose L1 is very close to Catalan (as is the case of pupils from Latin America whose

L1 is Spanish). From our perspective, these conclusions point to the need for serious reflection on the part of all educational agents.

Introduction

The phenomenon of migration has become one of the fundamental characteristics of the beginning of the third millennium. This circumstance, in the case of Spain, has led to a break away from a 'country of emigrants' to an 'immigrant country'. According to the Statistical Office of the European Communities (Eurostat, 2010a), during 2009, Spain has become the second state on the continent with regard to number of resident foreigners (5,651,000 in absolute figures), only surpassed by Germany (7,185,900), and well above figures for countries with a long tradition of receiving other nationalities and with a higher population, such as the United Kingdom (4,020,800), Italy (3,891,300) and France (3,737,500).

In addition, in percentages, if we exclude some small countries, unique for their sociodemographic characteristics, such as Luxembourg, Cyprus or the Baltic Republics of Estonia and Latvia, Spain is clearly in the lead among member states of the European Union with regard to the number of foreigners compared with total population. Thus, with a rate of 12.3% of foreigners, it exceeds larger countries such as Germany (8.8%), the United Kingdom (6.6%), Italy (6.5%) and France (5.8%) and also other medium-sized countries, which are normally immigration receivers, such as Austria (10.3%), Belgium (9.1%), Sweden (5.9%) and Holland (3.9%).

In any case, the real differentiating factor in comparison with any of these countries is the rapid increase of this group, which has multiplied its presence six-fold since 2000, with Spain becoming the largest receiver of immigrants in the European Union year after year (Eurostat, 2010b). The phenomenon has not had the same effect on the different regions that comprise the state, and Catalonia with 1,182,957 registered foreigners, 15.7% of its population, is the autonomous community that receives the largest number of recent arrivals (Spanish National Institute of Statistics, 2011).

Consequently, as has occurred in other Western societies (Cummins et al., 2007), family regrouping processes, births in the destination society and movements owing to political reasons or war have caused a radical transformation in our classrooms with regard to their linguistic and cultural diversity (Vertovec, 2007).

In this regard, in the specific case of Catalonia, foreign student figures have evolved spectacularly. According to data from the Catalan Department of Education (2010), at the start of the 2010/2011 academic year, the number of foreign students in non-university education represented 13.3% of the total (around 153,000 in absolute figures), while a little more than a decade ago, in the 1999/2000 academic year, the figure was only 2.1% (less than 20,000 in absolute figures).

As is well known, this new reality is far removed from the traditional bilingual differentiation of Catalan society with the presence basically of two linguistic groups: Catalan speakers and Spanish speakers. In the 1980s, this sociolinguistic configuration led to the organisation of the education system based on the parameters of bilingual education. In addition to a profound command of Catalan, the language of Catalonia and that commonly used as the vehicular and teaching language throughout the education system, an equivalent knowledge of the Spanish language, the official language of the State as a whole, was pursued. This hugely successful approach has been verified by numerous research projects (Arnau, 2003; Arnau & Vila, this volume; Huguet, 2007; Vila, 1995).

However, returning to the current situation and within the context of linguistic and cultural diversity to which we have previously referred, guaranteeing a good command of the language or languages of the receiving society is, without a doubt, one of the central objectives of schooling (Met, 2008). Aware of this fact, the teachers themselves tend to emphasise how decisive the command of the language used at the school is on the student's success or failure, and, as a result, in order to achieve this objective, considerable effort is dedicated to it. In spite of this, on numerous occasions, the results obtained do not correspond with either the expectations generated or the dedication invested (Huguet & Navarro, 2006).

It can be said that among the teachers there are prior beliefs and ideas that condition the educational response, and do not always lead to the necessary process of reflection on actual classroom practices (García & Velasco, 2011). There is, for example, a tendency to believe that immigrant children schooled in the first academic years acquire the language naturally, simply by 'immersion' in our education system, without the need for specific activities or programmes.

Either way, the diversity of languages of origin and, particularly, the different level of ability in the language of instruction of recent arrivals are probably some of the elements that cause most concern in our schools today (Arnau & Vila, this volume). In many cases, the origin of a large part of the difficulties that arise in the teaching–learning processes aimed at these pupils are attributed to this, which, in short, translates into a higher level of school failure among them in comparison to their native peers, with a higher incidence in cases of late incorporation (Navarro & Huguet, 2005, 2010).

In this regard, it is worth noting some of the contributions from Cummins (1981, 2000) when suggesting the enormous difference that exists in the skills involved in language use in informal situations (Basic Interpersonal Communicative Skills – BICS) and in formal situations (Cognitive Academic Language Proficiency – CALP). In other words, the ability to do things with the language in a face-to-face, conversational situation, where an endless number of non-linguistic signs appear that allow the meaning and sense of the speaker's linguistic productions to be accessed, is not the same as in a formal situation (e.g. in reading and writing activities) where the speaker is not present and his/her intentions can only be accessed through linguistic procedures. As is evident, in both cases the necessary skills are very different.

However, returning to the subject of school results among immigrant students, and focusing on the Catalan context, we should point out that unfortunately the general conclusions do not differ substantially from what occurs in other countries with more tradition in studies on school performance and immigration (Huguet & Navarro, 2006).

A short review of some research carried out at the different stages of compulsory education provides conclusive data. With regard to preschool education (three to six years of age), we refer to the study by Vila (2008) in which the author analyses the effects of schooling at this educational stage in relation to the acquisition of the school's language (Catalan). The study, carried out in 50 educational centres around Catalonia, comparatively analysed the process of acquisition of the Catalan language by 567 native schoolchildren and 434 immigrants (including L1 speakers of Arabic, Soninke and Spanish). The most important conclusion is that, regardless of the language of origin, at the end of this educational stage, the native student obtained significantly better results compared with the pupils of immigrant origin.

In primary education (7–12 years of age), we refer to the research by Oller and Vila (2008), which evaluated the knowledge of Catalan among immigrant students. In this case, the study was carried out in 47 schools, with pupils from the final year of this educational stage: 626 natives (267 Catalan speakers, 298 Spanish speakers and 61 bilingual Catalan–Spanish speakers) and 486 immigrants, speakers of 27 different languages. In general, the results show that when analysing knowledge of the Catalan language, immigrant students never reach the same level as their native peers whose L1 is Catalan, and only those whose L1 is a Romance language are able to reach similar levels as their native peers whose L1 is Spanish, but after a minimum of six years living in Catalonia.

Finally, with regard to compulsory secondary education (13–16 years of age), we can cite the work by Navarro and Huguet (2010), carried out in a single school on a sample of 121 students (93 natives and 28 immigrants). Among the native students there were three common linguistic groupings with regard to the L1 in Catalonia: Catalan speakers, Spanish speakers and bilingual speakers; and among the immigrants there were speakers of Romanian, Ukrainian, Bulgarian, Arabic, Spanish, Portuguese and Wolof. The study assessed the knowledge of Catalan and Spanish of all the students, again showing significantly poorer results in both languages for immigrant students compared with their native peers.

Certainly, the data obtained in the research described is coherent with that carried out in Spain in other contexts different from Catalonia (Huguet *et al.*, 2012), and also with results of international reports such as the Programme for International Student Assessment (PISA) (Organisation for Economic Cooperation and Development, 2010), indicating that difficulties in language use condition the results of curricular learning and content, translating into school failure, which particularly affects students that have recently arrived in our schools.

The students' 'length of stay' and 'family language' (L1) are possibly two of the most researched variables for explaining the conclusions of these studies and research projects (Jarvis & Pavlenko, 2008). With regard to the first, based on an analysis of research carried out in contexts with a longer tradition in the reception of immigrant students, mainly developed in the English-speaking environment, Cummins (2000) is clear:

> Research studies since the early 1980s have shown that immigrant students can quickly acquire considerable fluency in the dominant language of the society when they are exposed to it in the environment and at school. However, despite this rapid growth in conversational fluency, it generally takes a minimum of about five years (and frequently much longer) for them to catch up to native-speakers in academic aspects of the language. (Cummins, 2000: 34)

With regard to this, within our context, we should mention the pioneering study by Maruny and Molina (2000), carried out in the Catalan region of the Baix Empordà (Girona). This research, based on an interview situation, analysed the process of acquisition of Catalan by a group of students originally from Morocco, educated from third year of primary education to fourth year of secondary education, who were selected according to the amount of time they had lived in Catalonia (less than 18 months, 18 to 36 months and over 36 months). The results of the research show that at least three years are necessary for a sufficient conversational ability in the language of the school to be developed, five years for an acceptable reading comprehension and even more time with regard to writing and other skills that guarantee school success (none of the sample subjects reached an adequate level).

Also, more recently, Huguet *et al.* (2011) have emphasised the same question, analysing the influence of length of stay on the acquisition of the languages of the school (Catalan and Spanish). From a sample of 93 native students and 28 immigrants in secondary education, a lower degree of linguistic knowledge is registered in both languages among immigrants in comparison with their native peers of the same age and school level. These differences are significant when referring to those who have been in Catalonia for less than three years, and they continue to register far from negligible values even for those who have exceeded three years of stay (in fact, after three years in Catalonia the differences obtained with regard to both Catalan and Spanish range between 1.5 and 2 standard deviations). In other words, after three years of residence and schooling, immigrant students continue to show difficulties in accessing the languages of the school in relation to the average of their native peers.

As we have previously stated, in addition to 'length of stay', another variable that appears to be significant with regard to the level of linguistic development reached in the language of instruction for immigrant students is that of 'family language' (L1). Although still scarce, over the last few years some research contextualised in Catalonia has appeared that has a bearing on this matter. The work by Vila *et al.* (2009) examines the results of immigrant students who attend 'reception classrooms' created by the Catalan Department of Education in 2004. The sample included the group of students who attended all classes of this type provided during the 2005/2006 academic year.

Among the most relevant conclusions reached is the fact that one of the most significant factors in the explanation of knowledge of the Catalan language acquired was the L1 of the student under study. Specifically, it showed that students whose L1 was a Romance language found it easier to learn Catalan, compared with their peers of other linguistic origins (particularly Asian and specifically those whose L1 was Mandarin Chinese). In any case, the level of school adaptation was a catalyst in the explanation of the results. Arnau (2004) reached similar conclusions, stating that students of Asian origin, in general, had to overcome more obstacles than those whose L1 is an Indo-European language.

Later, Oller and Vila (2011) focused on the end of primary education and worked with a sample of immigrant pupils whose L1s were Arabic (131 subjects), Romanian (44 subjects) and Spanish (221 subjects). In this study, as well as analysing the relationship of interdependency between Catalan and Spanish, which changes in relation to oral and written language, the authors pointed out that the results were modulated by the sociolinguistic environment (Catalan or Spanish), the length of stay and the L1. Specifically, the Arabic-speaking students obtained the lowest results in both Catalan and Spanish when compared with the other linguistic groups,[2] which is attributed to the different level of education of their families compared with the other groups analysed, as well as to matters regarding the lack of possibilities to formalise their L1 and to use it for academic purposes.

Obviously, when explaining the ability achieved in the school's languages, referring to the two variables we have used does not suffice. In this regard, attitudes towards the languages present have also been explored by researchers. The work by Huguet *et al.* (2008) goes into more depth with regard to this question, describing and analysing attitudes towards Catalan and Spanish in a sample of 225 students of immigrant origin schooled in different places around Catalonia. The results obtained, as a whole, show positive attitudes towards both Catalan and Spanish. However, this affirmation was explained in the sense that linguistic origin clearly determined the attitudes manifested: the most relevant differences were noted among students from Latin America, whose L1 is Spanish, as they showed more positive attitudes towards Spanish and less favourable ones towards Catalan.

In further research on the previous study, Lapresta *et al.* (2010) went on to analyse the discourses on which linguistic attitudes are founded in some of the students of the sample. The most relevant conclusions showed that, beyond the area of origin and the L1, the variable that best enabled the discourses detected to be articulated could be termed as 'satisfaction and perception of school and social valuation and integration', such that the pupils of immigrant origin who feel most valued and integrated on a social and school level develop the best attitudes towards the Catalan and Spanish languages. Obviously, this circumstance should have clear repercussions with regard to the generalisations that link a certain area of origin with the correct attitudes towards the official languages of Catalonia, as well as towards the linguistic policy to follow and the linguistic ideologies of society in general.

With this background framework and focusing on the end of compulsory secondary education (16 years of age), the main objective of our research is to study the process of acquisition of the Catalan language by immigrant students educated in Catalonia. As determining factors of the process we consider some of the variables that have proven to be particularly significant in previous studies: length of stay and family language.

Method

Variables

According to the methodology commonly used in this type of study, we will provide a brief description of the different controlled variables (independent variables) and their respective categories.

- *Origin*, which includes two categories:
  - ○ Native students.
  - ○ Immigrant students.
- *Length of stay in Catalonia*: According to the methodology applied in previous studies (Huguet *et al.*, 2011, 2012; Maruny & Molina, 2000; Navarro & Huguet, 2005, 2010), and for purposes of a better handling of data, we have differentiated three categories of the variable:
  - ○ Less than three years.
  - ○ From three to six years.
  - ○ More than six years.

- *Family language (L1):* This variable allows us to control for the language that the immigrant student uses in the home environment, differentiating between some of the most numerous linguistic groups in Catalonia:
  - Spanish.
  - Arabic.
  - Romanian.
  - Chinese.
  - Others.

As is well known, in addition to the variables mentioned above, the social-professional level of families is another of the classic variables to consider when analysing the development of linguistic abilities. However, unlike the case of the native students, the level of occupation of immigrants does not tend to coincide with their cultural status, and as a result the *level of education of the families* is probably a more suitable variable for assessing the incidence of the family context regarding the linguistic progress of the students (Huguet *et al.*, 2011, 2012; Navarro & Huguet, 2005, 2010). Based on this, the following categories were established for this variable:

- University education.
- Secondary education.
- Primary education or lower.

Finally, our dependent variable is linguistic competence in the Catalan language, the numeric values of which are obtained from the instruments described in the corresponding section.

Participants

With regard to the sample of participants in the study, our objective was to ensure that this was representative of the different geographic origins of the immigrant student body in compulsory secondary education in Catalan schools. Therefore, using data provided by the Department of Education for the 2006/2007 school year as reference, we worked with the following groups: European Union (EU 25); Rest of Europe, which at that time included Bulgaria and Romania; the Maghreb; Rest of Africa; Latin America; Rest of America; Asia and Oceania.

Based on this, students studying the last year of compulsory secondary education in 10 public centres were selected: four in the region of Barcelona and two in each of the other Catalan regions (Tarragona, Lleida and Girona). According to this method, once those who did not meet the criteria for some of the sections of the test were excluded, such as immigrant students who had joined late and who had not been schooled in their country of origin or who had lived in Catalonia for less than a year, the resulting sample

Table 2.1 Distribution of sample of immigrants according to 'family language' (L1)

Family language (L1)	n
Spanish (Latin American varieties)	114
Arabic	40
Romanian	17
Chinese	14
Other languages (23)	77
Total	262

Table 2.2 The most numerous linguistic groups in the sample (Spanish, Arabic, Romanian and Chinese) according to variables 'family language' (L1) and 'length of stay' (number of subjects and percentage with regard to their linguistic group in brackets)

Linguistic group	Less than 3 years	From 3 to 6 years	More than 6 years	Total
Spanish (Latin American varieties)	44 (38.60%)	44 (38.60%)	26 (22.80%)	114 (100%)
Arabic	9 (22.50%)	11 (27.50%)	20 (50.00%)	40 (100%)
Romanian	8 (47.06%)	8 (47.06%)	1 (5.88%)	17 (100%)
Chinese	4 (28.58%)	5 (35.71%)	5 (35.71%)	14 (100%)
Total	65 (35.14%)	68 (36.76%)	52 (28.11%)	185 (100%)

Note: There are significant differences among these linguistic groups according to 'length of stay' (Chi-square = 15.834; $p = 0.0147$).

comprised 262 immigrant students and 341 native students, who attended the same reference classrooms as the former.

The distribution of the immigrants, considering their L1, is as shown in Table 2.1.

As can be seen in Table 2.1, the largest linguistic groups were Spanish, Arabic, Romanian and Chinese, with a total of 185 students and which are some of the languages most present in Catalan schools (in the sample 27 different languages were detected, the majority barely represented, which makes their statistical handling difficult and which were not considered in the final study).

Furthermore, given that in addition we were interested in analysing the results obtained by these groups according to length of stay in Catalonia, we distributed the aforementioned corresponding categories according to this variable: less than three years, from three to six years, and more than six years.

This data is shown in Table 2.2.

Materials

Basically, two types of instrument were used: the first, a questionnaire used in previous research (Huguet *et al.*, 2011, 2012; Navarro & Huguet,

2005, 2010), enabled the independent variables to be controlled for, while the second, a language test, allowed us to examine the linguistic skills in Catalan (dependent variable) of the students in the sample.

For this assessment of the linguistic knowledge of Catalan we used a widely recognised test (Huguet, 2008; Huguet *et al.*, 2011, 2012), which was prepared based on studies by Bel *et al.* (1991). This test analyses the following aspects: oral comprehension (OC), morphosyntax (MS), orthography (ORT), written comprehension (WC), written expression (WE), oral expression lexico-morphosyntax (LMS), oral expression information organisation (IO), phonetics (PhO), reading correctness (R-C) and reading intonation (R-I).

Each of the sections has a scoring that ranges from 0 to 100 points according to the number of correct or incorrect answers.

In its application, the test comprises two parts: a group test, which is carried out with the use of a response booklet and includes all of the written tests (OC, MS, ORT, WC, WE); and an individual test, which corresponds to the oral tests (LMS, IO, PhO, R-C, R-I) and is carried out with the help of specific materials for the oral part.

A time limit is applied to each of the sub-tests, and, with regard to the scoring, as well as that for each sub-test, two additional indices are obtained: SC1, which corresponds with the average of the five written sub-tests, and SC2, which is taken from the average of the five oral sub-tests and the five written ones.

The time used for the group and individual parts, respectively, was 75 and 20 minutes (in the latter case for each one of the tested participants).

Procedure

Once the objectives of the study had been extensively explained to them, the education authorities themselves guided us in the selection of the 10 secondary education centres considered to be ideal for our research. Based on this, we approached the authorities of each centre in order to clarify the content of the research and the phases it would involve.

The instruments described in the previous section were applied during the final term of the school year, under the responsibility of specialised personnel with a perfect knowledge of the tests and trained for this purpose. At all times the anonymity of the students was maintained and the confidentiality of the data obtained was guaranteed.

The collective part of the test on linguistic knowledge was applied to all of the native and immigrant students. With regard to the individual tests, they were given to all of the immigrant students and to a sub-sample of native students selected at random (approximately 25%).

Once the different tests had been given, they were corrected and the resulting numerical data was introduced into a statistics package for their corresponding analysis.

Table 2.3 Academic level of the families involved in the research (absolute data and percentages)

Origin	University	Secondary	Primary or less	Total
Native	118 (34.6%)	144 (42.2%)	72 (23.2%)	341
Immigrant	97 (37.0%)	119 (45.4%)	46 (17.6%)	262
Total	215	263	125	603

Data handling

In accordance with the quantitative nature of the data obtained, fundamentally analysis of variance (ANOVA) descriptive statistics and Scheffé's comparison of means method were used. While ANOVA allows the effects of the independent variables to be verified in the explanation of the differences found in the dependent variable, the Scheffé method helped us to specify these differences when the result of the variance analysis was significant.

Furthermore, the handling of the statistics was performed with the help of the Statview for Windows package, version 5.0.1, and the level of significance used was 0.05.

We should point out that, in order to check the level of coherence between the native and immigrant families with regard to their academic education[3] an analysis was carried out using the chi-square test, which allowed us to rule out differences between the groups: $\chi^2 = 2.838$ ($p = 0.2419$). Table 2.3 shows the level of studies of the families involved in the research, which was determined using the parent with the highest level as reference.

Results

We will begin this section presenting a comparison of the overall data corresponding to the knowledge of Catalan obtained from the four linguistic groups of the selected immigrants, considered as a whole ($n = 185$), in relation to the native students ($n = 341$). Subsequently, we will analyse the incidence of the 'length of stay' and 'family language' (L1) variables in more detail for the immigrant students of the above-mentioned linguistic groups: Spanish, Arabic, Romanian and Chinese.

Knowledge of the Catalan language: Native pupils versus immigrant pupils

To tackle this matter, an analysis was made of the variance comparing the results of native and immigrant students with regard to the different abilities assessed and the global SC1 and SC2 indices.

Table 2.4 Comparison of average Catalan scores and standard deviations obtained by the whole language groups of immigrants selected (Spanish, Arabic, Romanian and Chinese) and native students in sub-tests (OC, MS, ORT, WC, WE, LMS, OI, PhO, R-C, R-I) and global indices SC1 and SC2. Level of significance in each particular case

| | Immigrants (n = 185) | | Native (n = 341) | | | |
	Mean	SD	Mean	SD	F value	P value
OC	64.031	24.449	83.811	14.464	135.748	<0.0001
MS	44.349	25.492	79.616	15.836	381.622	<0.0001
ORT	69.110	21.668	87.148	15.002	125.515	<0.0001
WC	56.875	23.756	82.105	12.681	252.382	<0.0001
WE	71.330	29.340	89.182	12.078	96.293	<0.0001
SC1	61.139	21.004	84.372	10.207	290.175	<0.0001
LMS	61.803	19.042	81.364	10.834	81.172	<0.0001
IO	46.798	24.610	51.236	19.126	2.241	=0.1356
PhO	71.380	13.502	85.378	8.173	81.229	<0.0001
R-C	31.203	29.439	66.910	25.855	95.464	<0.0001
R-I	28.095	31.432	51.292	34.141	30.928	<0.0001
SC2	54.498	17.902	75.302	10.748	102.330	0.0001

Table 2.4 presents this data, together with its level of significance.

As can be seen, the scoring is notably lower in the case of immigrant students for all of the sub-tests and indices. In addition, the comparisons are significant in the majority of cases.

As we would expect, the above results translate into the derived indices from which we obtain values of $F_{1,524} = 290.175$ ($p \leq 0.0001$) for SC1 and $F_{1,272} = 102.330$ ($p \leq 0.0001$) for SC2. This data demonstrates that the immigrant students belonging to the selected groups have a substantially lower level of Catalan when compared with native students. In addition, the dispersal of the results is greater in the case of immigrants, as shown by the standard deviations obtained in each case, which determine a greater variability between them compared with a greater consistency among native students.

Length of stay in Catalonia and development of Catalan language skills

As can been seen when reviewing existing studies on the subject, in relation to the length of time in the receiving country there is a certain level of unanimity among researchers in that a long period of time is necessary for immigrant children to be able to use the language of the school in education and learning activities on an equal level with native students.

In order to better clarify the subject, considering the period of residency in Catalonia (less than three years, from three to six years, and more than

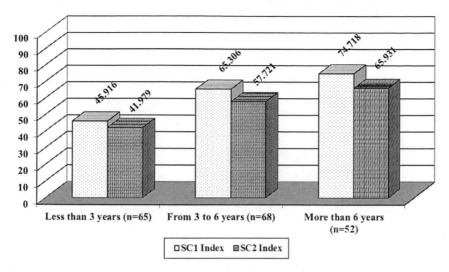

Figure 2.1 Average Catalan scores in SC1 and SC2 indices according to 'length of stay' (mean of the selected language groups: Spanish, Arabic, Romanian and Chinese)

six years), we decided to establish sub-groups of immigrant students for the four selected linguistic groups ($n = 185$).

Figure 2.1 shows the measures obtained in the indices SC1 and SC2 considering this categorisation of the variable.

As can be seen, considering all of the four groups of immigrants selected, those that arrived more than six years ago obtained higher averages than those who arrived between three and six years ago, and these obtained higher averages than those who arrived less than three years ago.

This translates into the derived indices from which we obtain values of $F_{2,182} = 42.242$ ($p \leq 0.0001$) for SC1 and $F_{2,182} = 39.001$ ($p \leq 0.0001$) for SC2.

In addition, significant differences can be found in the contrasts of all of the SC1 categories: '–3 years vs. 3–6 years' [$F_{2,182} = 42.242$ ($p < 0.0001$)], '–3 years vs. +6 years' [$F_{2,182} = 42.242$ ($p < 0.0001$)], and '3–6 years vs. +6 years' [$F_{2,182} = 42.242$ ($p = 0.0039$)]. The same occurs for SC2: '–3 years vs. 3–6 years' [$F_{2,182} = 42.242$ ($p < 0.0001$)], '–3 years vs. +6 years' [$F_{2,182} = 42.242$ ($p < 0.0001$)], and '3–6 years vs. +6 years' [$F_{2,182} = 42.242$ ($p = 0.0035$)].

Family language (L1) and development of Catalan language skills

With regard to the L1 of the immigrant students, in order to carry out a more suitable statistic analysis, we opted to focus our attention on the most representative linguistic groups of the sample: Spanish, Arabic, Romanian

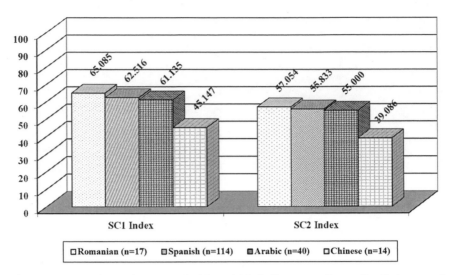

Figure 2.2 Average Catalan scores in SC1 and SC2 indices according to 'family language' (selected linguistics groups: Spanish, Arabic, Romanian and Chinese)

and Chinese (coinciding broadly speaking with the languages most common in Catalonia among the immigrant population).

Figure 2.2 shows the measures obtained in the indices SC1 and SC2 for students corresponding to each one of these groups.

As a whole, while the averages for the Romanian, Spanish and Arabic groups are fairly similar, they are much more distant from the case of the Chinese speakers.

Consequently, the analysis of results shows that there are significant differences with respect to SC1, with a value of $F_{3,181} = 3.165$ ($p = 0.0258$), and with respect to SC2, with a value of $F_{3,181} = 3.980$ ($p = 0.0089$). In all cases, the most specific differences are found in SC1, but only in the case of Chinese speakers with respect to the other languages: 'Arabic vs. Chinese' [$F_{3,181} = 3.165$ ($p = 0.0137$)], 'Spanish vs. Chinese' [$F_{3,181} = 3.165$ ($p = 0.0034$)] and 'Romanian vs. Chinese' [$F_{3,181} = 3.165$ ($p = 0.0082$)]. The same occurs for SC2: 'Arabic vs. Chinese' [$F_{3,181} = 3.165$ ($p = 0.0038$)], 'Spanish vs. Chinese' [$F_{3,181} = 3.165$ ($p = 0.0009$)] and 'Romanian vs. Chinese' [$F_{3,181} = 3.165$ ($p = 0.0049$)].

Interaction between 'length of stay' and 'family language' (L1) in the explanation of the development of Catalan language skills

Thus far we have presented the results on the incidence of the variables 'length of stay' and 'family language' (L1) in the development of Catalan language skills individually. In this section we will show its evolution according to the combined action of the two variables.

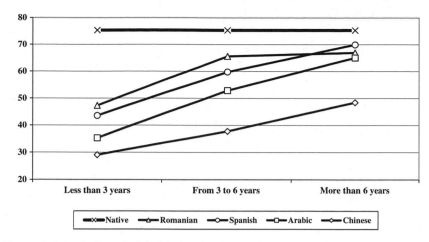

Figure 2.3 Evolution of global index (SC2) according to 'length of stay' and 'family language'. Selected language groups of immigrants (Spanish, Arabic, Romanian and Chinese) are presented in contrast with native students. Average scores in each particular case appear as additional data

	Native	Romanian	Spanish	Arabic	Chinese
Less than 3 years	75.302	47.275	43.558	35.291	29.060
From 3 to 6 years	75.302	65.597	59.772	52.858	37.770
More than 6 years	75.302	66.945	69.938	65.047	48.423

Figure 2.3 shows the averages obtained by each one of the linguistic groups in the more global index (SC2), but also considering the progress obtained owing to the years of residency and schooling in Catalonia.

As can be seen, in general, and independently of the linguistic group, considerable progress is connected to the 'length of stay' variable. However, the contrast with native students shows that only after a length of stay of over six years do the scores become close to those obtained by the native students, and from this statement we must exclude the Chinese speakers.

Furthermore, except for the aforementioned case of the Chinese, this occurs with the rest of the languages analysed, be they typologically 'closer' languages (Spanish or Romanian) or more 'distant' (such as the case of Arabic).

The analysis of the interaction between the variables 'length of stay' and 'family language' (L1) confirms this statement: again independently each one is significant in the explanation of the results on Catalan language skills, $F_{3,173} = 8.807$ ($p < 0.0001$) in the case of 'family language', and $F_{2,173} = 15.995$ ($p < 0.0001$) in the case of 'length of stay', but the same cannot be said for their combined action, obtaining a value of $F_{6,173} = 0.248$ ($p = 0.9595$).

In other words, our data appears to indicate that speakers of each one of the languages progress in the knowledge of the Catalan language during their residency and schooling in Catalonia, and this is independent of the linguistic group they belong to, although the L1 seems to influence the speed and intensity of the process towards the target language.

Discussion

At the beginning of this section we should point out that the data presented here must be handled with maximum caution, as it is taken from the analysis of partial variables that are unlikely to cover the reality of the whole.

With the limitations derived from the previous paragraph, we are able to confirm that in our research the linguistic knowledge of Catalan by immigrant students belonging to the language groups selected is, as a whole, below that shown by their native peers, with these differences being statistically significant. This circumstance is not at all new, and our results fall in line with conclusions suggested by previous studies carried out in other regions of Spain (Huguet *et al.*, 2012), and in international reports (Organisation for Economic Cooperation and Development, 2010). It appears obvious that the complete development of skills in an L2 by immigrant students is a long and complex process (Cummins, 2000), from which recent arrivals to Catalonia are not exempt (Huguet *et al.*, 2011; Navarro & Huguet, 2010; Oller & Vila, 2008; Vila, 2008).

As expected, these difficulties in the use of language condition their results in learning and school content as a whole, and this translates into higher levels of school failure in comparison to their native peers (Huguet & Navarro, 2006).

On the other hand, our data reveal how the length of stay variable in a receiving country influences linguistic development in the languages present in the new society (an aspect that coincides with research recently carried out in Catalonia: Huguet *et al.*, 2011; Oller & Vila, 2011). The fact that immigrant students need more than six years of residency and schooling in the receiving country to reach the levels of scoring obtained by their native peers should make us rethink certain beliefs in this regard, and particularly in terms of the long periods necessary to obtain those skills that Cummins (1981, 2000) refers to as cognitive-academic, which allow for the use of a more formal and decontextualised language, compared with the conversational-type skills marked by the presence of a speaker who provides non-linguistic signs that enable the meaning and sense to be understood in informal face-to-face situations.

We must point out that this previous statement also affects the large Spanish-speaking group, despite the typological closeness of their L1 to Catalan. As we have seen, their knowledge of the Catalan language is not far off that shown by other non-Spanish speaking groups, with the exception of those whose L1 is Chinese. In other words, the argument of linguistic 'proximity' between the language of origin and the target language does not explain alone, or in all of the cases, the levels of linguistic competence achieved (as we have seen, Spanish speakers have significantly higher results compared with the Chinese group, but not in comparison to the Arab or Romanian groups, although the latter is a closer Romance language).

In this sense, research exists in our context that confirms the difficulties that a student whose L1 is Chinese faces (Arnau, 2004), and we also have other contributions that suggest that the speakers of languages that are typologically very distant from Catalan could present difficulties comparable with other 'closer' groups from a linguistic point of view, although the L1 plays a fundamental role, and part of the errors produced tend to come from the structure of the first language (Chireac *et al.*, 2011). In addition, the results finally obtained appear to be modulated by the sociolinguistic environment in which the student is integrated, according to whether the dominant language in the context is Catalan or Spanish (Oller & Vila, 2011).

On the other hand, the analysis of the data from our research with regard to the interaction of the 'length of stay' and 'family language' (L1) variables appears to indicate that speakers of each of the four languages on which we have focused, progress in their knowledge of the Catalan language during their residency and schooling in Catalonia, and this is independent of the language group they belong to, although the L1 appears to influence the speed and intensity of access to the target language.[4]

Before we conclude we would like to once again take up the discussion regarding the Latin American group of origin, and we should point out the logical interest that it has caused among researchers, both for its size and also for the fact that its L1 coincides with one of the official languages of Catalonia. The study by Huguet *et al.* (2008) reveals that in comparison to other linguistic groups it shows the most positive attitude towards Spanish and the least favourable one towards Catalan. One conclusion that was explained in a continuation of the same study (Lapresta *et al.*, 2010) was that the subjects' satisfaction and perception of their valuation by and integration into the school and society is more consistent than the area of origin or the linguistic group in the determination of attitudes or identities adopted.

These and other questions that have not been covered in this research should be taken into account when analysing educational practices and teaching–learning processes that affect the students of different linguistic origins, and at the same time we should make an effort to include them in the reflections on the current educational training of teachers (Arnau & Vila, this volume). In this regard, beyond the quantitative data we have contributed in our study, we consider more qualitative and in-depth research to be necessary, focusing on the analysis of educational practices developed with immigrant students. With this we would like to emphasise the current interest in the study of the same and of interaction in the classroom, a focus motivated by the growing importance given to the classroom context, owing to the increasingly greater acceptance of sociocultural approaches, and to the crisis of the model that establishes a hierarchical and one-way epistemological relationship between academic research and professional practice.

Notes

(1) This work is part of a larger research project funded by the Spanish Ministry of Science and Innovation, with project number EDU2009-08669EDUC.
(2) As is to be expected, the Latin-American students obtained better results in Spanish and the Romanians in Catalan. This last piece of data is consistent with previous studies carried out with Romanian language students in Catalonia (Chireac *et al.*, 2011).
(3) Among the four linguistics groups of immigrants selected, a similar procedure was followed in order to compare the level of consistency of the families in relation to their education. The analysis, carried out using the chi-square test, showed significant differences [$\chi^2 = 25.348$ ($p = 0.0003$)], with the Romanian and Spanish language groups being placed above the Chinese and Arabic groups with regard to levels of studies obtained.
(4) In this sense, even taking into account the education of the families according to the linguistic groups, the Chinese language group seems to be the one that encounters the most difficulties. Thus, although a lower level of studies among the families of Chinese origin could be related to less progress in the acquisition of the Catalan language, this situation does not occur in parallel among the Arab language group, despite sharing a similar level of academic training.

References

Arnau, J. (2003) Llengües i educació a Catalunya: Valoració de l'experiència realitzada i perspectives de futur. In J. Parera (ed.) *Plurilingüisme i educació. Els reptes del segle XXI* (pp. 115–137). Barcelona: ICE de la Universitat de Barcelona.

Arnau, J. (2004) El aprendizaje de la L1 y la L2: relaciones e implicaciones para la política y práctica educativas. In Á. Huguet and J.L. Navarro (coords.) *Las lenguas en la escuela* (pp. 35–45). Huesca: Gobierno de Aragón.

Bel, A., Serra, J.M. and Vila, I. (1991) *El coneixement de llengua catalana i castellana en acabar l'ensenyament obligatori el 1990*. Unpublished manuscript. Barcelona: Departament d'Ensenyament-SEDEC.

Catalan Department of Education (2010) *Dades de l'inici del curs 2010-2011. Dossier de premsa*. Barcelona: Generalitat de Catalunya.

Chireac, S.-M., Serrat, E. and Huguet, À. (2011) Transferencia en la adquisición de segundas lenguas. Un estudio con alumnado rumano en un contexto bilingüe. *Revista de Psicodidáctica* 16 (2), 267–289.

Cummins J. (1981) The role of primary language development in promoting educational success for language minority students. In California State Department of Education (ed.) *Schooling and Language Minority Students: A Theoretical Framework* (pp. 3–50). Los Angeles, CA: Evaluation, Dissemination and Assessment Center – California State University.

Cummins, J. (2000) *Language, Power and Pedagogy: Bilingual Children in the Crossfire*. Clevedon: Multilingual Matters.

Cummins, J., Brown, K. and Sayers, D. (2007) *Literacy, Technology, and Diversity*. Boston: Pearson Education Inc.

Eurostat (2010a) Population of foreign citizens in the EU27 in 2009. *News release* 129/2010. Online at http://epp.eurostat.ec.europa.eu/cache/ITY_PUBLIC/3-07092010-AP/EN/3-07092010-AP-EN.PDF

Eurostat (2010b) *Eurostat Yearbook*. Luxembourg: Office for Official Publications of the European Communities. Online at http://epp.eurostat.ec.europa.eu/portal/page/portal/product_details/publication?p_product_code=KS-CD-10-220

Garcia, O. and Velasco, P. (2011) Observando, colaborando y describiendo: Devolviéndole el poder a los docentes bilingües. In A-M. de Mejia and C. Hélot. (eds) *Empowering Teachers across Cultures. Enfoques críticos. Perspectives croisées.* (pp. 29–44). Frankfurt am Main: Peter Lang.

Huguet, À. (2007) Minority languages and curriculum. The case of Spain. *Language, Culture & Curriculum* 20 (1), 70–86.

Huguet, À. (2008) Interdependencia lingüística y práctica educativa. Un estudio con escolares de origen inmigrante. *Infancia y Aprendizaje* 31 (3), 283–301.

Huguet, À. and Navarro, J.L. (2006) Inmigración y resultados escolares: Lo que dice la investigación. *Cultura y Educación* 18 (2), 117–126.

Huguet, À., Chireac, S-M., Navarro, J.L. and Sansó, C. (2011) Tiempo de estancia y aprendizajes lingüísticos. El caso de los escolares inmigrantes en Cataluña. *Cultura y Educación* 23 (3), 355–370.

Huguet, À., Janés, J. and Chireac, S.M. (2008) Mother tongue as a determining variable in language attitudes. The case of immigrant Latin American students in Spain. *Language and Intercultural Communication* 8 (4), 246–260.

Huguet, À., Navarro, J.L., Chireac, S-M. and Sansó, C. (2012) Immigrant children and access to school language. A comparative study between Latin American and non-Latin American students in Spain. *VIAL – Vigo International Journal of Applied Linguistics* 9, 85–106.

Jarvis, S. and Pavlenko, A. (2008) *Crosslinguistic Influence in Language and Cognition.* New York: Routledge.

Lapresta, C., Huguet, À. and Janés, J. (2010) Análisis discursivo de las actitudes lingüísticas de los escolares de origen inmigrante en Cataluña. *Revista de Educación* 353, 521–547.

Maruny, L. and Molina, M. (2000) Adquisició del català i competència comunicativa en alumnes d'origen marroquí a l'ensenyament obligatori. Unpublished research report. Barcelona: Fundació Jaume Bofill.

Met, M. (2008) Paying attention to language: Literacy, language and academic achievement. In T.W. Fortune and D.J. Tedick (eds) *Pathways to Multilingualism. Evolving Perspectives on Immersion Education.* (pp. 49–70). Clevedon: Multilingual Matters.

Navarro, J.L. and Huguet, À. (2005) *El conocimiento de la lengua castellana en alumnado inmigrante escolarizado en 1° de ESO. Un estudio empírico.* Madrid: MEC-CIDE.

Navarro, J.L. and Huguet, À. (2010) Conocimiento del catalán y castellano por parte del alumnado inmigrante. *Revista de Educación* 352, 245–265.

Oller, J. and Vila, I. (2008) El conocimiento del catalán y el castellano del alumnado de origen extranjero, tiempo de estancia en Cataluña y lengua inicial al finalizar la enseñanza primaria. *Segundas lenguas e inmigración en red* 1, 10–24. Online at http://letra25.com/ediciones/2Li/2li-1/

Oller, J. and Vila, I. (2011) Interdependencia entre conocimiento de catalán y castellano y efectos de la lengua familiar en la adquisición de las lenguas escolares. *Cultura y Educación* 23 (1), 3–22.

Organisation for Economic Cooperation and Development (2010) *Programme for International Students Assessment – PISA 2009.* Online at http://www.pisa.oecd.org/

Spanish National Institute of Statistics (2011) *Avance del Padrón municipal a 1 de enero de 2011.* Notas de prensa, 4 de abril de 2011. Online at http://www.ine.es/prensa/np648.pdf

Vertovec, S. (2007) Super-diversity and its implications. *Ethnic and Racial Studies* 30 (6), 1024–1054.

Vila, I. (1995) *El català i el castellà en el Sistema Educatiu de Catalunya*. Barcelona: Horsori.

Vila, I. (2008) Lengua familiar y conocimiento de la lengua escolar en Cataluña al finalizar la educación infantil. *Revista de Educación* 346, 401–424.

Vila, I., Canal, I., Mayans, P., Perera, S., Serra, J.M. and Siqués, S. (2009) Las aulas de acogida de la educación primaria de Cataluña el curso 2005–2006: Sus efectos sobre el conocimiento de catalán y la adaptación escolar. *Infancia y Aprendizaje* 32 (3), 307–327.

3 Language Attitudes of Latin-American Newcomers in Three Secondary School Reception Classes in Catalonia

Mireia Trenchs-Parera and Adriana Patiño-Santos

This chapter presents a qualitative study on the language attitudes of secondary school students of Latin-American backgrounds in three Reception Classes in Catalonia, the classes aimed at welcoming newcomers into the school system and at facilitating their learning Catalan, both as the language of school and of social relations. Participant observation and interviews with students and teachers involved in the reception process have allowed us to observe that the implementation of reception policies vary depending on social and educational contexts, as well as on individual factors. We found out that teachers have to face various challenges in their job, such as the predominantly Spanish linguistic practices in the neighbourhood, the continual arrival of newcomers throughout the school year, the weight of ideologies in favour of international languages and the pedagogical ideologies of the staff. Besides, students' positive attitudes towards Catalan seem to be related to their first experiences with the language at school, as well as their future expectations of continuing formal education in Catalonia.

Introduction

The purpose of this chapter is to present the results of a qualitative study on the language attitudes of young Latin-American newcomers in three secondary-school Reception Classes (RC), the main resource offered by the

Administration in Catalonia in order to welcome multicultural diversity in schools and to promote social integration in a multilingual society.[1] To do so, we have focused on three schools that have similar intakes in terms of ethnic origin and socio-economic status. We have chosen to investigate those attitudes in relation to the daily educational reception practices that teachers bring into play.

Even though Catalan society is officially bilingual (Catalan/Spanish) and inhabitants of all ages are able to practice everyday bilingualism, government policies have chosen Catalan, the non-international language, as that of schooling and as the means to promote young newcomers' integration. This choice brings consequences for practices within such institutional settings as schools, since educational agents – both teachers and students – have to deal, among other challenges, with the teaching of Catalan in the context of an extended use of Spanish among both autochthonous and immigrant students (Boix, 1993; Galindo I Solé, 2008; Marshall 2006, 2007; Vila-i-Moreno et al., 2004).

Our interest in language attitudes springs from the fact that, as Garrett puts it:

> Language attitudes and the socio-cultural norms they relate to are an integral part of our [in the present study, young newcomers'] communicative competence (Hymes, 1971), so in terms of our everyday use of language, language attitudes would be expected not only to influence our reactions to other language users around us, but also to help us anticipate others' responses to our own language use and so influence the language choices that we make as we communicate. (Garrett, 2010: 21)

Attitudes are developed and transformed in socialisation processes, and it is in such processes that they should be studied if the language is seen as a means for social integration in multilingual contexts.

Thus, we became interested in investigating the pedagogical reception strategies implemented in Catalan schools and, more specifically, their RCs, as the first – and often only – socialising spaces where youths of Latin-American Spanish-speaking backgrounds may be in contact with Catalan in all (formal and informal) its registers. The RC and their teachers, therefore, become important – though not exclusive – factors in the conformation of these young newcomers' language attitudes towards the language of schooling Catalan.

We are specifically concerned with the language attitudes of young Latin-American newcomers since, upon arrival in Catalonia, they already know Spanish (in their own varieties), and consequently show a preference for this language for social relations, often using Catalan exclusively in certain school contexts (Codó & Patiño Santos, 2010; Huguet et al., 2008; Newman, 2011; Unamuno & Patiño Santos, 2009). Besides, Latin-Americans currently represent the biggest minority group in secondary schools in

Catalonia after students of Moroccan and Romanian backgrounds (Domingo & Vidal Coso, 2011), a group mainly composed of children of Dominican, Ecuadorian, Colombian and Argentinean families and, more recently, of people from Venezuela and Bolivia.[2]

Their presence in schools as Spanish speakers has been a point of debate in educational contexts where different discourses circulate. Some teachers and school administrators consider that Latin-Americans can easily integrate, mainly because they speak a Romanic language close to Catalan in structure. Those teachers inform us that Latin American students may be heard in playgrounds speaking Catalan with both autochthonous and other immigrant classmates, especially when in playful interactions. On the other hand, other teachers consider that the linguistic integration of these students becomes difficult precisely because of their previous knowledge of the Spanish language. For these teachers Spanish-speaking newcomers feel that Spanish is sufficient for them to establish social relationships in Catalonia and, therefore, reserve the use of Catalan only for classroom interaction and conversations with teachers.

Our study on language attitudes within this sociolinguistically complex educational context (see Woolard, 2008, 2009, for further description) will be introduced as follows: first of all, we present the objectives that guided our study ('Objectives of the Study') and the methodology we used in order to gather and analyse data ('Methodology of the Study'). After that, we offer a contextualisation of various studies carried out in RC in Catalonia that, from different perspectives, have paid attention to this programme as a site for multicultural education and the management of multilingualism ('The Reception Class in Catalonia as a *Locus* for the Management of Immigration and Multilingualism'). The analysis, in 'Three Ways of Organising the Reception Class' and 'To Learn or Not to Learn Catalan: What do Latin-American Students Say?', triangulates fieldwork data (i.e. observation of the three RC with teachers and students' voices in interviews) in order to present the ways in which language attitudes emerge in these particular contexts. A final discussion and some reflections about linguistic educational practices in RC conclude this chapter.

Objectives of the Study

The present study intends to address the following questions.

(1) What attitudes are displayed by young secondary school students of Latin-American origin towards Catalan and Spanish and towards bilingualism in Catalonia?
(2) What attitudes are displayed by young secondary school students of Latin-American origin towards the reception process in their school?

(3)   What ideologies are displayed by teachers involved in the reception process in secondary schools with regard the educational strategies to be
implemented?
(4)   How do school reception practices relate to the development of attitudes
by students of Latin-American origin towards Catalan and Spanish and
towards bilingualism in Catalonia?

Methodology of the Study

Our methodological approach combines participant observation in RC
and in free-time spaces such as the playground, the cafeteria and the hall-
ways, with both formal interviews (one per teacher and student participant)
and informal encounters with RC and mainstream teachers and with students of Latin-American backgrounds, in three state secondary schools in
Barcelona's metropolitan area. Thus, observation throughout the 2008/2009
year has allowed us to identify some of the didactic strategies and materials
teachers use when welcoming Spanish-speaking newcomers into the Catalan
educational system. In interviews with RC and mainstream teachers, we
asked about language attitudes and uses observed in the students, as well as
the strategies carried out in the school to promote the use of both languages
and the integration of newcomers. The interviews with Latin-American
youth were carried out in ten focus groups to collect opinions, beliefs and
anecdotes.

Data analysis has consisted of thematic, recursive analyses of interviews
and of field notes to investigate students' and teachers' attitudes towards
Reception and towards the teaching and learning of Catalan and Spanish by
newcomers in their schools. We also explored students' interviews to investigate their attitudes towards Catalan and Spanish and towards bilingualism
in Catalonia.

As the specific context for our study, we have chosen the following
schools.[3]

•   Institut d'Ensenyament Secundari (IES) – i.e. secondary school – Marc
Aureli (located near the centre of Barcelona).
•   IES Inca Garcilaso (located in a peripheral neighbourhood within
Barcelona).
•   IES Josep Vicens (located in a small satellite city 35 minutes from
Barcelona).

All schools were located in working-class neighbourhoods. As for the
make-up of the predominant immigrant student population, many are of
Latin-American origin although there is also a strong presence of students
from Morocco and, in the first school, from Pakistan as well.

The Reception Class in Catalonia as a *Locus* for the Management of Immigration and Multilingualism

One basic resource implemented by the Catalonian Government in order to welcome social and linguistic diversity took shape officially in 2004 with the Plan for Language and Social Cohesion (Generalitat de Catalunya, 2009). One of its educational initiatives was the *Aules d'Acollida* ('Welcoming Classes' or RC (Woolard, 2009: 129)) aiming at linguistic, social and educational integration for the 13.07% of young immigrants in schools (Generalitat de Catalunya, 2009: 21).

The RC in Catalonia intend to cover the initial needs of these students in all curricular areas, as well as in their learning the language of the school (for a complete overview, see Arnau & Vila, this volume). It involves the designation of 'newcomers' teachers' who manage the RC, which can be of an 'open' or 'semi-open' nature. The RC are understood as a flexible resource that schools adapt to their organisational criteria and number of newcomers. It aims at a maximum of 12 immigrants who have arrived over the previous 24 months, who have no prior knowledge of Catalan and who have not followed a similar curriculum before, as might be the case of Romance-language speaking European students. In Catalonia, no student can spend more than 50% of school time in the RC, and it is recommended that they remain there for no more than two years, when they should have reached level A2 (basic oral and written communication) of the Common European Framework of Reference for Languages (CEFR) linguistic ability index. This is why, since their arrival, all newcomers attend regular classes with lower linguistic demands such as physical education or arts and, often, specially is the case of Latin-American students, spend much school time in mainstream classrooms.

From an official methodological point of view, the key priorities of the RC are linguistic immersion, the encouragement of teamwork, the negotiation of meanings, the development of oral competence, personal attention given to students and families, and the establishment of positive affective relationships between students and teachers. At the end of each term, the process of language acquisition should be evaluated, along with the students' level of integration and their progress in a number of curricular areas. The main objective is that newcomers should be able to establish extensive social relations with the students of local origin and with the teaching staff in general. Both in the process of creating a RC and in its operation, the schools can take advantage of the methodological support and resources provided by the supervision teams from the Education Services of the Autonomous Government (see more information in the Plan for Language and Social Cohesion (Generalitat de Catalunya, 2009)).

All these general educational guidelines take different shapes in each school and thus the actual implementation of RC has become a focus of interest for both educational and language researchers. In relation to these issues, researchers have investigated the actual implementation of RCs and in Alegre *et al.* (2008) found two predominant organisational models. The first one sets an independent timetable for RC attendance for each immigrant student in relation to mainstream class attendance so that their Reception time – and thereby language learning – is prioritised over the learning of other contents. One consequence is that students cannot always attend classes in mainstream subject areas. The fact that they work separately at tasks adapted to their ability – 'differentiated classroom model' (Tomlinson, 2004) – brings with it a certain social isolation. The second predominant model establishes that students will follow as many subject lessons in the mainstream class as possible and will only attend the RC when the content proves too challenging. This arrangement raises timetabling and evaluation conflicts, but shows the intention of standardising the education of newcomers. The positive side of this model has been confirmed by the results of the investigation conducted by Vila *et al.* (2009) on the effectiveness of RC in promoting linguistic knowledge and the adjustment to the educational system. In general, knowledge of the language of schooling was found to be tied to a successful period of adjustment to the school and students who performed best were those who had spent fewer hours in the RC.

RC organisation is just one of the factors to take into account when investigating the verbal behaviour of immigrant students. The interactional and ethnographic research by Nussbaum and Unamuno (2006) looking at the RC of primary and secondary schools and studying the development of competence in Catalan, Spanish and English, documented how the development of situated oral competence among newcomers was related to their degree of commitment to school activities. In this regard, researchers noted that the desire to belong to the new school community implies for immigrant students 'a process of socialisation that includes the learning of a new identity which makes the person in question a member of the community' (Nussbaum & Unamuno, 2006: 61).

In this socialisation process, language attitudes of young newcomers are also to be taken into account. In the case of Catalonia, Newman and Trenchs-Parera have conducted research on the language attitudes of both young newcomers and their autochthonous peers. The results of their first, quantitative study (Newman *et al.*, 2008) show that students of immigrant backgrounds, regardless of their mother tongue, display an overall preference for the international language Spanish, thus confirming results of previous studies (Huguet *et al.*, 2008). Considering that such behaviour on the part of people who have been in a Catalan RC called for further examination, in a follow-up qualitative study, Trenchs-Parera and Newman (2009) explored attitudes and ideologies of Latin-American students. They found out that they were mainly concerned with maintaining their linguistic Latin-American identity in opposition to the Peninsular Spanish variety. The non-international language, Catalan, was not a matter of particular concern to them; rather, the negative attitudes displayed were based largely on their viewing Catalan as a practical obstacle to success in classes and so such attitudes were less frequent in those student who had higher linguistic competence (Newman, 2011). Again, the role of the daily school practices was highlighted as relevant in relation to students' language attitudes. A further statistical analysis of the 2008 data (Trenchs-Parera, n.d.) also pointed at a probable relationship between school practices and the language attitudes and behaviour of young people.

However, these studies do not inform sufficiently about the possible influence of RC practices in the development of newcomers' language attitudes in bilingual societies. For us, the RC in state secondary schools becomes the ideal context where to study the management and negotiation of multilingualism and multiculturalism, the formation of language attitudes and the complexity of the processes of teaching and learning second languages in bilingual settings.

Three Ways of Organising the Reception Class

Marc Aureli School: Two linguistic norms in conflict

Marc Aureli School is located in an area of Barcelona with more than 15,000 inhabitants, of whom over 30% are of immigrant origin. Of the three contexts studied, this school has the highest proportion of recently arrived immigrants and the lowest level of economic resources, as the average income per capita is only 51.4% of the one registered in Catalonia.[4] The school was founded in the 1980s when, as the other two schools, it began receiving the children of Spanish-speaking immigrant families from Southern Spain. Today, the presence of students of migrant backgrounds is highly significant and in the year 2008/2009 123 out of the 231 students had been born abroad. All students come from low-income households since, as in the other two schools, the scarce middle class families in the neighbourhood – many of them Catalan-speaking – send their children to partially state-supported private schools.

In Marc Aureli School, two teachers are responsible for the reception programme. Even though they have degrees in sciences, they were trained in second language teaching by the Catalonian Government.[5] The RC programme in the school is designed into two streams, based on the newcomers' primary languages: 'Romance-based' and 'not Romance-based'. In turn, each stream is divided into two levels, *beginners* and *intermediate–advanced* and other teachers from the school are involved in this division. At the *beginners* level, students learn basic grammar and vocabulary, using materials and resources provided by the administration. They attend the RC for 12 hours per week and return to their mainstream classrooms for other subjects. The classes observed were from the Romance-based stream at both its levels, *beginners* and *intermediate–advanced*. The *beginners* level takes place in a classroom located at the very top of the building, separate from other classrooms. The number of RC students throughout the year varies as new students arrive and others are then moved out to attend mainstream classes.

At the time of data collection, the *beginners* group was comprised of five students: three Colombian girls and two boys from the Dominican Republic. Within the class, the teacher organised reading aloud and reading comprehension activities. It was a controlled practice in which the teacher corrected pronunciation, explained grammar or posed reading comprehension questions, a methodology that promotes little interaction in the L2. Students are allowed to speak in Spanish whereas Catalan is incorporated gradually. The teacher addresses everyone in Catalan while the students mostly respond in Spanish.

The *intermediate-advanced* level Romance-based group consists only of a boy and a girl from Brazil and a boy from Chile. The insistence on the use of both oral and written Catalan increases in this group. The activities are more communicative and the resources are artefacts taken from everyday life, such as newspapers, TV programmes and advertisements. This encourages the students to talk, albeit with grammatical errors, thus promoting the development of communicative and verbal fluency. Code switching is continuously present, acting as a learning resource (Nussbaum & Unamuno, 2006).

The school promotes intercultural activities along with the use and knowledge of the students' languages of origin. However, we observed that in the playground students organised themselves into locals and newcomers, who split up into different subgroups based on language and culture. Besides this self-separation, RC teachers face two more challenges: (1) the constant arrival of newly registered students and (2) the fact that Spanish – not Catalan – continues to be the language of social relations in all areas of the school apart from the classrooms. With regards to the constant arrival, teachers find working in the RC difficult because the constant and open admission of students complicates the organisation planned at the beginning of the school year. Newcomers, with particular characteristics and needs, as well as wide-ranging academic levels, need to be incorporated into the class immediately, in many cases calling for the redistribution of participants. In this sense, the continuous mobility into the school and between classes makes it difficult to make sense of the group.

The second challenge relates to the language choice that the majority of the students of the RC make to conduct their social relationships. Both mainstream and RC students use Spanish in all areas outside the classroom, relegating Catalan as the language of the classroom (see a comparable case reported by Huguet *et al.*, this volume). A similar situation was reported in the studies carried out by Heller (2006) and Goldstein (2003), since children of minority backgrounds relegated French and English as the languages of instruction, ignoring institutional efforts to make them use such languages in their social relations. Similarly, we find that this preferred use of Spanish complicates the learning of Catalan by reserving it for institutional and instructional uses. As the RC teacher explains below, because of the characteristics of the school population, giving classes in Catalan does not suffice to promote its everyday use:

> Yes, the language for all things social in the school is Spanish, that's how it is shall we say. (...) Within the classroom it's Catalan because the teachers teach in Catalan; (...). In terms of the hallways, as far as the school yard is concerned the language you hear mostly is Spanish; in the context of the neighbourhood you don't [hear Catalan] either. (Interview with the RC teacher at Marc Aureli School)

This quote shows the tension between what the teachers' goal regarding linguistic practices is and what students effectively do. Thus, a conflict is revealed: (a) the use of Catalan as an institutional language promoted by teachers within the classroom and (b) the use of Spanish as the preferred language out of the classroom. The confrontation of the two linguistic norms reflects ideological positions regarding the value speakers give to each language which, in turn, echoes local historical and sociopolitical struggles in the relationship of Catalonia with the Spanish state.

Josep Vicens School: The Reception Class as an island

The students from Josep Vicens School come from a town in the metropolitan area of Barcelona of about 70,000 inhabitants, of whom 16% were born abroad, mostly in Latin America or Africa. The disposable family income per capita is just a bit over 75% of the average household income per inhabitant in Catalonia. Its socio-economic level is therefore a little higher than that of the catchment area feeding Marc Aureli School. However, Josep Vicens School rarely receives students from middle class families as they prefer to send their children to either another nearby state school with higher academic reputation or to partially state-funded schools. During the year 2008–2009 the school, which offers all compulsory secondary education levels, pre-university grades and four vocational training programmes, had around 660 students and 19 of the 25 newcomer students in Compulsory Secondary Education had arrived from Latin America.

From the point of view of the school's aims, personalised education is seen as one of the key elements and it is precisely this characteristic that defines their RC. The school's RC is located on the second floor in an annex building which, upon entrance, displays the machines and gadgets used in the training programmes, such as electricity and welding. In fact, one can see that the RC classroom was originally dedicated to electrical engineering workshops as it still shows walls adorned with posters having to do with engineering, technology and electro-mechanics. There is no reference to language teaching materials, unlike the other two classrooms observed, with the exception of a calendar and a worn-out world map.

RC classes are taught by a single teacher with training in teaching Spanish as a second language and with extensive teaching experience inside and outside Spain. He organises the RC into two levels, *beginners* and *intermediate–advanced*. At beginners' level, students work on the subjects Catalan language, natural sciences, mathematics and social sciences, as stated in the institutional guidelines for RC, and, in the case of speakers of non-Romance languages, Spanish. Seven students from various origins belong to this class: five of them attend classes regularly and two occasionally. Students carry out activities by working with worksheets or materials from the LIC Space (*Espai LIC*, LIC standing for *Llengua i Cohesió Social*, namely, Language and Social Cohesion), an online didactic resource centre run by the Catalan Government. They attend this class 12 hours per week, following the language policy regulations.[6] The methodology emphasises individual work with little interaction between the participants, except when they work in pairs on a single task. So, for example, in one of the classes observed, we saw that Adham from Morocco was working on Catalan vocabulary at *beginners' level*, Marimar from Venezuela on the food guide pyramid, and Inaya from Morocco and Munir from Bangladesh on mathematics, all of them working on Catalan while Lin from China works on vocabulary activities in Spanish. Meanwhile, the teacher was moving from table to table checking their work. As a result, students primarily interact with the course materials, secondarily with the teacher and rarely, if at all, with classmates.

This same space is transformed an hour later to give way to the *intermediate–advanced* group, with four Latin-American students and one from Bangladesh. Even though this latter student does not have the language level to participate in the class, after weeks of observation, we realised that he was in this class because he was a troublemaker in the mainstream classes. Once the RC is underway, the activities become communicative; the methodology changes and the teacher organises speaking, reading and writing activities by using fun resources, such as vocabulary games and role plays. In addition to the LIC Space, the teacher works with photos of the city, figures, drawings and games to promote teamwork. The rules of interaction change with respect to the beginners' level and students exchange information using Catalan. The use of Spanish is discouraged and the reminder of 'just in Catalan' is often heard. This raises some resistance from some students who are not confident to speak the language.

In contrast to Marc Aureli School, the Reception activities in Josep Vicens School are limited to the RC, and no specific activity aims at promoting the use of Catalan outside this classroom. Moreover, the efforts of this teacher do not seem to be reinforced by other teachers. According to the data collected from teachers not directly involved in the RC, many of them consider that cultural and linguistic diversity should be reserved to the RC. In addition, students that represent a disciplinary problem are sent to the RC, as the case of the boy from Bangladesh or of Adham who attends both beginners and intermediate RC because the rest of the teachers – as one teacher acknowledged – 'cannot stand his bad behaviour'. As in Marc Aureli, youngsters tend to cluster by nationalities in the playground without interacting with autochthonous students.

The challenges of the RC teacher here are the academic differences between some of the newcomers, especially in maths and reading comprehension in Catalan, as well as the lack of interest that some display when it comes to learning and integration, something that is manifested visibly in the playground. Differences between learning styles and the knowledge brought from previous educational systems complicate the class:

> Let's say that after last year 15 pupils were chosen, we could drop the others, I had to deal with that lot, which was impossible. So it was impossible for a reason. John, his progress is very slow and he doesn't realise that here in the reception class we have a deadline and I have to assess them (...) and, you can't just become an endless and bottomless toolkit (...) I, I'm an expensive resource and you're privileged, so either you take advantage 100% or next year your adaptation period will be officially over and you'll have to look for something else. (...) well, the problem is that they haven't realised that. (Interview with the RC teacher in Josep Vicens School)

In this quote, diversity is categorised as a problem that should be isolated in order not to disturb the mainstream class. Such a vision of diversity poses some responsibilities over the students categorised by teachers as 'slow' and 'unaware' of the resources offered by the institution to learn Catalan and the so-called basic subjects (mathematics and sciences). Such ideologies on diversity are similar to those of the Bridging Classes in Madrid, designed by the administration for newcomers to learn Spanish as the language of schooling (Martín Rojo, 2010; Pérez-Milans, 2007). Coincidentally, the metaphor of the classroom as an 'island' (Pérez-Milans, 2007: 115), verbalised here by the RC teacher, extends to that of the contents learned in these classes, making the passing from a compensatory class to a mainstream one difficult.

Inca Garcilaso School: Mainstreaming from day one

In the 2008–2009 academic year, out of the 576 pupils in Inca Garcilaso School, 200 were immigrant students, 140 of whom were from Latin America. Of these, 43 attended the RC. The school's population actually reflects quite faithfully the sociocultural make-up of the neighbourhood. Although this school, located in a peripheral neighbourhood within Barcelona, receives a small minority of students of Catalan origin, the vast majority of the autochthonous population in the neighbourhood consists of immigrants coming from Spanish-speaking areas in Spain in mid-20th century and, therefore, Spanish is the language predominantly used in the homes of the school's autochthonous students. The disposable family income per capita in the neighbourhood is just 62.6% of the average household income per inhabitant in Catalonia. It is therefore at a socio-economic level very similar to the population that makes up the social context of Josep Vicens School, as families with higher incomes in the neighbourhood tend to send their children to other schools with a higher academic reputation.

At first sight, Inca Garcilaso School resembles Josep Vicens School and offers the same academic trajectories. However, once we take a closer look, this school demonstrates a distinct way to provide for diversity, as the two teachers who run the reception programme in Inca Garcilaso School have been building, for over six years, a particular approach to reception. The RC teachers – one of them with a degree in Catalan Philology and the other one trained in Classical Philology – base their work on the belief that newcomers should not be isolated from their mainstream classrooms. Instead, they should work with their mainstream classmates right from their arrival. This type of welcome policy implies, however, a number of functional changes that are not always understood by other teachers in the school, mostly accustomed to RC models in which the student leaves the mainstream classroom to learn Catalan in isolation.

These RC teachers have organised the areas of Catalan and Social Sciences according to educational levels, which means that for eight hours a week both newcomers and locals are divided into classes corresponding to their levels. This means that the RC does not exist in a separate classroom. Instead, it is a classroom for both local and immigrant students with low levels of ability in those subjects. For that reason, we can find local and immigrant students together doing either initial or advanced Catalan lessons. The RC teachers take charge of the lowest levels in Catalan and Social Sciences, as well as the optional subjects, in a three-year welcome programme that surprisingly extends beyond the 24 months that the Government recommends.

Here, newcomer students are seen simply as students that have extra needs in reading or writing, as any of the rest of their colleagues of local origin might have, and, like all the others, deserve individual attention. As one RC teacher explained: '*Exactly the same just as other students who are of local origin might also attend if they have these needs and thereby we work at the level of the student with more individualised attention; even at times [their level is] much higher than that of the students from our country, and clearly we achieve something else which is the affective aspect, which is very important*'. In this way, the idea of the RC role as an integrating resource is widened, giving relevance to that 'affective' component, an aspect that teachers here value far higher than the mere learning of the language of instruction.

Unlike in the other two schools, newcomers in these bottom level classes use the same materials and textbooks as the rest of their classmates, but activities and explanations are adapted so that they can follow and learn the same content. In the sense that these teachers teach the language of the school through curricular content, their methodology is related to the content and language integrated learning (CLIL) approach described by Escobar Urmeneta and Evnitskaya (this volume). Thus, we can understand the words of the teachers interviewed when they explain that, from the very start, newcomers never leave their mainstream classroom and their local classmates. According to their experience, this reception ensures that newcomers are recognised as pupils with the same social-educational status as their classmates, and this allows their skills to be developed and evaluated in line with the level of knowledge, maturity and interests to be expected at their age.

Aspects that are highlighted here are newcomers' motivation to stay on at school and complete pre-university studies, a situation that contrasts with the other schools studied where teachers complained that students were de-motivated as far as learning the language of instruction because they did not want to move on to higher education. The two RC teachers describe this as a key emotional factor for the reception programme, an affective aspect which, according to other teachers in the school, makes the RC in Inca Garcilaso School a success, both academically and in terms of integration.

The challenges identified for the RC at this school were not the 'language or academic deficiencies' of the newcomer students but the resistance of other teachers for whom diversity seems to be related to both being of immigrant background and behaving disruptively in the classroom. Thus, these teachers would also send disruptive immigrant students to the RC teacher, as happened in Josep Vicens School. For them, welcoming the immigrant students did not seem to be a collective ideology at the school, even if its director – extremely supportive of the two RC teachers – meant it to be. An excerpt from an interview with a mainstream teacher allows us to see these tensions between ways of interpreting the role of the RC:

> Well I think these kids feel very welcomed, that if it's true, the work that our two colleagues do in this regard is very good because I think they do feel thoroughly welcomed and they act as an important point of reference for them (. . .) Organisationally it could probably be done a better way (. . .) there are kids who have severe learning difficulties and on top of that are newcomers and maybe they ought to be in another group that's not A or B where basically there are students who don't have these problems. (Interview with a Mainstream Class Teacher from Inca Garcilaso School)

Although the integrating role of the RC teachers is valued, we find that there are aspects of the welcome policy that not all teachers agree to. At first, the teacher defines the integrating role of his colleagues in terms such as 'they really love them' and 'they are a point of reference for them,' considering the affective component as a fundamental element in the welcome programme. However, these evaluations contrast to what she says about the structural organisation of the RC. Indeed, it is here that we see this tension between the point of view of the RC teachers and that of their colleagues who, like this one, show discontent that students with low academic levels do not go to a RC. Thus, we find at least two confronting ideologies on diversity: one that stresses early integration and a segregationist one that puts the language in the centre of reception, ignoring that it is in the exchange with peers that newcomers learn quickly and meaningfully (Martín Rojo, 2010).

To Learn or Not to Learn Catalan: What do Latin-American Students Say?

This section is devoted to the analysis of the voices of the Latin-American students who had attended RC at these schools. Our intention was to explore their attitudes towards Catalan and Spanish and to relate those attitudes to the educational practices they experience.

Attitudes of students in semi-open Reception Classes

We observed similarities in the views of students participating in the semi-open or 'pull-out' RC at Marc Aureli and Josep Vicens schools. Those students interviewed say that they use Catalan mainly with the teachers and in academic activities, but not with schoolmates. Their use of Catalan within the family is shown to be for recounting anecdotes or poking fun; it is therefore something 'artificial' (Frekko, 2009). The following interview with a group of three third-year Ecuadorian girls from Josep Vicens School shows these issues, confirming previous results (Newman, 2011; Trenchs-Parera & Newman, 2009): the resistance by Latin-American students to speaking Catalan, even by those who have known the language since primary school and who should have developed total fluency:

Alix: no, I remember one time, the first time I came here, yeah, it was to the reception class ... 'cos everyone when they come from another country goes to the reception class, they're really keen on the kids, speaking Catalan and stuff ... but I don't normally speak it, just when:: [you've got to], I mean Catalan.

Thus, even though students recognise that they quickly learn to speak Catalan, they do not use it in their daily lives, only when they have to, pointing to an institutional use:

Alix: . . . and with the teacher you speak in Catalan . . . because . . . I dunno, nothing . . . even in Catalan [class] we speak Spanish

Lilian: we read in Catalan and they even explain things in Spanish (. . .)

Rocío: (. . .) where my family lives . . . no, in my house I don't speak Catalan, it's just where my family lives . . .

Researcher: but:: you don't speak Catalan with anyone? And not you guys either?

Alix: with my parents but I'm just joking.

This excerpt shows the explanation of the students' linguistic uses inside and outside the classroom. The categorisations that emerge allow us to see a linguistic distribution based on the students' preferences: Catalan as the language of instruction, but Spanish as the language of family and of leisure spaces. Catalan is seen as the language of informal exchanges only when joking, a phenomenon similar to the *crossing* studied by Rampton (1995) in British schools and by Woolard (2003) as regards Spanish-speaking locals in Catalonia. If this is the case, code-switching in such jocular situations indexes students' distancing from Catalan and, therefore, the fact that they do not recognise it as their own language, but rather that of others.

This same idea is reinforced by other reasons Latin Americans provide to explain why they do not use Catalan in their daily lives. Some of them say it is 'embarrassing' not to speak it well ('¡Porque me da vergüenza!' [*It embarrasses me!*], shouted Colombian Rocío, visibly uncomfortable when asked about the issue). This feeling among the newest arrivals is linked to low language competence and low self-esteem at their own language abilities. Among the teenagers who have been at primary Catalan schools, such embarrassment is usually related to another explanation given for their unwillingness to speak Catalan: that they do not find swear words as strong as in Spanish, a phenomenon very recently described by Woolard (2009) as regards local Spanish speakers. Spanish is the language of home, which provides them with enough linguistic resources to express themselves in different registers, whereas the use of Catalan is something that they feel is only possible in formal contexts:

Researcher: and you? Why [don't any of you speak in Catalan in the street]?

Lilian: because I don't like it (. . .) I don't like it because:: it seems more:: I dunno

Alix:	And the swear words are less::
Lilian:	=yes=
Alix:	strong than in Spanish

These ideas are echoed among students in Marc Aureli School. In the following interview with one Dominican boy who has spent less than six months in the RC, he shows a preference for learning languages other than Catalan. Behind his views we are able to recognise some quite common linguistic prejudices, which have also been found in other contexts where a non-international language coexists with an international one (Ibarraran *et al.*, 2007) in the Basque country:

Jose:	No: I mean me:: no, I don't prefer Catalan, I prefer another language like:: French
Researcher:	ah::
Jose:	although it's even more difficult

Attitudes of students in the open classroom

Contrary to what happens in Marc Aureli and Josep Vicens Schools, in Inca Garcilaso School many Latin-American students find meaning in the use of Catalan. In this open 'push-in' system, the language is not just used academically, but for personal reasons, such as those related to future professional expectations, the completion of the integration process, and socialisation inside and outside the school. As an example, the interviews with one Latin-American group in this school were conducted in Catalan at the request of the students themselves, despite the fact that the interviewer was Latin American.

The excerpt from the following interview conducted at Inca Garcilaso School shows that positive attitudes towards Catalan are related to the way this school works with newcomers. First, integration has a positive effect beyond the classroom. Newcomers are seen as students who simply need language support and are able to understand and follow daily school life just like their local classmates. This view means that reception is geared not only towards linguistic incorporation into the school, but also towards the importance of students' social life in school. Second, and in consequence, students express the idea of feeling valued and integrated. They develop positive personal expectations and stay at school, at least until finishing compulsory education, as RC teachers explained. On the whole, such expectations are not found in the other two schools. In the interview excerpt, 18-year-old David from Colombia accounts for his first days at school four years ago. His experience demonstrates the importance of the welcome programme in this school and the central role of the teachers in the process. Unlike the other schools studied and despite the initial difficulties experienced on arrival, students integrate into their school and see a connection between what they do in the RC and what they do in other classes:

Researcher: you the first day how was it, d'you remember your first day? ...

David: well I had a very sad story when I started studying, you know why, in the old days, I mean I still, that they say that the school has become a lot more Spanish speaking and before it wasn't, (...) Here in Inca Garcilaso School everyone then the teachers spoke Catalan, the students, my classmates spoke to me in Catalan, so I felt a bit mm left out, d'you know what I mean. When Montse (the RC teacher) came she's my (...)

Joaquin: she's like everyone's second mother

David: she's like a little angel (...) the two, the two of them

Researcher: when you say Montse, who is Montse?

David: Montse Márquez, Montse Márquez, because she's the first who arrived and said to me 'David Garcia come, come with me.' I was a bit surprised and thinking what's happening, where's she taking me. So then we went to the Reception Class, really fantastic. I got to know Montse and some other teachers who have left now, ages ago, and really excellent.

This story of David's allows us to see, on the one hand, the experience of a Spanish-speaking newcomer in a Catalan school. David explains he felt lost during his first day at school until the teacher's invitation to the RC where she had prepared a welcome itinerary for him, as for all newcomers. From his explanation, we can see the active role of the teacher and the way in which she invites the new students to become involved in the school. Such invitation starts the first day with a welcome routine that includes the introduction to the school's norms and spaces. We note the co-construction involving interviewees in the assessment of their teacher, explaining her efforts to include them on an emotional level, something that she herself stressed as important (see section '*Inca Garcilaso School: mainstreaming from day one*').

Students' comments show affection that we do not observe in the other schools. The teachers' objective behind linguistic immersion in mainstream classes upon arrival is actually understood and approved of by newcomers. Another Inca Garcilaso student who did not use Catalan much outside class did not mind instruction in that language:

Rulfo: In a way it's good [that classes are given in Catalan] because that way you learn to understand them and to speak it. And words you don't know, that you don't understand, well, you can ask the teacher and that way you learn little by little.

The impact of this reception programme can be seen in the plans of the students as they find personal advancement through education is possible. Thus, some Latin Americans express their wish to continue studying or do so already. Johan from Ecuador, already in the pre-university course, wants to eventually become a journalist, as did Sebas from Uruguay. Guillermo from Argentina says '*I want to go to the university. Many people feel they have to, but I want to go. However, I haven't decided what I want to study*'. Such intentions did not appear in any of the interviews held in the other two schools.

Conclusions and Discussion

We have presented the educational practices within which teachers and students carry out official reception policies in a complex in three classrooms with similar sociocultural conditions within a multicultural society such as the Catalan one. This process entails a set of challenges for the schools responsible for the reception of the children of migrant workers who do not speak the language of instruction. Even though this situation is common to different contexts where at least two languages with different status coexist, what becomes relevant from the studied context is the fact that the language of the school is not that one of wide international communication. In the particular case of Catalonia, the local government has proposed the Reception Programme as the educational resource for integrating newcomers into the educational system, a programme that focuses on the learning of the language of the school as well as the local curricular contents of subjects, such as mathematics, sciences and social sciences.

The differing expectations, both for locals as for newcomers, lead to a complex situation that has consequences for both groups. Challenges are faced using a number of tools and strategies which, managed by participants in their daily practices, give rise to a set of language attitudes. Our comparative case study of language attitudes of participants of three RC in the metropolitan area of Barcelona has shown that a variety of factors, such as the schools' particular backgrounds, shape some of the teachers' ideologies underpinning the organisation of the RC programme in each one of them. Such ideologies become an important factor that has an impact in newcomers' attitudes towards Catalan, which plays a central role in socialisation processes in Catalonia as the language of the school. Those ideologies have manifested themselves in: (1) the way in which the teachers in charge of the RC describe their practice and their immigrant students; (2) the mainstream teacher's perceptions of the RC programme and (3) the educational strategies used in the classroom.

The study has allowed us to detect at least four challenges faced daily by reception. The first challenge is a structural one since they have to address three issues: (a) increasing presence and continual arrival of newcomers (as in the three schools observed), a fact teachers cannot change; (b) scarce structural and staff resources at disposal (as in Josep Vicens School) and (c) mainstream teachers' lack of experience or sufficient specialised training in receiving newcomers (as in Marc Aureli School).

The second of these challenges is resolved by teachers in accordance to their ideologies about the concepts of 'integration', 'welcome programme' and language teaching–learning processes, giving rise to different organisational practices. Where linguistic diversity is understood 'as a problem' (in one of the teachers' words) – as in Marc Aureli and Josep Vicens Schools – such diversity is concentrated in one classroom where mainstream teachers may send students with academic problems. Where diversity is understood as an everyday situation – as in Inca Garcilaso School – all students belong to the same mainstream classes for most subjects except for Catalan and Social Sciences, for which all students – not just newcomers – are grouped according to linguistic competence in Catalan. Thus, immigrants who need it throughout their studies are attended to by reception teachers, without being sent to a distinct group. Each of these conceptions has consequences reflected in the attitudes expressed by the students who have passed through the RC.

A first consequence is that a young newcomers' first experience with reception at school is essential when they come to assess the relevance of the language of the school (Newman, 2011). On the one hand, regardless of schools' differences in organisation, we observe similarities in the language attitudes and communicative practices of students participating in semi-open RC. Bearing in mind that the three schools studied receive large proportions of students with very similar socio-economic backgrounds, one might expect that the students of the three schools would display similar attitudes towards the two official languages, with a probable preference for Spanish. This study reveals a difference where the organisation of the RC involves the newcomers' separation or isolation: the discontinuity between communicative practices demanded in and out of the school. In such schools, newcomers do not see the non-international language as a language of communication in all its registers (Frekko, 2009; Woolard, 2009) and so, in general, they do not feel it is a language that they can make their own. The linguistic practices of the neighbourhood and, often, the family seem to strongly influence practices and attitudes of students who do not see a need to use the language taught in the RC when socialising. Consequently, the RC becomes the only space where newcomers have contact with the language of instruction, relegating it to formal and academic situations. The efforts of reception teachers, working in isolation, may not suffice to counteract the weight of ideologies in favour of international languages (Dorian, 1998).

It is true that the attitudes of some students at Inca Garcilaso echoed such ideologies. However, in this school, with an inclusive reception system, we also detect positive attitudes – invisible, at least to us, in the other two schools – towards the non-international language. For some, Catalan is not a mere language of instruction – a function they approve of – or one exclusive to a higher or more prestigious social class (Trenchs-Parera & Newman, 2009; Woolard, 2009) or to autochthonous students; rather, they approve of it mattering to Catalans as a sign of their identity and spontaneously use it in the school when relating both to other newcomers and to autochthonous students.

A second consequence of this inclusive approach is that it appears to generate positive attitudes towards schooling and academic culture. The number of Latin-American students who, in interviews or corridor conversations with researchers, express the intention to stay in school with the prospect of moving on to higher education is very high in comparison with those schools with semi-open programmes. The fundamental difference seems to lie in the attitude – described by themselves as 'the affective component' – of those responsible for the reception programme valuing the potential and background expectations of students who join the system late and promoting the students' confidence in their academic abilities and in their abilities for bilingual language absorption.

In sum, the study has revealed key factors in educational practices for integration in bilingual contexts: (a) the structural importance of diversity within the school; (b) the value of students' competences recognised by both reception and mainstream teachers; (c) the immediate integration into mainstream classes according to academic – not necessarily linguistic – levels; (d) the continuous monitoring and support of newcomers in basic subjects; (e) a pedagogical attitude on the part of the RC teachers to involve the rest of the staff and (f) an affective factor involving individualised attention.

However, even where such educational practices are present, challenges in relation to the reception programmes at schools in sociolinguistically complex contexts remain, namely (a) the lack of active involvement in the reception programme of mainstream specialised teachers and (b) the self-division between local students and newcomers in leisure spaces, which makes the establishment of intercultural networks difficult. Such attitudes, if not consciously attended to within the schools, become key factors that hinder the achievement of the linguistic, social and educational integration.

For us, this study has, first, allowed us to better understand the linguistic consequences of the educational strategies in secondary schools receiving young immigrants of Latin-American origins. Second, it has provided information to support schools in evaluating and redesigning their socio-educational strategies with the aim of integrating newly arrived students into the language of instruction. Finally, the study has partially contributed to the description of the sociolinguistic situation in Catalonia as a multilingual host society.

Acknowledgements

This study was financed by research grants 2008ARIE-00018, 2010ARAFI-000017 from Generalitat de Catalunya and Recercaixa 2010ACUP 00344 from Obra Social 'la Caixa'. We would like to give special thanks to Dr Michael Newman, our research colleague, for the interviews he conducted and his comments on early drafts. Finally, we would like to thank the participating teachers and students for generously sharing their time and opinions. We hope that they will recognise themselves along these lines and that the results reported will be of use in their daily efforts to construct the best schools possible.

Notes

(1) In the year 2009/2010 there were 662 Reception Classes in primary education and 401 in secondary education, while in the 2004/2005 year there had been, respectively, 378 and 225 (Generalitat de Catalunya, 2009: 22).
(2) For more information, see IDESCAT (2010), the official statistics website of Catalonia at http://www.idescat.cat/en/ and at the Spanish Ministry of Education website at http://www.educacion.gob.es/dctm/ministerio/horizontales/estadisticas/no-universitarias/alumnado/matriculado/2009-2010/extranjeros09.pdf?documentId=0901e7 2b80d24971.
(3) All names of schools and participants are pseudonyms.
(4) Average income per capita of the catchment areas feeding each of the schools has been taken or calculated from the official websites of Barcelona's city council (http://www.bcn.es) and IDESCAT (2010).
(5) RC teachers do not necessarily have a language teaching degree. They are permanent teachers chosen by the staff and trained by the Government.
(6) *Espai LIC* or LIC Space includes interactive materials addressed towards newcomers learning Catalan, http://www.xtec.cat/lic/index.htm.

References

Alegre, M.A., Benito, R. and González, S. (2008) *De l'Aula d'Acollida a l'aula ordinària: processos d'escolarització de l'alumnat estranger.* UAB: Bellaterra.
Boix, E. (1993) *Triar no és trair. Identitat i llengua en els joves de Barcelona.* Barcelona: Edicions 62.
Codó, E. and Patiño-Santos, A. (2010) Language choice, agency and belonging at a multilingual school in Catalonia (Comunicación). *SS18 (Sociolinguistics Symposium 18).* University of Southampton, September 2010.
Domingo, A. and Vidal Coso, E. (2011) Migracions i llengua als territoris de parla catalana. Una perspectiva demogràfica. *L'Avenç,* November 1st
Dorian, N. (1998) Western language ideologies and small-language prospects. In L. Grenoble and L. Whaley (eds) *Endangered Languages: Language Loss and Community Response.* Cambridge: Cambridge University Press.
Frekko, S. (2009) 'Normal' in Catalonia: Standard language, enregisterment and the imagination of a national public. *Language in Society* 38, 71–93.
Galindo i Solé, M. (2008) *Les llengües en joc, el joc entre llengües: L'ús interpersonal del català entre els infants i joves de Catalunya.* Lleida: Pagès Editors.
Garrett, P. (2010) *Attitudes to Language.* Cambridge: Cambridge University Press.

Generalitat de Catalunya (2009) *Pla per a la llengua i la cohesió social. Educació i convivència intercultural.* Barcelona: Generalitat de Catalunya.

Goldstein, T. (2003) *Teaching and Learning in a Multilingual School: Choices, Risks and Dilemmas.* New Jersey: Lawrence Erlbaum.

Heller, M. (2006) *Linguistic Minorities and Modernity: A Sociolinguistic Ethnography.* London and New York: Continuum International.

Huguet, A., Janès, J. and Chireac, S.M. (2008) Mother tongue as a determining variable in language attitudes. The case of immigrant Latin American students in Spain. *Language and Intercultural Communication* 8 (4), 246–260.

Ibarraran, A., Lasagabaster, D. and Sierra, J.M. (2007) *Inmigración y aprendizaje de lenguas en un contexto bilingüe.* Bilbao: LETE Argitaletxea.

IDESCAT (2010) *Institut d'Estadística de Catalunya, Enquesta de la població activa.* http://www.idescat.cat. Last accessed 18 November 2011.

Marshall, S. (2006) Spanish speaking Latin Americans in Catalonia: reflexivity and knowledgeability in contructions of Catalan. In C.M. Molinero and M. Stewart (eds) *Globalization and Language in the Spanish-Speaking World: Macro and Micro Perspectives* (pp. 158–177). London: Palgrave.

Marshall, S. (2007) New Latino diaspora and new zones of language contact: A social constructionist analysis of Spanish-speaking Latin Americans in Catalonia. In J. Holmquist, A. Lorenzino and L. Sayahi (eds) *Selected Proceedings of the Third Workshop on Spanish Sociolinguistics* (pp. 150–161). Somerville, MA: Cascadilla.

Martín Rojo, L. (2010) *Constructing Inequality in Multilingual Classrooms.* Berlin: Mouton De Gruyter.

Newman, M. (2011) Different ways to hate a language in Catalonia: Interpreting low solidarity scores in language attitude studies. In J. Michnowicz and R. Dodsworth (eds) *Selected Proceedings of the 5th Workshop on Spanish Sociolinguistics* (pp. 40–49). Somerville, MA: Cascadilla Proceedings Project.

Newman, M., Trenchs-Parera, M. and Ng, S. (2008) Normalizing bilingualism: The effects of the Catalonian linguistic normalization policy one generation after. *Journal of Sociolinguistics* 12 (3), 306–333.

Nussbaum, L. and Unamuno, V. (eds) (2006) *Usos i competències multilingües entre escolars d'origen immigrant.* Bellaterra: Servei de Publicacions de la UAB.

Pérez Milans, M. (2007) 'Las aulas de enlace: un islote de bienvenida'. In L. Martín Rojo and L. Mijares (eds) *Voces del aula. Etnografías de la escuela multicultural* (pp. 95–120). Madrid: CREADE.

Rampton, B. (1995) *Crossing: Language and Ethnicity Among Adolescents.* London/NY: Longman.

Tomlinson, C.A. (2004) *How to Differentiate Instruction in Mixed Ability Classrooms.* Alesandria, VA: Association for Supervision and Curriculum Development.

Trenchs-Parera, M. and Newman, M. (2009) Diversity of language ideologies in Spanish-speaking youth of different origins in Catalonia. *Journal of Multilingual and Multicultural Development* 30 (6), 509–524.

Trenchs-Parera, M. (n.d.) Incidència de les estratègies educatives en les actituds i ideologies lingüístiques dels adolescents nouvinguts a l'educació secundària pública de Catalunya. Unpublished report for the research project 2008ARIE-00018. Barcelona: Generalitat de Catalunya.

Unamuno, V. and Patiño Santos, A. (2009) 'Aquí no parlem català': multilingualism and borderlines in urban high schools in Barcelona. (Comunicación). *AILA Migration and Language Research Network. 3th International Seminar on Language and Migration.* UAB, 2–3 February 2009. Barcelona.

Vila, I., Canal, I., Mayans, P., Perera, S., Serra, J. M. and Siqués, C. (2009) Las aulas de acogida de la educación primaria de Cataluña el curso 2005–2006: sus efectos sobre el conocimiento de catalán y la adaptación escolar. *Infancia y Aprendizaje* 32 (3), 307–327.

Vila-i-Moreno, X., Vial, S. and Galindo, M. (2004) Language practices in bilingual schools: Some observed, quantitative data from Catalonia. In X. P. Rodríguez-Yáñez, A. M. Lorenzo Suárez and F. Ramallo (eds) *Bilingualism and Education: From the Family to the School* (pp. 317–329). Munich: Lincoln Europa.

Woolard, K.A. (2003) 'We don't speak Catalan because we are marginalized': Ethnic and class connotations of language in Barcelona. In R. Blot (ed.) *Language and Social Identity* (pp. 85–103). Westport, CT: Praeger.

Woolard, K. A. (2008) Language and identity choice in Catalonia: The interplay of contrasting ideologies of linguistic authority. In K. Süselbeck, U. Mühschlegel and P. Masson (eds) *Lengua, nación e identitad. La regulación del plurilingüismo en España y América Latina* (pp. 303–323). Frankfurt am Mein/Madrid: Vervuert/Latinoamericana.

Woolard, K.A. (2009) Linguistic consciousness among adolescents in Catalonia: A case study from the Barcelona urban area in a longitudinal perspective. *Zeitschrift für Katalanistik* 22, 125–149.

4 Training a Primary Education Teacher to Teach Expository Text Comprehension Strategies[1]

Núria Castells, Isabel Solé, Cristina Luna, Eva Lordán, Esther Nadal, Mariana Miras and Sandra Espino

The present research project was aimed at promoting teachers' professional development in teaching content-area reading. The intervention case study involved one primary education teacher (level 1) and her class as the experimental group, and another teacher and her class as the control group (25 pupils each, aged 6). The main purpose of the intervention was to help the teacher to teach reading comprehension strategies. To obtain the initial information about the way the teachers implemented reading comprehension, semi-structured interviews and classroom observations were conducted and were jointly analysed with the teacher of the experimental group. The texts and strategies to be implemented were selected, discussed and designed with the teacher over a six-month period, in order to scaffold her practice. Furthermore, the teacher in the experimental group was asked to prepare and carry out an activity on her own, six months after the intervention had ended. Students from the two groups were given the Avaluació de la comprensió lectora (ACL) reading comprehension test (Català *et al.*, 2005), both before and after the intervention, and samples of their production in terms of reading comprehension were collected. Qualitative analyses were carried out on classroom observations and intervention interviews, and statistical analyses of the students' data were performed. The results indicate that the teacher was able to incorporate and implement reading comprehension strategies. The results also show some differences in the comprehension level that the students in the experimental group attained when compared with the control group.

Introduction

The ability to understand written information is fundamental for ensuring the acquisition of many of the competences required by today's society. As has been mentioned by Arnau and Vila (this volume), in Catalonia, the *Llei d'Educació* (Education Law) highlights the importance of teaching language competences in every content area of the curriculum. For the first two years of primary education, the curriculum establishes that 'reading is a fundamental factor for developing basic competencies and must be included in the development of every content area' (Generalitat de Catalunya, 2007: 21824). The legislative proposal, however, seems to be rather elementary in its approach and is therefore unlikely to be free of problems.

Apart from the Programme for International Student Assessment (PISA) (Catalan students' results can be examined in the work of Arnau & Vila, this volume), another international study on reading, PIRLS (Progress in International Reading Literacy Study) (Mullis *et al.*, 2007) demonstrates that fourth-year primary education students in Spain have significant problems in understanding informational or expository texts as opposed to literary texts. This reality, which has also been identified in other countries (Duke, 2000), poses a major challenge when we consider that most educational contents that students must learn at compulsory education levels involve reading expository texts (Bernhardt *et al.*, 1995). The results of the PIRLS study indicate, however, that Spanish students manage to adequately understand literary texts. Therefore, it seems that the teaching task aimed at promoting the comprehension of narrative texts, stories and tales, among others, is providing results. However, we wonder what is happening to the teaching of reading comprehension using expository texts.

Being able to read and understand expository texts, which provide knowledge about concepts of different levels of abstraction, represents a challenge for students. Unlike narrative texts, expository texts present unfamiliar contents, which are explained through abstract logical relations (Stein & Trabasso, 1981). Apart from the complexity of ideas they contain, the structure of expository texts can vary: sequence, description, compare–contrast, problem–solution and causation (Meyer & Freedle, 1984; Meyer *et al.*, 2002; Simonsen, 2004). Usually these structures appear in combination (Meyer & Poon, 2001), which complicates their understanding even further.

The aforementioned characteristics may perhaps lead some to consider expository texts to be more complex than narrative texts (Goldman & Rakestraw, 2000), and for that reason, their presence in the classroom seems to be somewhat anecdotal, to the extent that students can approach reading simple narrative texts almost independently. Various studies, however, demonstrate that kindergarten and early primary education students are capable of recognising certain characteristics in expository texts, some linguistic structures contained therein (Carlino & Santana, 1996; Pappas, 1993) and at the same time, can remember the content of an expository text they have read (Moss, 1997). Furthermore, different studies reiterate the need to promote the comprehension of texts with an expository structure and incorporate this instruction into the content areas (Guthrie & Ozgungor, 2002; Pressley, 2002).

Comprehension of expository texts and intervention

Intervening in the comprehension of expository texts requires possessing a wider vision of what this process means. Van Dijk and Kintsch (1983) and Kintsch (1998, 2009) propose a model in which they distinguish three different reading comprehension levels that students can achieve when reading a text. These different levels involve representing the text information in different degrees of depth along a continuum that goes from a more surface representation to a deeper one: surface memory, representation of the textbase and of the situation model.

The surface memory representation involves storing words and sentences from the text in a more or less literal manner. Elaborating the textbase requires building propositions, based on the information contained in the words and sentences of the text, to obtain a hierarchical and coherent representation of the text. This representation involves elaborating inferences to understand the text's contents, integrating the information that this offers at superstructure level (text structure, graphical information), the macrostructure of the ideas and the microstructure. The situation model, on the other hand, requires integrating the textbase with the reader's prior knowledge and goals. Therefore, the construction of a situation model depends on a much wider range of factors: the individual's background knowledge, personal experiences, interests, purposes for reading (Palincsar & Schutz, 2011; Sánchez, 2010). At the same time, it requires the creation of a textbase.

To date, interventions in research on expository text education have focused on the second year in primary education upwards. Apart from this convergence, some of the studies carried out have attempted to stress specific aspects in the construction of the textbase, taking first and foremost, and individually, elements such as the structure of the text, the comprehension of the different words of the text and the establishment of inferences. On the other hand, other research has attempted to promote the construction, by the learner, of the situation model in relation to the text being read (Beck et al., 1996; McKeown et al., 2009).

Going further into the differences between both intervention proposals, in the first research group, more associated with the construction of the textbase, the interventions were directed towards studying the characteristics of expository texts in a detailed and concrete manner. Specific effort and time is dedicated to each aspect, such as structure and content. Although many studies focus on the structure of the text, they also incorporate attention to the content and its comprehension, leaving the importance of knowledge that the reader can bring to the comprehension of the text on a second level, or even omitting it.

In this subgroup, we find the pioneering intervention by Danner (1976). From reading expository texts to his second-year students, Danner concluded that they could benefit from the text's organisation to remember and cluster sentences by topic. Students remembered the paragraphs that were topically organised better than those that were disorganised. Lauer (2002) made second-grade students read texts with a problem-solving structure. She found that the most appropriate answers and the better summaries were related to texts that had a better structure. Also in second grade, Williams et al. (2005) and Williams et al. (2009) carried out interventions regarding the reading of expository texts with a compare–contrast structure. They divided the students into three groups: in one group they taught the structure (and the context of the text); another one placed emphasis on the content, without addressing the structure; and in the third one no specific intervention was carried out. The results demonstrated that the intervention that took the structure of the text as reference, as well as emphasising the content, enabled students to achieve a better comprehension than the intervention that only stressed the comprehension of the contents. Hence, these studies argue the importance of addressing structural components of the texts despite the fact that there were no differences when transferring this knowledge between an intervention exclusively centred on the content and an intervention that, in addition, covered its structure (Williams et al., 2009).

The second perspective, which is more interested in encouraging a deeper comprehension among students, focuses its attention on a comprehensive, integrated study of the text, stimulating dialogue, discussion and reflection about the meanings that the text transmits and incorporating strategies throughout the discussion without working on them separately. Among the research that could be placed within this second perspective, we find those of Beck et al. (1996) and McKeown et al. (2009). These researchers have developed a proposal in which teachers guide the discussion on the meaning of the text, encouraging active student participation in this process. Their point of departure is the idea that texts can present various challenges for comprehension, and the ideal situation is to help students to think and reflect together on the meanings that the text transmits or suggests. Through dialogue on the text in the classroom, the teacher can address the validity of the meanings that the students draw from the text, helping them realise what they understand and do not understand, encouraging them to re-read and search for evidence in the text that supports their ideas, and giving attention to the structural components of the text (Beck & McKeown, 2006). In this second perspective, there are no differentiated activities for teaching each strategy; rather all are integrated within the course of the activity. There are few studies that explicitly compare these two ways of teaching reading comprehension, and those that do exist have been carried out on the later years of compulsory primary education. Thus, the longitudinal study carried out by McKeown et al. (2009), has demonstrated that the integrated teaching of reading comprehension strategies favours, in fifth-year primary education students, the recall of both expository and narrative texts.

Characteristics of this intervention

A large part of the research reviewed provides a teaching programme prepared by investigators for participating teachers. Although some studies claim that teachers 'enjoyed the programme and thought that the children had benefited from it' (Williams et al., 2005), they do not provide reliable data on whether the teachers are capable of using what they have learned during the intervention with other texts, and in an independent manner. Therefore, it does not guarantee that the changes caused by the intervention are maintained after completion.

The intervention we propose assumes that teachers have broad theoretical, practical and tacit knowledge (Atkinson & Claxton, 2002; Grossman, 1990) that constitutes the basis for their future learning, as well as for introducing changes in the way they teach. For this reason, any intervention that aims to introduce new educational strategies must consider the teachers' knowledge as the starting point for anchoring the new proposals. In addition to this, from a socioconstructivist perspective, any intervention aimed at having an influence on teachers' ideas and practices should be conceptualised, with caution, as a guided participation process (Rogoff, 1993) or a process related to the metaphor of scaffolding (Wood et al., 1976). Consequently, we assume that the intervention needs to take into account the educational practices that teachers have designed to teach social sciences and reading comprehension, in order to guide, accompany and help them to become more competent professionals. Therefore, the intervention is designed as a gradual process, which requires successive discussions and negotiations of the meanings and proposals, together with sharing the emotions and effects that emerge in the educational practice. At the same time, the researcher adopts the role of an expert who collaborates with the teachers (Kurpius & Fuqua, 1993), so that they can share their perspectives about the object of the intervention. As McKeown and Beck (2004) point out, improving teachers' practices requires cooperation between teachers and researchers.

Assuming the ideas presented, the intervention carried out has considered, first, the principles provided by Palincsar and Schutz (2011) on what the teaching of reading comprehension strategies that favour the construction of increasingly wider and related situation models should involve. The principles entail:

- Using related texts to teach reading comprehension.
- Helping children to understand the text in terms of the goals, questions or speculations that they have decided to tackle by reading it. This requires prior analysis by the teacher to identify reasonable learning goals, as well as any challenges that the text may present for students' comprehension and the manner in which the teacher can help students to overcome them.
- Guiding the students in building knowledge, which involves helping them to specify their prior knowledge and see how it is related with the new information, as well as identifying the relationships between the different ideas presented in the text according to the initial goals. On a deeper level, helping the students to become aware of the strategies they are using.

These principles are defined in an intervention proposal in which evidence from other research on learning to read is also included, such as the importance of considering writing activities as complementary activities to those focused on text comprehension (Spivey, 1997) and the importance of working in small groups (Johnson, 1981). Hence, the final intervention proposal was configured as follows:

- At an organisational level: encourage interaction between equals in order to stimulate students to discuss the meanings that they do not understand.
- At a task-type level: from the tasks that the teacher develops, prioritise those that have a major potential for helping students to understand the text and avoid those that have scant potential, and encourage the inclusion of activities that promote the use of reading for learning.
- Regarding the strategies focused on promoting text comprehension: from the methodological strategies the teacher already used, promote those that have a clear purpose and function for encouraging expository text comprehension; transform those of little function; and help the teacher to incorporate others. These strategies were organised according to the three stages that can be established in any reading activity: before, during and after reading.

Objectives

The objectives that we set out were the following:

- Promote the inclusion of reading comprehension strategies for expository texts beginning with first-year primary education, by the teacher.

- Assess the degree to which the teacher is capable of using reading comprehension strategies independently, at a point in time after having completed the intervention.
- Assess the impact of these strategies on the overall comprehension and specific comprehension of the contents learnt by students through reading expository texts.

We hoped that the reading comprehension strategies introduced by the teacher had an impact on the comprehension level measured by the ACL test and, especially, on the comprehension and learning level of the specific content worked on.

Method

Design and participants

The study as a whole lasted for two school years. The intervention was carried out in a first-year primary education class in a school that had Catalan as the vehicular language (see Arnau & Vila, this volume).

Two teachers in a public school in a city in Catalonia, who volunteered to participate in the study, were randomly assigned to the two experimental conditions: the reading comprehension programme or the control group. Each class had 25 students ($n = 50$). The families of the students in both classes were middle to upper class, most of them spoke Catalan at home or knew this language well enough to understand and speak it fluently, and they signed an authorisation indicating they agreed to let their children participate. Six per cent of the students were enrolled in part-time or full-time special education services. The teachers' and students' characteristics are shown in Table 4.1.

In the second year of primary education, we suggested to the teacher of the reading comprehension programme that she prepare, individually and six months after the completion of the intervention, a teaching session for an expository text. We also asked her to implement it with her students. In this second year, the teachers themselves continued to participate with the same groups of students.

Table 4.1 Student and teacher characteristics for each classroom

Teacher	No. of years of experience	No. of students in the class	Female	Male	Special education
A (experimental)	15	25	10	15	2
B (control)	17	25	11	14	3

Significant efforts were made to ensure that the planned intervention proposal met the ecological validity requirements to be considered when an intervention is carried out in a natural context (Cook & Reichardt, 1986).

Materials and instruments

During the project, different materials were used:

- To identify the reading comprehension level of students, the ACL (reading comprehension assessment) test was used (Català *et al.*, 2005). More specifically, the forms ACL-1, for first-year primary education, and ACL-2, for second year, were used. This test is standardised for the Catalan population and has an acceptable reliability index. It identifies four dimensions of reading comprehension: literal comprehension (recognition of what explicitly appears in the text); inferential or interpretative comprehension (exercised when the reader's prior knowledge is activated and suppositions are formulated on the text's contents); information reorganisation (ability to synthesise the information received and outline it); critical or judgement assessment (involves forming one's own judgements and responses of a subjective nature). Therefore, it is a complete test that has clear parallels with other tests (PIRLS, PISA) regarding the dimensions analysed and the type of texts presented (narrative, expository, etc.).
- Specific tests were prepared to assess the learning level achieved by students regarding the expository texts studied in the classroom. More specifically, for the last text covered in the first-year class, '*Les Formigues*', a table was prepared that students had to complete (see Appendix 4.1). For the second-year text ('*Els Sectors*', see Appendix 4.2), the teacher prepared a test with three different types of questions: retrieve literal information from the text; integrate information present in different parts of the text and a question to integrate information and elaborate on it (see Appendix 4.3).
- Regarding the expository texts covered in the classroom, to ensure the ecological validity of the intervention as far as possible, the point of departure taken was from the curriculum for the environment, society and culture knowledge area subject. Both teachers used the same textbooks and trade books to prepare the classes. The expository texts used by the teachers to develop the reading and comprehension activities were the same for both groups and were chosen by the teachers themselves according to the topic to be studied. Nonetheless, the activities implemented during the intervention were designed and agreed on in conjunction with the research team and the teacher of the reading comprehension programme.

Regarding the instruments used, the interviews conducted with the teachers were recorded on tape, while the classroom sessions were recorded using audio-visual means.

Procedure

The procedure followed for the intervention included various actions, some of which were related with the students, others with the teachers and others with both students and teachers in a classroom. For this reason, so that the process followed is easy to understand, the actions performed with each of the participating collectives are presented below.

Teacher of the comprehension programme (A) and her class

With the teacher of the comprehension programme, several semi-structured interviews and meetings were held. The first interview focused on determining the teaching practices for reading comprehension and the reading situations of expository texts that she carried out. Its aim was to determine the point of departure for guiding the mentoring and intervention proposals. This interview was followed by the observation and recording of a teaching session for an expository text.

After this, a total of four meetings were held, which make up the core of the intervention. At the first meeting, the teacher and the researcher watched and analysed the expository text comprehension session previously recorded, for which the intervention would be developed, in order to identify aspects that could be changed.

The three other meetings were used to review some of the texts that the teacher would work on with the students and to jointly devise a proposal for increasing comprehension. Prior to each intervention meeting, the teacher sent the researchers the text that the primary education team had decided to teach in class. The three texts chosen were on the following topics: weather, mammals and ants (Figure 4.1).

The team of researchers reviewed the texts, analysed possible difficulties that students might find and planned proposals that enabled them to study the content of the text in depth, with dialogue and interaction, following the criteria presented in the introduction section. The teacher also gave her proposal during the meeting, which was discussed and analysed. From the combination of the two proposals, a plan that respected the teacher's vision of the class group, the material being taught and the tools already available was agreed on, introducing changes or new aspects that favoured students' learning of strategies for expository texts (see the example proposed for the 'Les Formigues' text in Table 4.2).

The teacher carried out her classes according to the agreements made on the activities to implement in the classroom during a long session for each of the texts selected. Once the intervention process was completed, a new interview was conducted to assess the experience and to look at the changes achieved in depth.

At the start of the new school year (second-year primary education), another follow-up interview was conducted in order for the teacher to

Figure 4.1 'Les Formigues' text (Ortoll, 2010)

Table 4.2 Work proposal agreed on with the teacher of the reading comprehension programme

Phase	Agreements
Before reading	Discuss mammal characteristics from memory, contrasting them with those of ants.
	On the blackboard, write down the questions about ants that the students come up with.
During reading	Read in silence and think of questions.
	Identify differences between this text and others.
	Reading by the teacher and clarification of questions.
	Collective reading.
After reading	Answer questions orally with the class and focus on how they can find the answer. Students write down the answers in pairs.
	Texts with blanks to complete individually

prepare a teaching session for expository text comprehension without help. The proposal that the teacher prepared individually was also implemented in her classroom with the students that she had had the previous year.

Control group teacher (B) and her class

The teacher of the control group was also interviewed at the start of the project to investigate her teaching practices for reading. For this teacher, an initial session and an intermediate session were recorded and observed. The teacher of the control group used the same expository texts as the teacher of the experimental group. The first observation determined the point of departure of this teacher and ensured that there were no significant differences between her and the teacher of the experimental group. The second observation determined that no substantial changes had occurred in her way of teaching.

At the end of the project, a meeting was held with both teachers (experimental and control groups) to share the intervention process carried out.

Students (control group and experimental group)

Before the intervention (January) and at the end of the school year (June), the reading comprehension level of the first-year students was assessed using the ACL-1 and ACL-2 tests, given by the teachers with the help of the researchers.

During the intervention process (March–April–May), tests that the teachers (of the experimental and control groups) had prepared with the researchers' support to assess the learning of the contents studied were given out. In the second year, the test of the 'Els Sectors' text that the teacher of the experiment group had prepared individually was given.

Procedure for analysing the data

Qualitative and quantitative analyses were performed on the data obtained from the different participants.

Analysis of the observations made

The content of the different interviews, meetings and observations was transcribed and qualitative analyses were performed using different instruments created *ad hoc* for the analysis. To identify changes in the actions of the teacher of the experimental group within the classroom, categories were drawn up (in a deductive–inductive process) regarding three theoretically and conceptually relevant dimensions: social organisation in the classroom; type of activity implemented; specific strategies focused on improving reading.

- For the dimension of social organisation in the classroom, the following categories were established: teacher works with the classroom; teacher works with individuals; children work in pairs or groups and the teacher helps them.

- As regards possible activities, some of them were associated with the type of reading that students could do (silent; aloud – better if they have read silently before; line by line – activity that the teacher implemented before our intervention); with the teacher's activity (explains the content of the text; reads the text) or with the proposal that she made to the students (identify difficult concepts/words; answer oral questions on the text to help students build their understanding; write words related with the text; fill in blanks with information about the text; write sentences about the text; copy what she or some of the pupils wrote).

- Regarding reading strategies, the teacher could ask students to: underline or highlight unknown words (the teacher told them the words to underline); pay attention to the text structure, e.g. the title; attend to paratextual components, e.g. pictures, images; make hypotheses, predictions and questions the text will answer; retrieve information (asking literal questions); integrate information (relate information from different parts of the text; construct information) combining text information and previous knowledge; reread to detect parts of the text that the students did not read carefully or to make them think about the meaning of the text. The teacher could also contextualise text content and ask for previous knowledge; explain the meaning of unknown words, concepts or sentences; recapitulate or ask students to do so; supervise comprehension of the task; or show how to write something.

The categories associated with strategies for studying reading are theoretically supported, although more have been added as a result of the observations made. The categories are exhaustive in terms of the dimensions selected and are mutually exclusive. At the analysis level, the presence/absence of a certain category at each of the sessions observed (total: 7) was coded.

The categories were applied by two of the researchers. They independently coded three of the sessions to determine the level of agreement achieved (Cronbach's alpha: 82%). Having resolved any discrepancies by agreement, they continued to divide up the remainder of the sessions, which they coded independently, resolving any questions collaboratively.

Analysis of the text comprehension tests

The two tests given after the students had studied reading comprehension were analysed and the number of correct answers was identified. For the 'Les Formigues' text, students could obtain a maximum of 10 points, 1 point per correct answer.

For each of the answers to the question aimed at retrieving literal information in the 'Els Sectors' text, a mark of 0.25 was given (1 point in total). The second question, which required integrating information, was scored as 0.5 for each correct answer (1 point in total). In the last question, to integrate and elaborate on information, the information cores were analysed and their appropriateness was assessed. If students indicated *'they transform material into products or things'*, a score of 1 was given; if they said *'they do things for people'*, 0.5; if the answer was different from those given previously: 0. The analysis of this question, carried out by two researchers, obtained an 80% agreement rate.

The results of the ACL-1 and ACL-2 tests, as well as the results of the tests prepared to assess the students' learning, were introduced into the database of the statistic program SPSS15 to calculate the descriptive and significance statistics through the Student *t*-test for independent samples.

Results

Teacher's incorporation of strategies in the experimental group versus control group

In line with the first objective set, which attempted to encourage teachers to include reading comprehension strategies for expository texts in first-year primary education, there is evidence that this goal has been fully achieved. An important and notable change that occurred from the first stage of the intervention was that the first-year primary teachers included texts on environment, society and culture in their classes and they suggested to their respective students that they read them.

The initial interviews carried out with the teachers indicated that it was not usual for them to suggest texts and ask their students to read them, and even less so with texts that were the subject of reading comprehension teaching in this area. The teachers confirmed that they tended to explain the content rather than make the students read it:

> Teacher A (initial interview): 'What happens...., is we find ourselves, that in Catalan we have plenty of texts, we read, we look for strategies to help comprehension, we make it gradual... The type of comprehension that is studied in Catalan is gradual. Then of course, however, when you change to the topic of the Environment... you find that you have very, very few texts because we study it visually and orally.'

> Teacher B (initial interview): 'In the Environment and Society, we explain the topics orally. At times, the texts are accompanied by exercises and we ask the students to do them.'

Regarding the usual practices of teachers when teaching reading comprehension, Table 4.3 shows the similarities and differences between teacher A and B, using the same text with their respective class group before the

Table 4.3 Social organisation, activities and strategies used by Teacher A (experimental group) and B (control group) prior to intervention, and by Teacher A, individually six months after the intervention

Dimensions	Categories	Teacher A (pre)	Teacher B (pre)	Teacher A (post)
Social organisation	Teacher (T)-classroom	x	x	x
	T-pupil	x	x	x
	T-pairs or group			x
Activities	T explains	x	x	
	T reads	x	x	x
	Children read silently	x	x	x
	Children read aloud		x	x
	Children read a text line by line	x		
	Children identify difficult concepts/words			x
	T asks oral questions on the text	x	x	x
	T asks pupils to write words related with the text read			x
	T asks pupils to fill in blanks with information about the text		x	
	T asks pupils to write sentences on the text			x
	T asks pupils to copy what teacher/pupils wrote		x	x
Strategies	T asks pupils to underline, highlight unknown words	x		x
	T asks pupils to pay attention to text structure	x	x	x (title)
	T asks pupils to watch for paratextual components			x
	T contextualises text content and asks for previous knowledge	x	x	x
	T asks for hypotheses, predictions and questions			x
	T explains the meaning of unknown words, concepts, sentences	x	x	x
	T assigns activities for retrieving information	x	x	x

(*Continued*)

Table 4.3 (*Continued*)

Dimensions	Categories	Teacher A (pre)	Teacher B (pre)	Teacher A (post)
	T assigns activities for integrating information	x		x
	T assigns activities for constructing information combining text information and previous knowledge	x		x
	T asks pupils to reread			x
	T recapitulates	x		
	T and students recapitulate together			x
	T supervises comprehension of the task			x
	T shows pupils how to write something			x

intervention. As can be seen, the initial situation was similar, if not identical, for both groups.

As we see in Table 4.3, before the intervention and in the same way as teacher B, teacher A organised the activities in such a way that she tended to interact with students at whole-group level or individually. Regarding reading, she usually provided explanations about what they would read, and the students would read quietly and afterwards aloud, line by line, stopping at the end of each one regardless of whether or not there was a full stop or any other punctuation mark. Next the teacher would also read the text again and then ask oral reading comprehension questions. Unlike the control group teacher, teacher A did not propose any activity that related reading and writing.

Analysis of this first session, together with the explanations that teacher A had given in the first interview, led us to devise a proposal that this teacher could incorporate into her teaching practice: working in small groups; more meaningful reading for the students (not line by line, but taking into account punctuation); activities that combine reading and writing, and therefore, deepening the combined use of both tools. At a strategy level, she already used several, but they did not help the students make predictions or hypotheses on what they might expect to find in the text, nor did they emphasise the importance of re-reading. Furthermore, it was also considered important that she be able to ensure that the students understood the purpose of the activity, and that she led them to take into account paratextual elements to establish more relationships and understand the text in greater depth.

We also appear to have achieved the second objective we set for ourselves, assessing to what degree the teacher is able to use the reading comprehension strategies independently some time after having completed the intervention. Table 4.3 shows the difference between the initial session with teacher A and the session that she prepared individually a year after having started the intervention (and six months after having completed it).

Table 4.4 shows the sessions in which teacher A incorporates some of the strategies suggested to her, as well as the proposals she abandoned in order to encourage a better understanding of texts by her students. The data presented in this table enables us to determine the level of transformation in the teacher's teaching practice and the level of 'consistency' in the intervention agreed on with her. These changes are shown, for example, in the strategies incorporated, such as working in pairs, writing based on the text, attention given to paratextual elements and formulation of hypotheses.

Equally relevant is the teacher's awareness of the change that participating in the intervention has had on her practice. In the closing interview of the intervention, she was asked her opinions on the experience, what had surprised her, what she had realised and what changes she had identified in her class group, among others. Some of her statements literally collected are:

Teacher 1 – experimental group (final interview)
- 'It's not just that they have a different level of comprehension. In terms of our approach ... they are more participative, it means that they master it more, the fact of analysing what they do and what they are looking for forces them to be closer to the text.'
- 'Before I wondered whether I needed to be so literal or whether I wanted them to discover for themselves ... They discovered ... they said that they found the answer in the text themselves, they were happy. You think that you have to tell them what you want them to learn, but it is also important that they discover it for themselves, that they search for it ...'
- 'I've seen them change. Once they understood the dynamics, they raised their hands more ... after they knew, they looked for the answer in the text. The group is more motivated, they participate more.'

Teacher A's statements illustrate that the change in her educational practices has been detected not only in the students' involvement in understanding the text, but also in the more emotional side of the students, with the teacher seeing them to be more motivated and participative.

Impact of the intervention on the students' comprehension

The results obtained regarding the third objective, to assess the possible impact of the intervention carried out with the students, demonstrated

Table 4.4 Social organisation, activities and strategies used by Teacher A (experimental group) before the intervention (1) during the intervention (2–3–4) and in the session afterwards (5)

Dimensions	Categories	Sessions observed				
		1st (pre)	2nd	3rd	4th	5th (post)
Social organisation	Teacher (T)-classroom	X	x	x	x	x
	T-pupil	X	x	x	x	x
	T-pairs or group		x	x	x	x
	Pupils working on their own	X			x	x
Activities	T explains	X	x		x	
	T reads	x	x	x	x	x
	Children read silently	x	x	x	x	x
	Children read aloud		x	x	x	x
	Children read a text line by line	x				
	Children identify difficult concepts/words				x	
	T asks oral questions on the text	x	x	x	x	x
	T asks pupils to write words related with the text read				x	
	T asks pupils to fill in blanks with information about the text		x	x	x	
	T asks pupils to write sentences on the text		x	x	x	x
	T asks pupils to copy what teacher–pupils wrote		x			x
Strategies	T asks pupils to underline, highlight unknown words	x	x			x
	T asks pupils to pay attention to text structure	x	x		x	x (title)
	T asks pupils to watch for paratextual components		x	x	x	x
	T contextualises text content and asks for previous knowledge	x	x	x	x	x
	T asks for hypotheses, predictions and questions		x	x	x	x

(Continued)

Table 4.4 (*Continued*)

Dimensions	Categories	Sessions observed				
		1st (pre)	2nd	3rd	4th	5th (post)
	T explains the meaning of unknown words, concepts, sentences	x	x	x		x
	T assigns activities for retrieving information	x	x	x	x	x
	T assigns activities for integrating information	x	x	x		x
	T assigns activities for constructing information combining text information and previous knowledge	x	x		x	x
	T asks pupils to reread		x		x	x
	T recapitulates	x	x	x		
	T and students recapitulate together				x	x
	T supervises comprehension of the task				x	
	T shows pupils how to write something				x	x

different aspects. The ACL-1 test (see Table 4.5) showed that there are no significant differences between the experimental and control groups in the pre-test, indicating that the groups had an equivalent level when the process was started. In the post-test where the test corresponding to second-year primary education was used, there were no significant differences either. The experimental group's average was slightly above that of the control group before the intervention, except for critical comprehension questions, for which it was slightly below. Once the intervention was completed, the scores of the experimental group continued to be slightly higher than that of the control group in areas of reorganisation and inferential comprehension and also in critical comprehension. Given that there are no significant results, they are considered tendencies that are difficult to interpret.

These results are qualified slightly when consideration is given to the answers provided by the students for the final questions they were asked on the specific texts that the teachers had agreed to study (see Table 4.6).

Table 4.5 Results of the Student t-test for the pre- and post-tests of the ACL test, control group and experimental group (first year)

ACL dimensions	Pre-test (ACL-1)				Post-test (ACL-2)			
	Experim. X (σ)	Control X (σ)	t	p	Experim. X (σ)	Control X (σ)	t	p
Literal comprehension	6.92 (2.61)	6.12 (2.74)	1.05	0.30	4.12 (2.04)	4.12 (1.85)	0.00	1.00
Reorganisation	2.96 (1.54)	2.80 (1.50)	0.37	0.71	3.12 (2.00)	2.96 (1.81)	0.29	0.77
Inferential comprehension	4.64 (2.06)	3.96 (1.90)	1.21	0.23	2.88 (1.74)	2.84 (1.72)	0.08	0.93
Critical comprehension	1.40 (0.76)	1.52 (0.82)	−0.53	0.59	1.56 (1.29)	1.36 (1.18)	0.57	0.57

*$p < 0.05$

Table 4.6 Results of the Student t-test for the experimental group and the control group on the text test 'Les Formigues' (first year) and 'Els Sectors' (second year)

Assessment tasks	First grade				Second grade			
	Experim. X (σ)	Control X (σ)	t	p	Experim. X (σ)	Control X (σ)	t	p
'Les Formigues'	9.22 (1.23)	8.68 (1.77)	1.21	0.23				
'Els Sectors' Retrieving					0.91 (0.17)	0.85 (0.22)	1.08	0.28
Integrating					0.94 (0.17)	0.77 (0.25)	2.67	0.01*
Integrating elaborating					0.83 (0.35)	0.21 (0.37)	5.85	0.00**

*Not interpretable, as it does not comply with normality (Levene's test).
**$p < 0.001$

For example, for the first-year text, *'Les Formigues'*, students in the experimental group achieved an average of 9.2 correct answers, as opposed to students in the control group, who had an average of 8.6, although this result is not significant.

For the *'Els Sectors'* text, the results obtained demonstrated that the students in the experimental group were capable of answering questions of greater complexity (integrating and developing the information) significantly better than students in the control group. In the other two questions, there appear to be no significant differences that could be interpreted.

Conclusions and Discussion

The objectives that we had set in this study, involving intervening in the reading comprehension study of first-year primary education students, seem to have been largely achieved. First, thanks to a respectful intervention process with text comprehension practices that the teacher already had a solid command of and focused on discussing new proposals with her, the teacher incorporated and/or maintained the teaching strategies for reading comprehension that, from a research point of view, are essential in encouraging an adequate comprehension of texts (Palincsar & Schutz, 2011).

More specifically, she incorporated strategies linked with teaching the content of texts in pairs, generating hypotheses, re-reading texts, asking students to recapitulate contents read and activities that associate reading with writing. At the same time, the intervention process carried out ensured that the teacher was able to maintain and transfer the strategies studied to another reading situation with a different text.

This data indicates the importance of a shared, collaborative and maintained approach between researchers and teaching staff (Kurpius & Fuqua, 1993), to ensure that interventions focused on improving reading with expository texts can be maintained beyond the intervention process.

On the other hand, regarding the impact of the strategies on the students' comprehension, the data from the activities associated with the texts studied in the intervention seem to indicate that the third objective has also been achieved. The data from tests taken subsequently to the work done on the texts in the classroom demonstrate that the students in the experimental group show a tendency to achieve better results than those in the control group, especially on questions where they have to include information appearing in the text and use their own knowledge (processes linked with a deeper representation of the content).

Unfortunately, the ACL-2 tests, which we hoped would show differences between both groups, revealed very similar data. This fact may be owing to the tests being designed for second-year primary education level and having items that were too complicated for students to solve, regardless of what they might have learnt. An indication of this fact is the low averages obtained. This result could also be attributed to the difficulty in transferring comprehension strategies learnt through specific texts to a test that had to be carried out individually and that included different text types. We found that, once the ACL-1 tests had been used to ensure the equivalence of the groups at the start, a different test needed to be used. In Catalan, we were unable to find other reading comprehension tests that were standardised.

Another of the limitations of our study is associated with the short duration of the intervention, caused by factors beyond the researchers' control.

In this regard, perhaps more resounding results could have been observed in an intervention that covered a full school year, a greater number of classes and using a measurement instrument adjusted to the possibilities of the students.

Despite these limitations, our study demonstrated that, at least in our sociocultural context, it is viable to propose the possibility of working with expository texts and encouraging their comprehension from the second half of the first year in primary education. As opposed to other studies in other contexts, such as the United States (Williams *et al.*, 2005, 2009), it is possible to favour a reading comprehension study among younger students. It also points to the importance of training teachers in the specific linguistic context in which they have to teach, a challenge as it has been mentioned in Arnau and Vila, this volume.

Note

(1) Research Project: '*Ensenyament d'estratègies per comprendre textos expositius als primers dos cursos de primària*' (2008ARIE00020) (Castells, N., Solé, I., Luna, C., Lordán, E., Nadal, E., Miras, M., Espino, S.)

References

Atkinson, T. and Claxton, G. (eds) (2002) *El profesor intuitivo*. Barcelona: Octaedro.

Beck, I.L. and McKeown, M.G. (2006) Encouraging young children's language interactions with stories. In D. Dickinson and S. Neuman (eds) *Handbook of Early Literacy Research* (Vol. 2). New York: Guilford.

Beck, I.L., McKeown, M.G., Sandora, C., Kucan, L. and Worthy, J. (1996) Questioning the author: A yearlong classroom implementation to engage students with text. *The Elementary School Journal* 96 (4), 385–414.

Bernhardt, E., Destino, T., Kamil, M. and Rodriguez-Munoz, M. (1995) Assessing science knowledge in an English–Spanish bilingual elementary school. *Cognosos* 4, 4–6.

Carlino, P. and Santana, D. (coords) (1996) *Leer y escribir con sentido. Una experiencia constructivista en Educación Infantil y Primaria*. Madrid: Visor.

Català, G., Català, M., Molina, E. and Monclús, R. (2005) *Evaluación de la comprensión lectora*. Barcelona: Graó.

Cook, T.D. and Reichardt, C.S. (1986) *Métodos Cualitativos y Cuantitativos en la Investigación Evaluativa*. Madrid: Morata.

Danner, F.W. (1976) Children's understanding of intersentence organization in the recall of short descriptive passages. *Journal of Educational Psychology* 68, 174–183.

Duke, N.K. (2000) 3.6 minutes per day: The scarcity of informational texts in first grade. *Reading Research Quarterly* 35, 202–224.

Generalitat de Catalunya (2007) Decret 142/2007, de 26 de juny, pel qual s'estableix l'ordenació dels ensenyaments de l'educació primària. *Diari Oficial de la Generalitat de Catalunya*. Retrieved from http://www.gencat.cat/eadop/imatges/4915/0717 6074.pdf

Goldman, S.R. and Rakestraw, J.A. Jr. (2000) Structural aspects of constructing meaning from text. In M.L. Kamil, P.B. Mosenthal, P.D. Pearson and R. Barr (eds) *Handbook of Reading Research* (Vol. 3, pp. 311–335). Mahwah, NJ: Erlbaum.

Grossman, P. (1990) *The Making of a Teacher.* New York: Teachers College Press.

Guthrie, J.T. and Ozgungor, S. (2002) Instructional contexts for reading engagement. In C.C. Block and M. Pressley (eds) *Comprehension Instruction: Researcher-Based Best Practices* (pp. 275–288). New York: Guilford Press.

Johnson, D.W. (1981) Instructional goal structure: cooperative, competitive, or individualization. *Review of Educational Research* 44, 213–214.

Kintsch, W. (1998) *Comprehension: A Paradigm for Cognition.* New York: Cambridge University Press.

Kintsch, W. (2009) Learning and constructivism. In S. Tobias and T. Duffy (eds) *Constructivist Instruction* (pp. 223–241). New York: Routledge.

Kurpius, D.J. and Fuqua, D.R. (1993) Fundamental issues in defining consultation. *Journal of Counseling & Development* 71 (6), 598–600.

Lauer, K.D. (2002) The effect of text structure, content familiarity, and reading ability on second-graders' comprehension of text. Unpublished doctoral dissertation, Columbia University.

McKeown, M.G. and Beck, I.L. (2004) Direct and rich vocabulary instruction. In J.F. Baumann and E.J. Kame'enui (eds) *Vocabulary Instruction* (pp. 13–27). New York: Guilford Press.

McKeown, M.G., Beck, I.L. and Blake, R.G.K. (2009) Rethinking reading comprehension instruction: A comparison of instruction for strategies and content approaches. *Reading Research Quarterly* 44 (3), 218–253.

Meyer, B.J.F. and Freedle, R.O. (1984) Effects of discourse type on recall. *American Educational Research Journal* 21, 121–143.

Meyer, B.J.F. and Poon, L.W. (2001) Effects of structure training and signaling on recall of text. *Journal of Educational Psychology* 93 (1), 141–159.

Meyer, B.J.F., Theodorou, E., Brezinski, K.L., Middlemiss, W., McDougall, J. and Bartlett, B.J. (2002) Effects of structure strategy instruction delivered to fifth-grade children using the Internet with and without the aid of older adult tutors. *Journal of Educational Psychology* 94 (3), 486–519.

Moss, B. (1997) A qualitative assessment of first graders' retelling of expository text. *Reading Research and Instruction* 37 (1), 1–13.

Mullis, I.V.S., Martin, M.O., Kennedy, A.M. and Foy, P. (2007) PIRLS 2006. International Report. Chestnut Hill (Lynch School of Education, Boston College): TIMSS & PIRLS International Study Center.

Ortoll, C. (2010) Nou Saltamartí 1. Cicle Inicial de Coneixement del Medi. Barcelona: Editorial Barcanova.

Palincsar, A.S. and Schutz, K.M. (2011) Reconnecting strategy instruction with its theoretical roots. *Theory into Practice* 50 (2), 85–92.

Pappas, C.C. (1993) Is narrative "primary"? Some insights from kindergartners' pretend readings of stories and informational books. *Journal of Reading Behavior* 25, 97–129.

Pressley, M. (2002) *Reading Instruction That Works: The Case for Balanced Teaching* (2nd edn). New York: Guilford Press.

Rogoff, B. (1993) Observing sociocultural activity on three planes. In J.V. Wertsch, P. del Río and A. Alvarez (eds) *Sociocultural Studies of Mind* (pp. 139–163). New York: Cambridge University Press.

Sánchez, E. (2010) (coord) *La lectura en el aula. Qué se hace, qué se debe hacer y qué se puede hacer.* Barcelona: Graó.

Simonsen, S. (2004) Identifying and teaching text structures in content area classrooms. In D. Lapp, J. Flood and N. Farnan (eds) *Content Area Reading and Learning* (pp. 59–75). Mahwah, NJ: Erlbaum.

Spivey, N.N. (1997) *The Constructivist Metaphor. Reading, Writing and the Making of Meaning.* San Diego, CA: Academic Press.

Stein, N.L. and Trabasso, T. (1981) What's in a story: An approach to comprehension and instruction. In R. Glaser (ed.) *Advances in Instructional Psychology* 2, 213–267. Hillsdale, NJ: Erlbaum.

van Dijk, T.A. and Kintsch, W. (1983) *Strategies of Discourse Comprehension*. New York: Academic Press.

Williams, J.P., Brooke Stafford, K., Lauer, K.D., Hall, K.M. and Pollini, S. (2009) Embedding reading comprehension training in content-area instruction. *Journal of Educational Psychology* 101 (1), 1–20.

Williams, J.P., Hall, K.M., Lauer, K.D., Stafford, K.B., DeSisto, L.A. and deCani, J.S. (2005) Expository text comprehension in the primary grade classroom. *Journal of Educational Psychology* 97 (4), 538–550.

Wood, D.J., Bruner, J.S. and Ross, G. (1976) The role of tutoring in problem solving. *Journal of Child Psychology and Psychiatry* 17, 89–100.

Appendix 4.1

Test on the 'Les Formigues' text

Write yes or no

	Does it have a skeleton?	*Does it breathe using lungs?*	*Does it suckle when it is young?*	*Does its mother give birth to it?*	*Does it live in the ground?*	*Can it fly?*	*Do they live together?*	*Is it an insect?*
The ant								

Appendix 4.2

'Els Sectors' text (second-year primary)

'The people that produce products such as clothes, shoes, food, furniture, cars, etc. work in factories or workshops. (Picture of an assembly line where the word 'OPERATOR' appears).

In factories, material is transformed with the help of machines and a new product is made. Many people work there and they create many products. (Picture of a person working on a clay jar. Above it, is the word 'CRAFTSMAN'.)

In workshops, material is taken and transformed with the help of hands, tools or simple machines. The products obtained are handcrafted.'

Appendix 4.3

Test set on the 'Els Sectors' text (second-year primary)

1. Complete the following sentences based on what you have read in the text.

	Factory	Workshop
How many people work there?		
What do they use to transform the material?		

2. Fill in the missing word.
   An operator is a person who works in a ....
   A........................ works by transforming material with his hands.
3. What do these workers do?
   ....

5 Teacher Training in Literacy Instruction and Academic Achievement in a Multilingual Classroom

Joaquim Arnau, Haridian M de Aysa and Sonia Jarque

This research is based on an intervention programme in literacy instruction in a multilingual classroom. A secondary-school social sciences teacher and an instructional coach have designed and taught two lessons within the curriculum. The teacher's practices in literacy instruction in one of his classrooms before training (non-intervention group) were compared with the practices provided by both the teacher and the coach after the training process in another classroom (intervention group). The academic achievement of both groups of students was subsequently compared using pre-tests and post-tests. The study shows how the quality of literacy instruction improved after training and how this quality has also improved the academic achievement of the students (conceptual richness, academic vocabulary and quality of writing). This research confirms that teaching vocabulary and reading and writing strategies related to academic language are valuable practices for academic achievement. Other aspects of literacy instruction (context, language and knowledge) are discussed.

Introduction

Knowledge is constructed through the school's language, and it is through this language that school content is taught, understood by pupils and evaluated. As the curriculum moves on, as pupils progress towards higher levels, this becomes more abstract, and literacy becomes an increasingly fundamental instrument for understanding and expressing academic contents, and pupils are required to demonstrate their learning using their literacy resources.

Reading and writing academic texts is difficult because academic registers are dense, with information presented in different ways from the way meaning is constructed in everyday language (Schleppegrell, 2004).

Academic texts incorporate a specialised technical vocabulary from the various disciplines, and they are organised around logical relationships between ideas involving 'different ways of using language'. Each discipline has its own linguistic 'genres' or registers that can vary depending on the different communicative objectives. In natural sciences or physics there is, for instance, 'describe' (divide a phenomenon into its parts, components or stages, list its properties), 'explain' (express why and how it happens) and 'discuss' (argue, persuade, etc.) (Lemke, 1997). In history, the two most common genres are 'explanation' (of past situations, examining the causes and consequences) and 'argumentation' (defending a particular interpretation of the past, putting forward a range of positions and arguments for analysis and debate). Depending on the choices the historian or natural scientist makes, they create a text with its own 'macrostructure' (organisation of the processes or events, showing how one leads to another, and a selection of nouns, verbs and specific connectors). A whole collection of grammatical resources help with explaining the events (Schleppegrell, 2004, *op. cit.*).

Pupils' difficulties in understanding and expressing knowledge may be due to the specific characteristics of the language. If they have difficulties, they will not be able to express their knowledge accurately. Many students have little academic success at school, especially students whose language is not the language of instruction (Echevarria *et al.*, 2006).

To overcome these difficulties, teachers 'also need a better understanding of the features of the language they aim for students to develop' (Schleppegrell, 2004, *op. cit.*: 44). Based on this comprehension, they have to develop strategies for teaching vocabulary and the processes of reading and writing academic texts.

Reading comprehension and academic performance improve with knowledge of vocabulary. Pupils with limited vocabulary are not only readers with difficulties; they are also reluctant to read (Flood *et al.*, 2003; Stahl & Nagy, 2006). Vocabulary affects students' comprehension, fluency, writing, speaking, thinking, learning and achievement, as well as their confidence (Fisher & Frey, 2008; Met, 2008). Studies carried out in upper elementary classrooms indicate that teachers devote little time to teaching vocabulary and that the methods they use to teach it (basically definitional) are not very appropriate (Scott *et al.*, 2003). New approaches to teaching vocabulary have placed more emphasis on other methods: providing opportunities to use the words in context, teaching strategies for finding out the meaning of unknown words, etc. (Fisher & Frey, 2008, *op. cit.*).

For both reading and writing, pupils have to be provided with the right strategies so that they can understand the dense logical relationships shown in the texts, as well as the linguistic resources allowing them to express these relationships precisely.

As for writing, the teacher has to explain 'what' and 'how' they have to write, the ideas to be included, the structure of the text and the linguistic elements belonging to scientific discourse that have to be considered. Some provide 'models' (Quinquer, 2010) and others compare and contrast different types of text (Macken-Horarick, 1996).

Reading is a link in the learning process connected with writing and, like writing, also with oral discourse. The teacher has to 'select the texts' that will contribute to constructing knowledge and decide the 'purposes' or aims of reading. The idea is that the pupils should become increasingly competent readers, through teaching them 'cognitive strategies' (predicting, identifying important information, etc.) and 'metacognitive' ones (knowing what to do when there are comprehension problems, deciding on the right strategy depending on the purpose of the reading, etc.). A text students have to read might be the opportunity for comprehension of its structures, textual characteristics and vocabulary that they can later incorporate into the texts they write (Carrasquillo *et al.*, 2004).

Literacy instruction must be carried out in a context in which the activities are motivating and meaningful; a context in which pupils read and write to learn, and where the construction of knowledge is based on students' own ideas, on discussion and on interaction with one another; a context in which speech – oral discourse – is a first opportunity for the move from ordinary to academic language (Gibbons, 2003) and where it is practised in a way that is interrelated with reading and writing.

Observations made in the American context show that content area teachers tend not to provide literacy instruction because their training in this area is minimal (Tharp *et al.*, 2000). Professional development is needed so that teachers can put these ideas into practice when planning and teaching the curriculum (Fortune & Tedick, 2008). In this context, training programmes are being developed, aimed at teachers who have pupils with limited competences in English. The SIOP model (Sheltered Instruction Observation Protocol) includes the development of academic literacy as one of the important dimensions of the programme (Echevarria *et al.*, 2004).

In our context, in Catalonia, teacher training is no better. Secondary content-area teachers go into teaching with minimal teacher training and no training in literacy. Catalan is the predominant language of instruction and there are classes of pupils with various first languages who have limited capabilities in Catalan (see Arnau & Vila, this volume).

Literacy instruction training programmes, run by teachers of various subjects, are also beginning to be developed here (Quinquer, 2010, *op. cit.*). These programmes generally offer the following phases: reflection on practice itself, presentation of good practices, proposal for application in the classroom and shared evaluation of the new proposals.

Objectives and Hypothesis

This research assesses the effects of a literacy instruction intervention programme on the academic performance of pupils in a multilingual secondary school class where Catalan is the only medium of instruction and Spanish and English are taught as subjects (see Arnau & Vila, this volume). An instructional coach and a teacher shared the design and teaching of a thematic unit placing an emphasis on literacy. Together, the two processes constitute one of the first steps considered in teacher training.

The specific objectives of the research are as follows:

- To compare the differences in the quality of the literacy instruction received by pupils participating and those not participating in the intervention programme.
- To assess the effects of this intervention on pupils' academic performance.
- To evaluate the teacher training process.

The general hypothesis is that the pupils who receive teaching that places the emphasis on the quality of literacy instruction will achieve better academic performance than the pupils who do not participate. They will define concepts better and produce texts with greater conceptual richness, with greater presence of academic vocabulary and with more precise forms of writing (macrostructure, connectors).

The explanation of this process will consider the following sections: 'Methodology', 'Results Relating to Comparison of the Two Groups in Quality of Literacy Instruction', 'Academic Results', 'Conclusions' and 'Discussion'.

Methodology

Context

A secondary school, social sciences teacher, with two years teaching experience, very little teacher training and no training in literary instruction, is a representative profile of many teachers at this educational stage in terms of initial training. He teaches the subject to two multilingual second-year classes (13-year-old pupils). Catalan is the medium of instruction.

The class taking part in the programme (intervention group) is comprised of 26 pupils: 14 native Spanish speakers, three native Catalan speakers, seven immigrant Spanish speakers (from Bolivia, Ecuador, Peru) and two native Catalan–Spanish speakers. The immigrants have lived in Catalonia for an average of 4.7 years. They have a good oral understanding of Catalan and express themselves with some errors (average score of 3 on a 0–4 scale in basic conversational competences).

The class not taking part in the programme (non-intervention group) is comprised of 29 pupils: 12 native Spanish speakers, 10 native Catalan speakers, six immigrants (five Spanish speakers from Bolivia, Ecuador, Peru, and one Arab speaker from Morocco) and one native Catalan–Spanish speaker. The immigrants have lived in Catalonia for an average of 4.4 years. They have competences in Catalan similar to those of the intervention group (average score of 3).

The two classes are in a public school in the metropolitan area of Barcelona with working class pupils. The centre reflects the linguistic composition of this area: a predominance of native Spanish speakers over native Catalan speakers and a significant presence of immigrants who have arrived since 2000.

Characteristics of the intervention programme

The teacher and the instructional coach collaborated (team teaching) on the design and teaching of the first two lessons of the social sciences programme (population). The teacher agreed to teach the lessons first with one class without training in literacy instruction (non-intervention group) and then, after a month, with the other, after training (intervention group). During this period he taught a history unit to the intervention group while working with the instructional coach on the design and teaching process. The instructional coach observed the teaching process in the first class and then took part in the design and teaching process of the other.

The intervention programme was based on the following principles.

A governing idea

The contents are those specified in the students' textbook. However, they are extremely compartmentalised and there is little relationship between them. Experts in teaching social science consider that ideas cannot be taught independently of one another. One way of relating them is by selecting 'a case' or central idea, an excellent way of introducing a subject, making it possible to organise and integrate information (Seidlitz & Short, 2011).

Based on this idea, 'migratory movements' was selected as the central topic or theme. It was a subject likely to interest the pupils, as there are immigrants in the classes and the majority of Spanish-speakers are also descendants of immigrants. This central focal point made it possible to teach all the basic contents of the two lessons (demographic and economic characteristics of populations, level of development of countries, population movements, etc.) in an interrelated way. The sequencing of contents was based on the pupils' own references. They created and interpreted a survey on their origins, they read biographical texts about immigrants and migratory movements at a worldwide level, and they searched for information about demographic and economic characteristics and on countries of origin and receivers of immigration, focusing on countries close to them (those of the immigrants, Catalonia and Spain).

A synthesis task

All the pupils' activities resulted in a final product that was to include the fundamental concepts worked on and bring together all the preliminary tasks: a PowerPoint document created in pairs (an immigrant and a native, a Spanish speaker and a Catalan speaker), presenting and comparing the characteristics of two countries (a developed and developing one). In the case of interaction between immigrant and native, one of the countries would be the immigrant's country and the other Catalonia or Spain.

Text selection

The textbook would not be the only documentation source. Others would be included: adapted texts from a journalistic article on immigration and on the biographies of immigrants, other journalistic documents (social planning documents based on population pyramids, monographs on countries) and guides for searching for information on the internet.

Emphasis on literacy instruction involving

Reading: reading comprehension strategies (predictions, help for organising information and elaborating on the main ideas, metacognitive strategies for overcoming the incomprehension of certain technical terms), knowledge of text structure (content and language) and of different types of texts, and using reading for various purposes.

Writing: emphasis on the process (generating and organising the meaning of texts, asking for previous knowledge, information about text structure, attention to academic vocabulary, external support with guides and charts, revision, editing and writing for various purposes).

Vocabulary: selection of fundamental academic vocabulary, pupils' notebooks noting this vocabulary and pertinent definitions, reflection on the formal structure to be defined, monitoring words not understood in the texts and providing strategies for finding out the meanings of unknown words.

Integration of the four linguistic skills

Integrated practice in listening, speaking, reading and writing (reading a biography and taking notes to make an oral presentation, creating a text about the results of a survey, reading and sharing the text with the class and talking about it, etc.).

Interaction among students

Using 'think, pair and share' as a habitual grouping format; students of different origin (immigrant and native) are paired to collaboratively read or write a text and then to share it with the class.

Use of technology

As has been mentioned, the pupils searched for information on the internet about the different countries and created a PowerPoint document with a synthesis of all the information, which they presented to the class and the school's management team. Introduction to evaluating and selecting different sources of information, developing autonomous production and generating a new type of text are also ways of learning new forms of literacy.

As has already been mentioned, the teacher and the instructional coach shared the task of applying this programme. The teacher participated more in tasks where he felt more secure (preparation and interpretation of the survey details, preparation and elaboration of information on the internet, etc.). The instructional coach took on teaching support strategies for the reading and writing processes, although not exclusively. It was a question of the teacher seeing how these strategies are applied in practice. Both were present in the classroom during all sessions and the students accepted this process very naturally.

Procedures and criteria for comparing the quality of literacy instruction

Procedure

The way the teacher taught the lessons in the first of the two classes (non-intervention group) was observed and audio recorded. The way the teacher and the instructional coach taught the other class (intervention group) was also observed and video recorded. The recordings considered the communication between the teacher and the whole class. In the intervention group, some 'think, pair and share' actions were also recorded.

Criteria

For the comparison of the quality of literacy instruction in the two classrooms, the time, the type of literacy activities, the teacher's support strategies for the processes of reading, writing and comprehension and the expression of academic vocabulary have been considered.

The categories are as follows:

Time: activity length using teacher interactions with the majority of students.
Literacy: activities involving reading, writing and vocabulary.
Non-literacy related: teaching activities not involving reading, writing and vocabulary.
Management and others.

Reading

Includes the categories 'types of reading' and 'teacher support for the reading process' (categories adapted from Carrasquillo *et al.*, 2004, *op. cit.*).

Types of reading: 'reading aloud' (students read a text or a piece of text), 'guided reading' (teacher monitors and provides support for students in some of the reading phases) and 'independent reading' (students read without teacher's support). These types of reading can be 'individual' or 'shared' with one (paired) or more students.

Teacher support for the reading process: considers the strategies the teacher uses to facilitate reading comprehension at each of the three reading phases (pre-reading, reading and post-reading). 'Pre-reading phase' – knowledge about text structure, predicting, etc. 'Reading phase' – monitoring words not understood, asking questions, etc. 'Post-reading phase' – sharing what students have read, confirming predictions, revising vocabulary, etc.

Writing

Includes the categories 'types of writing' and 'teacher support for the writing process' (categories adapted from Carrasquillo *et al.*, 2004, *op. cit.*).

Types of writing: 'guided writing' (students engage in the writing process, with the teacher providing support and direction as required) and 'independent writing' (students carry out writing activities on their own). These types of writing can also be individual or shared with one (paired) or more students.

Teacher support for the writing process: considers the strategies the teacher uses at each of the three writing phases. 'Pre-writing phase' – generating text meanings, organising text meanings, knowledge about text structures, etc. 'Writing' – organising text meanings, highlighting words, etc. 'Post-writing' – sharing written texts, revising academic vocabulary, etc.

Vocabulary

Includes 'specific instructional methods' (categories adapted from Scott *et al.*, 2003, *op. cit.*) and 'other strategies'.

Specific instructional methods: 'definitional' (the teacher asks for a description or statement of a word and students try to answer by using a glossary or dictionary, or collaborating with one another; the teacher proposes writing the meanings of a list of words), 'contextual' (involves any instruction that provides information about how to use a word in context or how to use the context to figure out the meaning of a word), 'semantic' (the teacher uses some type of semantic analysis to discuss words/semantic maps; the students select key words and construct a web depicting relationships between words), 'structural' (deals with morphological structure or cognates of the words) and 'mnemonic' (emphasises remembering the word by linking key words with visual images).

'*Other strategies*': 'monitoring words not understood', 'revising words not understood', 'knowledge about text structures (language)', etc.

Some examples of previous categories (reading, writing and vocabulary) will be shown when the results of the comparison are presented.

Procedures and criteria for assessing pupils' academic performance

Participants

There were 26 pupils in the intervention group and 29 pupils in the non-intervention group, whose characteristics have already been described.

Assessment instruments

To assess the homogeneity of the two groups, two standardised tests were applied: the Raven Test, which measures intelligence without verbal and cultural contents and the Catalan verbal scale of the FEIA (Factorial Evaluation of Intellectual Aptitudes) test, a written test that evaluates capacity for understanding ideas and concepts expressed in writing and is also related with richness of vocabulary.

To assess the academic performance of students, written tests were used: one test on definitions and three texts. Defining is knowledge through 'generalisation', one of the five dimensions of vocabulary knowledge. Other types of knowledge are: 'application' through correct usage, 'breadth' through recall of words, 'precision', through understanding of examples and non-examples and 'availability', through use of vocabulary in discussion (Fisher & Frey, 2008, *op. cit.*). The testing of definitions consisted of six words of technical vocabulary from the lessons (migrant flow, income per capita, etc.). This subject includes a large number of technical terms of this kind. The precise definition of each word was scored with two points when it included both an adequate formal structure (1 point) and precise content (1 point).

The pupils wrote three texts with different contents: 'Description and comparison of two age pyramids' (two pyramids different from the ones they had described in class), 'Why is the birth rate lower in developed countries than in developing ones?' (one of the various comparisons that can be established between these two types of countries) and 'Migrations'. The teacher had specified that these areas of content, together with the definitions, were important objectives in learning about the topic. There was information highlighted in the textbook about these three pieces of content. In the three texts, 'conceptual richness' and 'academic vocabulary' were evaluated.

'Conceptual richness' refers to the quantity of precise ideas appearing in the text (notional function of the text) (e.g. 'the tree-shaped pyramid represents a young population, at the moment there is more demand than supply', etc.). One point is given for each precisely expressed idea.

'Academic vocabulary' refers both to 'technical' vocabulary (*migratory flow, life expectancy, country of origin of emigration,* etc.) and 'specialised' vocabulary common to a form of expression belonging to scientific disciplines (*represents, confirms, plans, predictions, heterogeneous,* etc.). One point is given for each different word with these characteristics. This criterion evaluates a second dimension in vocabulary knowledge that has already been mentioned (application through correct usage).

In the text 'Birth rate and development', the 'diversity of connectors' (causal and comparison/contrast) was valued, as it is a text based on this type of relationship. It is true that a very expert writer can write with almost no connectors (Schleppegrell, 2004, *op. cit.*) but we do not believe that this is within the capability of these pupils. 'Connector diversity' is an index relating the different 'causal and comparison/contrast connectors' (types) with all connectors in this category (tokens). A mathematical formula establishes correction criteria for whether a text is longer or shorter. A text with great diversity of connectors would include varied connectors (*however, but, on the other hand, while, not only...but, either*). A text with little diversity could be limited to a single connector repeated several times (*but*). Connectors can also be considered as more linguistic 'vocabulary', independent of the specific contents.

In the text on 'pyramids', the 'macrostructure' was also evaluated: the organisation and the extent to which the flow of ideas is logical and the text is connected. A score between 0 and 10 was given, considering the nature and number of relationships and the logical order in which they have to appear.

The quality of the written Catalan (grammar, spelling, punctuation) was not assessed because this programme did not place any emphasis on this dimension and it is not very likely that changes would be produced in the two groups in such a short time.

All the tests were applied in pre-test and post-test situations except for 'Birth rate and development'. It was not believed that the pupils would have precise previous knowledge on this topic, although they would of the subject of migrations and pyramids, as they had already studied them in primary school with more basic content. The pre-tests were applied to all the pupils before the teacher began work on the topic in the non-intervention group. The post-tests were applied immediately after each group completed the lessons.

Data analysis criteria

To determine the reliability of the measures (agreement between two assessors), Pearson's coefficient was used. To determine the homogeneity of the two groups, Student's *t*-test for independent groups was applied.

In all tests in which there was a pre-test and post-test measurement, mixed factorial variance analysis, the Student's *t*-test or the Mann-Whitney *U*-test were applied, according to whether the application conditions were met.

For the statistical decision, an alpha of 5% was established.

Results Relating to the Comparison of the Two Groups in Quality of Literacy Instruction

As can be seen in Table 5.1, the intervention programme lasted longer (13 sessions each of 45 minutes, compared with eight sessions in the non-intervention situation). The incorporation of technology (creation of the PowerPoint, the age pyramid with the computer system, searching for information on the internet) and the work on various texts required more time than normal. In the other classroom, the teacher focused all his work on the textbook.

As has been verified in other studies, the time devoted to literacy instruction is quite considerable in the two classes. Teachers devote many hours to activities related to reading, writing and vocabulary. As will be seen, the difference lies in the quality of the time devoted to it.

Table 5.2 shows that the intervention programme provided the students with practice in different types of reading, with 'guided' and 'shared' reading predominating. Many of the 'shared reading' activities were developed according to the 'think, pair and share' model. The time devoted to 'individual reading' was clearly greater than that shown in the table, but it is not recorded, because the time the pupils were reading outside the classroom (looking for information on the internet, synthesising the information from different documents, preparing for the assessment) was not counted.

The non-intervention situation provided practice in class only, in a single type of reading: 'reading aloud' from the textbook. Pupils read extracts from it consecutively, with subsequent clarifying comments from the teacher. The time the pupils devoted to 'individual reading' (preparing for the assessment) was not recorded here either.

It is also important to highlight the differences arising in the uses or purposes of reading in the two situations. In the intervention programme,

Table 5.1 Summary of time spent on activities

	Intervention		Non-intervention	
Activity	Total minutes	% total time	Total minutes	% total time
Literacy	486.45	74.95	334.25	85.56
Non-literacy related	110	16.94	41.40	10.59
Management and others	52.61	8.10	15	3.84
Total instructional time	649.06		390.65	

Table 5.2 Types of reading

	Intervention			Non-intervention		
	N	Total minutes	% total time	N	Total minutes	% time total
Guided reading (shared)	3	47.58	45.94			
Independent reading (shared)	2	39	37.66			
Reading aloud	10	9.8	9.46	122	65.45	100
Guided reading (individual)	1	6.13	5.91			
Independent reading (individual)	1	1.06	1.02			
Total	17	103.57		122	65.45	

the students read a text to create a diagram to facilitate comprehension, synthesised information from different texts, searched on the internet, made oral presentations, reviewed and improved the quality of the written texts (reading aloud) and confirmed predictions. In the non-intervention situation, the pupils used reading aloud as a means for the teacher to clarify the concepts in the textbook and to write a text (age pyramids). In the first situation, but not the second, there was a rich interrelationship between speaking, reading and writing skills.

There are differences in the variety and quality of scaffolding provided in the two situations (Table 5.3).

In the intervention programme there is a variety of cognitive strategies to facilitate reading comprehension. In the pre-reading phase, the outstanding features are 'knowledge about ideas from the text' (by considering underlined and printed aspects, graphic organisers, etc.) and 'knowledge about text structure' (in dialogue with the pupils on the type of relationships in the text: comparison–contrast, cause–effect, etc.). The text structure 'language' is also made explicit when it highlights the connectors (signal words) marking these relationships. For guiding both reading and writing, the teacher (or instructional coach) refers to charts on the walls of the classroom where the 'text structures' and 'text signals' are written. During the reading phase, on one occasion the pupils were asked to underline the words they did not understand (monitoring words not understood), words reviewed after reading. Most important at the post-reading phase was an 'extension activity', in which pupils transformed a read text (with graphic organisers) into a written text and a 'shared activity about what they have read' (presenting reading done in groups of four on biographies of immigrants) to the class. It was another of the activities they carried out based on 'think, pair and share'.

Non-intervention is characterised by the almost total absence of cognitive strategies. Only 'asking for previous knowledge' can be considered in this way. The teacher's predominant activity is focused on 'post-reading

Table 5.3 Teacher support for the reading process

	Intervention			Non-intervention		
	N	Total minutes	% total time	N	Time	% total time
Pre-reading						
Knowledge about ideas of the text	4	7.61	8.36			
Knowledge about text structure (content)	2	7.51	8.25			
Knowledge about text structure (language)	1	3	3.30			
Asking for previous knowledge	2	2.31	2.53	2	3	2.03
Predicting	1	1	1.09			
Asking questions	1	0.20	0.22			
Reading						
Monitoring words not understood	1	1.81	1.99			
Post-reading						
Transforming the read text through writing	1	25.33	27.83			
Sharing what they have read	1	21.22	23.3			
Revising words not understood	6	9.53	10.47			
Summarising	1	5.26	5.78			
Contextual vocabulary	2	3.01	3.30			
Structural vocabulary	2	2	2.19			
Confirming predictions	1	1.21	1.33			
Comments				63	55.51	37.63
Application activities				8	44.5	30.17
Revising definitions				11	17.13	11.61
Asking questions				9	16.58	11.24
Asking definitions				9	9.48	6.42
Highlighting vocabulary				1	1.31	0.89
Total reading	26	91		103	147.51	

The reading, writing and vocabulary categories are not mutually exclusive (e.g. 'transforming the read text through writing' is a category also included in writing).

aloud' comments and 'application activities' (when proposing calculations on demographics based on exercises in the book).

As can be seen in Table 5.4, the intervention programme provided a variety of types of writing. 'Guided and paired writing' activities predominated. The teacher scaffolded most of the writing activities. The highest degree of scaffolding occurred in a 'choral writing' activity, with the teacher and pupils

Table 5.4 Types of writing

	Intervention			Non-intervention		
	N	Total minutes	% total time	N	Total minutes	% total time
Guided writing (paired)	7	163	61.86			
Choral writing	1	32.86	12.47			
Independent writing (paired)	2	30	11.38			
Guided writing (individual)	1	25.33	9.61	1	49.16	92.91
Independent writing (individual)	2	12.30	4.66			
Dictation				1	3.75	7.08
Total	14	263.49		2	52.91	

writing a text together about age pyramids with the help of a text model. In this activity, the teacher applied a 'mediation strategy' characterised by a 'most support' to 'least support' process in writing the text: from choral writing on a pyramid to paired independent writing on another pyramid.

In the non-intervention programme, the pupils almost exclusively practised a single type of writing: 'guided independent writing'. The pupils read in the textbook about how to interpret a pyramid, the professor held a dialogue and commented with them about the ideas in the reading. Then, each pupil wrote his or her own text. This was the only text they wrote, except for a brief dictation on definitions.

The students in the intervention programme wrote a variety of texts: interpretation of the data from a survey they had drawn up; a script summarising the biography of an immigrant to be orally presented to the class; transformation of a read text into a written text; two texts on age pyramids, writing notes based on looking for information on the internet and a PowerPoint synthesis of all the information created to be presented in class. This variety of texts also shows the variety of the uses and purposes of writing in this programme.

The comparison between the two situations shows the differences in the level of support between the two of them for the writing process (Table 5.5).

In the intervention situation, there is a varied range of scaffolding at each of the three phases of the writing process. 'Generating and organising text meanings' predominates before and during the writing process. The teacher also applies other teaching strategies: he draws attention to the language of the structures of the texts that need to be written (connectors); he 'highlights' the importance of incorporating the academic vocabulary before writing and he 'revises' this vocabulary once the pupils have written the texts. Sometimes he also uses the 'sharing the writing' with peers resource as a means of also assessing and reviewing the general quality of the writing, a typical 'think, pair and share' activity.

Table 5.5 Teacher support for the writing process

	Intervention			Non-intervention		
	N	Total minutes	% total time	N	Total minutes	% total time
Pre-writing						
Generating texts meanings	5	20.63	24.25	2	17.08	77.74
Organising text meanings	2	2.50	2.93			
Knowledge about text structures (language)	1	1.90	2.23			
Highlighting words	2	0.58	0.68			
Reading aloud				2	4.89	22.25
Writing						
Generating text meanings	3	35.83	42.12			
Organising text meanings	2	13.86	16.29			
Post-writing						
Sharing written texts	2	8.3	9.75			
Revising academic vocabulary	1	1.05	1.23			
Revising important ideas	1	0.41	0.48			
Total	19	85.06		4	21.97	

In the non-intervention situation, the teacher limits himself at the pre-writing phase to 'generating text meanings' after 'reading aloud' the content of the book about which the text is to be created (population pyramids).

As seen in Table 5.6, the 'definitional' strategy is almost the only one used by the teacher in the non-intervention situation (92.58% of total time). The most frequent form is asking for the meaning of a word and, with the help of everyone, managing to define it or reading it in the textbook. This was because the teacher considered one of the most important objectives of the lesson to be gaining knowledge about how to define basic concepts. Here, as in the intervention situation, the students wrote down the definitions of the academic vocabulary in a notebook.

In the 'intervention situation', the 'definitional' strategy also predominates (46.40%), but there is a richer, more varied approach to vocabulary instruction. In relation to unknown words, other types of strategies are also used: 'contextual' (when asking for the meaning of the word *'recession'* the teacher asks the students to read fragments of text in which the word is included so that by themselves they come to associate its meaning with terms like *'lack of jobs'*, *'less industrial production'*, etc.); 'structural' (*'income per capita'*: associating this word with others from the same root such as *'capital'* and *'cap'* (the Catalan word for head), etc.) and 'monitoring words not understood' when the teacher is attentive towards the problems that can be created

Table 5.6 Teacher support for vocabulary

	Intervention			Non-intervention		
	N	Total minutes	% total time	N	Total minutes	% total time
Definitional	44	31.38	46.40	50	67.45	92.58
Revising words not understood words (post-reading)	6	9.53	14.09			
Contextual	4	8.19	12.11			
Knowledge about text structures (language)	2	4.90	7.24			
Teaching how to define	1	3.86	5.70			
Highlighting words	6	3.41	5.04	6	5.4	7.41
Structural	2	2	2.95			
Monitoring words not understood (before reading)	1	1.81	2.67			
Feedback on spontaneous language	3	1.50	2.21			
Revising academic vocabulary	1	1.05	1.55			
Total	70	67.63			72.85	

by the incomprehension of unknown words, asking the pupils to underline the words in the text they do not understand. As has already been mentioned when talking about reading and writing, the teacher provides 'the knowledge about text structures' (connectors) and highlights academic vocabulary the students could incorporate into their written texts. Oral discourse is also an opportunity for the teacher to occasionally provide feedback in academic language on the everyday language of the students (Student: *The countries who send emigrants*...; Teacher: *The countries of origin*...). In this situation, some time was devoted to 'teaching how to define', after which the pupils had to complete definitions in writing with the help of certain structures (...is the relationship between...). It was a question of raising the pupils' awareness of the structural characteristics of a good definition.

Research on teaching vocabulary indicates that it is inappropriate to place too much emphasis on definitions and that memorising them is not very motivating and provides only superficial knowledge. It is better to look for the meaning of a word in context and provide metacognitive strategies so that the pupils know what to do when they come across an unknown word. Above all 'making it usable' is effective in the right contexts (oral and written discourse) (Fisher & Frey, 2008, *op. cit.*).

A significant difference was observed in the use of academic vocabulary by the students in the two situations. In the intervention situation, the observations of the interaction between pupils (think, pair and share) indicated that they made frequent use of it in dialogues among themselves in order to negotiate the most precise language for writing up the results of a survey, presenting the written text in class, transforming a read text into a written text, describing a pyramid or preparing the PowerPoint document, etc. By contrast, in the non-intervention situation there was no negotiation among the students (the work was always individual), which limited the opportunities for use.

Up to now, a comparison of the quality of the literacy instruction in the two situations has been presented. A comparison will now be presented on the effect this has had on the academic performance of the pupils.

Academic Results

The agreement between the two assessors shows high, significant correlation indices, indicating that the correction criteria for the evidence are reliable (Table 5.7).

There are no significant differences between the intervention and non-intervention groups or in the intelligence or comprehension of concepts and ideas expressed in written Catalan. The two groups are homogeneous in these capacities (Table 5.8).

Table 5.7 Reliability of measures. Coefficient of correlation – intraclass (sample 10 students)

Tests	Correlation coefficient	Tests	Correlation coefficient
Definitions	0.959	Pyramids (conceptual richness)	0.972
Birth rate (conceptual richness)	0.973	Pyramids (vocabulary)	0.967
Birth rate (diversity of connectors)	0.973	Pyramids (macrostructure)	0.980
		Migrations (conceptual richness)	0.992
		Migrations (vocabulary)	0.838

Table 5.8 Homogeneity of the groups

	Group	N	Mean	Standard deviation	Student's t-test	p-value
Raven	Intervention	26	46.96	5.92	0.044	0.965
	Non-intervention	29	47.03	6.28		
FEIA	Intervention	26	15.77	4.38	0.276	0.784
	Non-intervention	29	15.45	4.26		

*$p < 0.05$

Table 5.9 shows that the results of the pre-test on the texts (birth rate and migrations) indicate that, before starting the learning process, the students in the two groups had similar levels of prior knowledge. There was only a slightly significant difference in favour of the intervention group in the pyramid texts. All the differences in the post-tests are significant in favour of the intervention group. The three texts written by this group show a much greater conceptual richness than that of the texts written by the non-intervention group. If the averages for this group in the pre-test and the post-test are compared, it can be seen that there are few differences on the migrations, birth rate and development topic. This indicates they have learned very little, even though they have read highlighted information about these two topics in the textbook.

One of the factors explaining the greater conceptual richness of the intervention group's texts is that these pupils have been able to relate and integrate general ideas from the lessons on each of the texts. In the writing about pyramids, they have referred to countries of origin and receivers of immigration, a topic worked on in the class survey, or to birth rate factors worked on based on a reading. The synthesis work done based on the PowerPoint has also provided an integrated vision, relating concepts from the lessons. These pupils have clearly read, argued and written more and with greater meaning than the pupils in the non-intervention group and they have appropriated more of the content because they have seen it as more meaningful.

Table 5.10 shows that in the pre-test there are no significant differences between the two groups in the use of academic vocabulary. The post-test

Table 5.9 Conceptual richness

		Group	n	Mean	Standard deviation	Comparison of differences	p-value
Text pyramids	Pre-test	Intervention	26	1.80	0.54	(Mann-Whitney U)	0.049*
		Non-intervention	29	1.31	1.31	Z 1.967	
	Post-test	Intervention	26	12.34	2.10	Z 3.101	0.002*
		Non-intervention	29	7.58	4.50		
Text migrations	Pre-test	Intervention	26	5.04	1.64	Student's t-test 0.888	0.378
		Non-intervention	29	4.55	2.32		
	Post-test	Intervention	26	15.15	5.10	Mann-Whitney U-Test	<0.001*
		Non-intervention	29	4.89	2.14	Z 6.135	
Text birth rate and development	Test	Intervention	26	4.11	1.94	Mann-Whitney U-Test	<0.001*
		Non-intervention	29	1.50	1.50	Z 4.168	

*$p < 0.05$

Table 5.10 Vocabulary

		Group	n	Mean	Standard deviation	Comparison of differences	P
Text pyramids Academic vocabulary (application, by use)	Pre-test	Intervention	26	1.69	0.93	Student's t-test	0.548
		Non-intervention	29	1.52	1.18	0.605	
	Post-test	Intervention	26	9.84	4.82	Mann-Whitney U-Test	<0.001*
		Non-intervention	29	5.06	3.20	Z 3.831	
Text migrations Academic vocabulary (application, by use)	Pre-test	Intervention	26	1.73	1.40	Student's t-test	0.582
		Non-intervention	29	1.93	1.28	0.554	
	Post-test	Intervention	26	9.07	3.81	Mann-Whitney U-Test	<0.001*
		Non-intervention	29	2.69	1.36	Z 5.769	
Definitions (academic vocabulary by generalisation)	Pre-test	Intervention	26	2.26	1.2	Factorial analysis of variance	<0.001*
		Non-intervention	29	2.50	1.4		0.007*
	Post-test	Intervention	26	5.81	1.96	F 48.742(repeated measure) 7.908	<0.001*
		Non-intervention	24	3.93	1.92	(group) 20.657 (interaction)	
Text (birth rate and development) Diversity of connectors (application by use)	Test	Intervention	26	1.38	0.28	Student's t-test 4.320	<0.001*
		Non-intervention	29	0.98	0.40		

*$p < 0.05$

results indicate that the pupils in the intervention group are significantly better than those in the non-intervention group in all written texts. They write texts with a greater quantity and variety of vocabulary, both technical, belonging to different contexts (*receiving country, country of origin of immigration, birth rate, life expectancy, primary sector,* etc.) and vocabulary of a more general 'scientific' nature (*prediction, belonging to, represents, increment, heterogeneous,* etc.). The pupils had more opportunities to negotiate this vocabulary in real usage situations, and the teacher also placed more emphasis on it.

In the 'definitions' test (vocabulary by generalisation) the pupils in the intervention group are also significantly better. It has also been mentioned that this was one of the most important objectives set by the teacher for the non-intervention group and to which he devoted the most time. It is probable that the reflection on 'how to define' improved the intervention group's skills. However, it is difficult to define certain words (such as *income per capita*), and these pupils' results were by no means outstanding (mean: 5.81, p: 0–12).

In the 'birth rate and development' text, a greater diversity of 'causal connectors' and 'comparison/contrast connectors' (*consequently, for this reason, that is why, by contrast, however, while, on the other hand*) can be detected (mean: 5.5). By contrast, there is little diversity in the texts by the pupils in the comparison group (mean: 1.75). This difference in diversity runs parallel with the quantity of relationships they are capable of establishing. In the intervention programme, the teacher encouraged reflection on the structure of the texts and on the 'signal words' (connectors) indicating this structure.

The students in the intervention group wrote a text with a macrostructure of greater quality, with an organisation in which the flow of ideas was more logical and the text was better connected (Table 5.11). The reasons for this are the ones already noted when talking about conceptual richness and vocabulary: the teacher's higher level of support for the writing process. The teacher's knowledge of the specific textual characteristics required by the

Table 5.11 Macrostructure

Variable	Group		n	Mean	Standard deviation	Comparison of differences	P
Text pyramids macro structure	Pre-test	Intervention	26	2.30	1.54	Factorial analysis of variance F	
		Non-intervention	29	1.96	1.64		
	Post-test	Intervention	26	5.26	1.39	54.200 (repeated measure)	<0.001*
		Non-intervention	29	3.48	2.02		
						5.888 (Group)	0.019
						4.977 (interaction)	0.030*

*$p < 0.05$

scientific description of an age pyramid, characteristics transmitted to the pupils using a model, was also important.

Conclusions

The comparison of the literacy instruction in the two classes indicates that the intervention group has received higher quality literacy instruction.

In relation to reading, a varied practice is observed, with different 'types' of reading, use of reading with 'diverse purposes' and a considerable degree of 'support' for the reading process. Similarly, a varied practice has been produced in regard to writing, with different 'types' of writing and diverse 'types' of text, with different 'purposes', and considerable 'support' for the writing process.

There has been considerable emphasis on teaching vocabulary, with the definitional approach predominating, but it has been combined with structural and contextual approaches, monitoring and reviewing words not understood. Observations of interaction between pupils have shown this use of academic vocabulary in negotiating the different tasks.

Literacy instruction has been developed in a context in which other factors activating learning and the motivation of the pupils have also been considered (in the proposal for an overall relational and meaningful idea, in the interaction activities, in the use of technology, etc.). The literacy instruction provided by the teacher before the training process (non-intervention group) has been of very poor quality. It could be said there has been almost no literacy instruction. Students have practised a very limited type of reading (reading aloud based only on the textbook). The same could be said of their writing, which has been limited to writing a single text. Support strategies have been virtually absent from the two processes. Vocabulary teaching has been limited exclusively to 'definitional' aspects, a method which, as is well known, demotivates and is not very effective. There have not been interaction tasks between pupils (only individual work), and knowledge has been presented as not very interrelated.

Pupils in the intervention group have shown better academic performance in accordance with the criteria considered here. Texts with greater conceptual richness and a greater presence of academic vocabulary have been written and the terms in this vocabulary have been defined with greater precision. A greater diversity of 'signal words' (connectors) has been used to relate the ideas of a text and they have been written in a more organised, logical way (macrostructure).

This research confirms that teaching vocabulary and reading and writing strategies, related with academic language, are valuable practices for academic achievement.

The team-teaching procedure used in this training process is based on the idea that a teacher, particularly if he or she has little training, cannot initially assimilate all the principles and resources of good practice. The training model put into practice here offers a general idea of all the dimensions that might be important for subsequently going more deeply into more specific aspects (conditions for effective group work support strategies for reading and writing, etc.). From this point of view, the assessment made by the teacher and the coach has been positive.

Concerning lesson design and planning, the joint conclusion is that too much time was allocated to teaching these two lessons and this could be reduced as the pupils become quicker at group work, using technology and researching information sources. This speed will undoubtedly be achieved if it is put into practice in successive lessons. Concerning the evaluation of the literacy instruction, it is recommended that the time devoted to individual work (work by the pupil and attention from the teacher) should be increased and more should be done on metacognitive strategies.

Discussion

This section will discuss the following points: the pupils' learning, relationships between language and academic performance and the literacy context.

What have the pupils learned?

From the data in this study it cannot be stated that the pupils have achieved basic literacy competences, if competences are understood as strategies and skills that they can easily transfer to other contexts, because this has not been tested. It can only be stated that what has been taught in a more appropriate way is what the students have learned more effectively. They will probably have acquired a certain awareness of what it means to read and write about the contents of the curriculum. This awareness can gradually be turned into skills if the teachers of all the subjects in the curriculum place the same importance on literacy.

In this experiment, the pupils have learned something more than aspects related to literacy. They have experienced and valued a new way of learning: interacting with each other and helping one another (*you help people who hardly talk; my partner has helped me a lot*); developing better ways of communicating, with more possibilities of providing ideas (*when you express yourself you become less shy and it's not the teacher who explains everything, we've participated more*); considering the pace and depth of learning (*you have more time to learn the concepts, you've done more work on it and it stays in your head better, it's easier, you learn more, not just what is in the book*); using technology (*I've learned IT*), and increasing interest and motivation (*more fun, lessons seem to go quicker*).

Relationships between language and performance

It is clear that not having their own academic language resources limits their performance. It is also true that academic language has to be used in a conceptually appropriate way, something pupils do not always do. However, if they do not have academic language available (vocabulary and other precise ways of expressing themselves such as the macrostructure of the texts) they will have more difficulties in expressing knowledge. In this experiment, a relationship has been observed between conceptual richness, academic vocabulary and macrostructure. The acquisition of specialised forms of academic language and the acquisition of knowledge are interrelated. When students are more knowledgeable about a concept and have the right forms of expression available, they have a better chance of showing this knowledge and understanding and producing quality texts.

The literacy context

To make literacy teaching effective, it must be established in a more general learning concept; in a class where the pupils' previous interests and knowledge are a guide for the development of the lesson; where there is shared conversation, and interaction among them is encouraged; where there is a variety of texts and materials, and a pace and time of learning make it possible for the pupils to achieve their objectives. This makes it necessary to break many of the routines established in the current curriculum (rigid timetables leaving little time for working in depth and paying individual attention to pupils, excessively compartmentalised knowledge). It calls for a curriculum that, as a priority, requires new forms of teaching, which means teacher training is a priority. This training must provide teachers with knowledge of the characteristics of the language they need to develop in the pupils, as well as the strategies for teaching it precisely.

Acknowledgements

This research was funded by the Institut d'Estudis Catalans (project IECSFCS2009-02ARN) and the Spanish Ministry of Science and Innovation (project EDU2009-11409).

We would like to acknowledge the guidance provided by Gemma Tribó, Professor of Didactics of Social Sciences.

References

Carrasquillo, A., Kucer, S.B. and Abrams, R. (2004) *Beyond the Beginnings. Literacy Interventions for Upper Elementary English Language Learners.* Clevedon: Multilingual Matters.
Echevarria, J., Vogt, M.E. and Short, D. (2004) *Making Content Comprehensible for English Language Learners: The SIOP Model.* Boston, MA: Pearson/Allyn and Bacon.

Echevarria, J., Short, D. and Powers, K. (2006) School reform and standard-based education. How do teachers help English language learners? *Journal of Educational Research* 95, 1–28.

Fisher, D. and Frey, N. (2008) *Word Wise and Content Rich, Grades 7-12: Five Essential Steps to Teaching Academic Vocabulary.* Portsmouth, NH: Heinemann.

Flood, J., Lapp, D. and Fisher, D. (2003) Reading comprehension instruction. In J. Flood., D. Lapp, J.R. Squire and J.M. Jensen (eds) *Handbook of Research on Teaching Language Arts* (2nd edn) (pp. 933–941). Mahwah; NJ: Laurence Erlbaum Associates.

Fortune, T.W. and Tedick, D.J. (2008) Integrated language and content teaching: Insights from the immersion classroom. In T.W. Fortune and D.J. Tedick (eds) *Pathways to Multilingualism. Evolving Perspectives on Immersion Education* (pp. 71–96). Clevedon: Multilingual Matters.

Gibbons, P. (2003) Mediating language learning: Teacher interactions with ESL students in a content based classroom. *TESOL Quarterly* 37 (2), 247–273.

Lemke, J.L. (1997) *Aprender a hablar ciencia. Lenguaje, aprendizaje y valores.* Barcelona: Paidós.

Macken-Horarick, M. (1996) Literacy and learning across the curriculum: Towards a model of register for secondary school teachers. In R. Hasan and G. Williams (eds) *Literacy in Society* (pp. 232–277). Longman: London.

Met, M. (2008) Paying attention to language: Literacy, language and academic achievement. In T.W. Fortune and D.J. Tedick (eds) *Pathways to Multilingualism. Evolving Perspectives on Immersion Education* (pp. 49–70). Clevedon: Multilingual Matters.

Quinquer, D. (2010) Aprendre ciències socials i experimentals. Parlar i escoltar, llegir, escriure. Unpublished manuscript, ICE, Universitat Autònoma de Barcelona, Bellaterra (Cerdanyola del Vallès), Spain.

Scott, J.A., Jamieson-Noel, D. and Asselin, M. (2003) Vocabulary instruction throughout the day in twenty-three Canadian upper-elementary classrooms. *The Elementary School Journal* 103, 269–286.

Schleppegrell, M.J. (2004) *The Language of Schooling. A Functional Linguistic Perspective.* New York: Routledge.

Seidlitz, J. and Short, D. (2011) SIOP U.S. History unit. In D.H. Short, M.E. Vogt and J. Echevarria (eds) *The SIOP Model for Teaching History-Social Studies to English Learners* (pp. 141–159). Boston: Allyn and Bacon.

Stahl, S.A. and Nagy, W.E. (2006) *Teaching Word Meanings.* Mahwah, NJ: Laurence Erlbaum Associates.

Tharp, R., Estrada, J., Dalton, S. and Yamauchi, I. (2000) *Teaching Transformed: Achieving Excellence, Fairness, Inclusion and Harmony.* Boulder, CO: Westview Press.

6 Production of Texts with Multimodal Resources by Two Groups of Primary Education Students

Aneska Ortega, Júlia Coromina and Ana Teberosky

The purpose of this research is to compare texts with multimodal resources produced by two groups of students in year four of primary education in the context of a teacher training process. The texts were the result of the guidance carried out using an instructional sequence for science in teaching a thematic unit. The students and teachers belong to two schools that encourage working with texts and multimodal resources. Catalan is the language of instruction. One of the schools is attended by native students, speakers of Catalan, and the other by students of immigrant families, speakers of different languages. The teachers at the two schools were given guidance on presenting and labelling resources of the texts used as input and on strategies for offering oral comments to guide their comprehension. They were also given guidance in the use of multimodal resources for language visualisation. The texts and the multimodal resources were used for comprehension and as models for producing documents (output) by the students.

From the documents produced by the students, we have selected 41 texts from both groups for this study. The texts were analysed according to linguistic criteria with regard to the level of productivity of the text, density and lexical richness and the number of nouns, verbs and adjectives, and also according to multimodal criteria with regard to the use of graphic and illustration resources, photos, formats, font types, paragraphs and headings. The results reveal greater differences in linguistic aspects than in multimodal aspects between the groups (immigrants and natives). These results are discussed on the basis of inferring that the differences are due not only to the textual use and encyclopaedic knowledge, but also to the direct and universal influence that digital media currently has on childhood.

Introduction

This research presents the integrated teaching of language and natural science contents, with particular emphasis on the use of multimodal resources. The integration of linguistic aspects and academic subjects is explained by the role of language in the construction of knowledge (Halliday & Martin, 1993). This study in particular deals with the language used in teaching texts from the subject unit on vertebrates. Multimodal resources form part of the material aspect and the technology used in informative texts, which current readers are accustomed to. This second point is justified by evidence that this media is currently the greatest instrument of cultural expression and communication among adults and children. Studies have shown that children spend a considerable amount of time watching television, using the computer, playing videogames and browsing the internet. Digital media currently has a more direct and universal influence on childhood than more traditional media (Buckingham, 2003).

The research was carried out on fourth-year primary education students, as educational literature insists on the importance of the mid-school years on language learning and on its relationship with a wide variety of subject contents, semiotic procedures, diversity of texts and technological resources (Allington et al., 2002; Bransford et al., 2000). In this literature, year four is considered a critical period in the primary education experience. Allington et al. (2002) maintain that during this school year some children without previous problems begin to experience difficulties, and Bransford et al. (2000) maintain that these are decisive times in the international assessment of primary school students. As schooling progresses, academic demands increase. Informative–expository texts on academic subjects are also a factor of difficulty because they present a structural organisation pattern of the information and relations between their sections that is very different from the structure of narrative text, which is more common in earlier school years.

Current assessments reveal that year four has become a crossing point for some children, in particular those with limited competences in the language of instruction. This is the case of students from immigrant families who fill many of the schools in Catalonia. Indeed, over the last few years in Catalonia there has been a significant increase in immigration within a very short period of time. The incorporation of these students into ordinary classrooms creates an extremely demanding situation for them and for the teacher, and is not without its difficulties. A simultaneous processing of the new language and of the concepts of the different curricula areas is required of the students, while they still have limited competences in the school language (L2). Several studies have revealed the difficulties that these students have in two basic aspects: in 'written and oral comprehension' (*input*) and in 'written and oral production' (*output*) (Huguet *et al.*, this volume). Comprehension is one of the basic requirements for acquiring L2 (Krashen, 1981), as well as a necessary condition for learning. Similarly, acquisition of L2 depends on the possibilities that the learner has of using the language (*output*) (Swain, 1985, 1995). The difficulties for students from immigrant families lie in their involvement in the learning of oral and written language and in the consideration of this population on behalf of the school to achieve their school success (Coelho, 2006).

Educational literature also suggests how to plan language intervention in ordinary classrooms that receive students with limited L2 competences. Coinciding with our objectives of integrating academic subjects, language and multimedia resources we have included proposals that follow a model of integration between language and curriculum content (Carrasquillo & Rodríguez, 2002; Echevarria *et al.*, 2004; Fisher & Frey, 2008; Vogt & Echevarria, 2008). We have also taken into consideration the proposals that emphasise the production, and not only the comprehension, of texts. In our experiment, this production was created as the result of a series of connected tasks within the instructional sequence (Swain, 1985, 1995).

The proposals are based on principles and practices that correspond to *textual and communicative aspects*:

- Include authentic information texts to awaken students' interest in the world, and not only fictional texts (Duke, 1999).
- Train teachers and students in the structure of informative–expository texts to facilitate reading (Duke, 1999).
- Place attention on oral communication through L2, with adaptations that make the oral messages understandable (Echevarria *et al.*, 2004, *op. cit.*).
- Present texts in a way that facilitates reading and comprehension, as well as access to their structure. These texts have a specific structure; they include technical and encyclopaedic vocabulary, and present a large amount of information, lexical and conceptual density (Pappas *et al.*, 2006).

Visual design aspects of the texts are also considered:

- Encouraging the visual design of the text and its structure, considering its layout, the number of words on a line, margins, paragraphs, font size and line spacing, among others (Walker & Reynolds, 2000).

- Facilitating the reading of texts and controlling the optimum length of lines and spacing (around 60 letters per line), in order to help develop a correct visual search (Spencer, 1969).

Finally, it considers the *production emphasis*:

- Developing written production competences through practices that focus attention on the explicit teaching of the language, practices focused on textuality, attention to errors and emphasis on vocabulary work (Nagy & Scott, 2000; Nation, 1990).
- Developing multimodal competences, showing students various models and how to use different resources (Walker & Reynolds, 2000).
- Helping students translate and represent the information from a textual source in a different semiotic form, such as a diagram or computer graphics, to increase comprehension (Manjarrez, 2007; Ogle & Blachowicz, 2002; Stead, 2002).

Objectives

Although there are several proposals for curricula integration, with descriptions of the integration of contents, attention to the constructive learning of students and focus on research results, there are no studies on the educational application of these principles, or there are very few. There are also few empirical research studies on learning processes under the above-mentioned school conditions. Therefore, our research develops a wider project of psycho-educational intervention to guide the practices of teachers and assist the learning of students. This study includes part of the results of this intervention in documents produced by the students.

- The first objective of the study was to analyse these texts as responses to the activities and to the stimuli, both from a linguistic and a multimodal resource point of view.
- The second objective consisted in comparing whether the students with more limited competences in Catalan, the language of instruction, displayed differences in the resulting texts or not.

The first objective responded to our interest in going into more depth in the learning process focused on text and multimodal resources; the second was more comparative and with it our aim was to find out to what extent the students' linguistic and sociocultural conditions influenced the results. Overall, we expected a larger influence of these conditions on the discursive aspects of learning than on multimodal aspects, given the evidence of a direct and universal influence of digital media.

Method

Participants

The sample of the current study comprised two groups of year-four primary education students, in total 41 students between 9 and 10 years of age from two public schools in Barcelona (School 1 and School 2), and two teachers, one from each educational centre. Catalan is the only medium of instruction, and Spanish and English are taught as a subjects (Arnau & Vila, this volume). The teachers' orientation sessions were given during the teaching of a thematic unit (vertebrates) on a weekly basis. The intervention was carried out as part of an educational innovation programme and within a research-action framework. Observations were recorded on video for all of the sessions. The following are details of the characteristics of these groups:

- *A group of year-four primary education students* at a school located in the centre of Barcelona (School 1), with a mainly native and Catalan-speaking population from homes with a medium socioeconomic level. Of a total of 20 students, 18 were native Catalan speakers and only two were foreigners (from Argentina). With regard to education results, approximately 90% of the students had a very high level of competences in the Catalan language.
- *A group of year-four primary education students* at a centre located in the old part of Barcelona (School 2), with an environment of linguistic and cultural diversity, made up of students from immigrant families, of a low and lower-middle socioeconomic class. There were immigrant students with differing lengths of residency in the country and varying levels of competence in Catalan. Of a total of 21 students, 12 were born in Catalonia but of immigrant families, and nine were foreign students from Pakistan, Bangladesh, Colombia, Mexico, Argentina, El Salvador, Brazil, Morocco and the Philippines. The students had diverse levels, with large individual differences that varied from medium to low, in Catalan language competences.

Procedure

Intervention programme

The intervention programme was developed taking the following aspects into account:

- Adaptation to the linguistic and cognitive needs of the two groups of students, but with particular attention to the level of competence for L2 learning.

- Use of multimedia resources for searching for and producing documents, in particular the combination of texts, drawings, photos, pattern and sequence diagrams representing natural science information.
- Consideration of the characteristics of the disciplinary content of Natural Sciences (vertebrates) in relation to the study materials and the teaching and learning process regarding this content. In particular, the following was valued:
  - Competences in informative text use that serve to teach these contents, both multimodal resources as well as vocabulary (general and specific, comprehension and production) in relation to conceptual development.
  - Incorporation of principles and practices recommended by the aforementioned literature on the integration of language and content teaching in ordinary classrooms with immigrant students.

Presented texts

The subject of vertebrates was presented in informative–expository type texts. From a discursive point of view, the structure of the text showed a variety of structural patterns such as definition, description, classification of parts, comparison and contrast, examples, and cause and effect.From a grammatical point of view, the informative–expository texts used verbs in the present tense (for example, 'is', 'are', 'have', etc.), generic nouns and technical terms (Pappas *et al.*, 2006).However, the information was not only found in the text, but also in the different modalities:illustrations, graphs, diagrams. Therefore, the informative–expository texts were multimodal; on one hand they had a pattern of illustrations, diagrams and text; and on the other, each text had a particular visual presentation with format, graphics and typographical resources.

Instructional sequence tasks

The tasks were organised into an instructional sequence with connected activities, taking into consideration the reciprocal nature of relations between contents, texts and semiotic resources, as well as the continuum between comprehension and production (and between reading and writing). Therefore, the tasks were designed from *input*, with the selection and manipulation of the informative texts that served as models, to final production of a multimodal document by the students. The instructional sequence tasks were the following:

- *Selection and manipulation of the text format* to aid comprehension. In an informative text, the graphics format was manipulated so that a certain standardisation was achieved between the line layout and the syntax (*cola and commata* type) to facilitate its reading out loud, comprehension and absorption of information (Blanche-Benveniste, 2008).

- Organisation of *listening* closely to the readings of the texts out loud by the teacher (emphasis on comprehension).
- *Labelling of the text* to highlight its structure and the organisation of information in terms of definition, description, classification of parts, comparison and contrast, examples, cause and effect (Rose, 2005). The labels included questions of the following type: 'what is it', 'what is this like', 'what comes next', 'what does it have', 'it is like', 'it is different', 'for example', 'why' (emphasis on comprehension).
- Subsequently, responding to questions and labels was encouraged, *locating the information in the text* for each metatextual question and label (emphasis on comprehension).
- A table *was used to organise the information in the text* and reference to other texts (transition between comprehension and production).
- *Retelling* or *rewriting* was encouraged to produce, through reconstruction, what was remembered of a text listened to or read (emphasis on production).
- Tasks were organised to *store and commit the words learnt to memory* and to recover them in definitions, reformulations, deductions and the creation of a glossary (emphasis on production).
- A *re-composition of information with format change* was also encouraged. In other words, summaries or paraphrases were made changing the form of representation: from text into a diagram or a conceptual map, etc. (emphasis on production).
- Finally, emphasis was put on *language visualisation* and on *multimodal representation*: font type and text organisation characteristics (blank spaces, paragraphs, graphics, tables, etc.), labelling that indicated the structure of the informative text (with description and questions: *definition* and *what is it?*, etc.), illustrations, graphs and photographs (emphasis on production).

Text analysis procedure

To analyse the texts, an assessment of graphs, semiotic aspects and multimodal criteria was made. The linguistic criteria considered took into account aspects related to expression in texts written by schoolchildren of this age.

- First, considering the type of text, an assessment was made as to whether the children's texts presented an adherence to informative–expository models.
- The other criteria was related to the construction of the text: productivity, number of words in the text, whole of the lexicon (content words: nouns, adjectives and verbs), type-token ratio (vocabulary diversity), lexical density (ratio of the proportion of content and functional words) and relative density of nouns, adjectives and verbs.

With regard to graphic features and multimodal criteria, we also considered the type of text:

- First, we assessed if the texts presented an adherence to the design of the models in aspects of text composition and visual language representation resources.
- Second, we considered the uniformity and organisation that gave unity and legibility to the text. In other words, we assessed whether the graphic features and multimodal criteria responded to the objective of discovering if the students' texts conformed to the design of the visual models provided, both in the patterns and the sequential order of the visual information presented, as well as in the layout of the elements (texts, images, diagrams, etc.).
- Third, we considered the texts' segmentation in terms of the presence of headings, separation of the text into paragraphs, use of subheadings, use of bullet points for subheadings or lists, visual emphasis of textual elements, such as the main heading, and use of key words. We wanted to analyse the students' acquisition of the visual language aspects related to the presentation of the text.
- Lastly, with regard to the design of the overall graphic resources, we analysed the texts' uniformity in design and organisation, and the distribution of the information that guaranteed legibility of the product.

Data analysis criteria

For the analysis of the texts with regard to word number, type-token ratio and lexical density, we used the AntConc 3.2.1 program (Anthony, 2007), which groups different textual corpus analysis tools together. For suitability to informative text types and the analysis of verb, noun and lexical density, a qualitative analysis was carried out. In addition, the statistical Student's *t*-test was performed, since the application condition according to the Levene test was met, and to analyse the graphic and multimodal criteria the chi-squared test was used.

Results

The 41 text productions responded to the instructions of preparing a digital document (PowerPoint) for presenting in class. This digital material originated from various notes, reports and compositions on paper. This study analyses the end result of the digital texts for public presentation. During the analysis and comparison of the text productions, linguistic and multimodal criteria were taken into consideration.

Results in relation to linguistic criteria

With regard to text type, the results reveal that the students from School 1 and School 2 produced informative–expository type texts. In both schools we found a predominance of the category of basic-level nouns, in other words, prototypical nouns common to the vocabulary of students of this age. Similarly, in the verbs category, there was a larger predominance of material- and relational-type verbs; specific action and relational verbs. With regard to the category of adjectives, there was a larger register of noun-qualifying, attributive-type adjectives.

Table 6.1 shows the average numbers of tokens, types and lexicon generated by each school group. To determine if these results were statistically significant, the independent sample Student's t-test was applied, comparing the averages of each group of words (tokens, types and lexicon) between Schools 1 and 2. For this test, first compliance with the condition of application was checked, verifying with the Levene Test that $p > 0.05$ (tokens: $p = 0.123$; types: $p = 0.575$ and lexicon: $p = 0.107$). Second, it was confirmed that the Student's t-test showed a $p < 0.01$ for each group of words and the significant difference between the averages of the two schools was assumed (tokens: $t = 6.428$, $df = 39$; $p = 0.000$; types: $t = 8.348$, $df = 39$, $p = 0.000$; and lexicon: $t = 6.793$; $df = 39$, $p = 0.000$).

In Table 6.2 we can observe that the total number of words produced, the variety and lexicon is greater in School 1 (Tokens = 3338; Types = 2242; Lexicon = 1557) than in School 2 (Tokens = 1874; Types = 1231; Lexicon = 897). Despite both groups producing texts of an informative type, School 1 students showed better precision, quality, specification and conciseness than those produced by School 2.

With regard to the percentage of nouns, verbs and adjectives, Student's t-test was performed for independent samples (see Table 6.3).

Table 6.3 shows the results obtained for the noun, verb and adjective densities, revealing that there are no differences. Similarly if we observe the

Table 6.1 Statistical analysis of tokens, types and lexicon between groups

		N	Average	Standard deviation	Standard average error
Tokens:	Sch. 1	21	158.95	36.279	7.917
Total written words	Sch. 2	20	93.70	27.959	6.252
Types:	Sch. 1	21	106.76	17.169	3.747
Total no. repeated words	Sch. 2	20	61.55	17.506	3.915
Lexicon: Total no.	Sch. 1	21	74.14	15.676	3.421
words that are not connectors, articles, prepositions, . . .	Sch. 2	20	44.85	11.504	2.572

Table 6.2 Descriptive analysis of token, type and lexicon counts between groups

| | Tokens | | | | | Types | | | | | Lexicon | | | | |
	Total N	Sum	Average	Standard Dev.	Variance	Total N	Sum	Average	Standard Dev.	Variance	Total N	Sum	Average	Standard Dev.	Variance
School 1	21	3338	159	36	1316	21	2242	107	17	295	21	1557	74	16	246
School 2	20	1874	94	28	782	20	1231	62	18	306	20	897	45	12	132

Table 6.3 Statistical analysis of the noun, verb and adjective density

		N	Average	Standard deviation	Standard average error
Noun density	Sch. 1	21	80.0690	8.51692	1.85855
	Sch. 2	20	78.4885	6.40051	1.43120
Verb density	Sch. 1	21	67.0876	7.91637	1.72749
	Sch. 2	20	69.3445	7.88003	1.76203
Adjective density	Sch. 1	21	87.2590	11.51210	2.51215
	Sch. 2	20	91.2225	11.77076	2.63202

percentages directly, there are no differences between the two schools. This is a result of the type of text studied being informative, where a greater presence is shown of nouns than of verbs and adjectives in both groups.

To analyse these results in more detail, an exhaustive study was made of the different grammatical categories generated (nouns, verbs and adjectives).

As can be appreciated in Tables 6.4, 6.5 and 6.6, it is clear that the texts produced by the students of School 1 present a wider range in all of these categories.

Results in relation to graphic and multimodal criteria

The three aspects considered were the design of the text composition model, the visual language resources, and the uniformity and organisation that gave unity and legibility to the text.

Table 6.7 shows the percentages of the graphics/multimodal aspect: students from both schools followed the model of the filing card provided at the start for presenting information in multimedia format. To verify if the validated variables (school and multimodal graphics aspect) were independent, the chi-squared test was used. In this case, as the minimum expected frequency is equal to 2.44 (less than 3), Fisher's exact statistical test was

Table 6.4 Linguistic analysis of the noun count in the student text productions

	School 1		School 2	
	N	*%*	*N*	*%*
Basic-level nouns	384	40.81	263	62.77
Proper nouns	31	3.29	38	9.07
Hyperonyms	93	9.88	43	10.26
General meronymy	53	5.63	16	3.82
Specific meronymy	172	18.28	55	13.13
Nominalisation	19	2.02	3	0.72
Abstract nouns	7	0.74	0	0.00
Metalanguage	9	0.96	1	0.24
Technical nouns	172	18.28	0	0.00
Derivatives	1	0.11	0	0.00
TOTAL	941	100.00	419	100.00

Table 6.5 Linguistic analysis of the verb count in the student text productions

	School 1		School 2	
	N	*%*	*N*	*%*
Existential	26	5.88	5	1.71
Discursive	7	1.58	7	2.39
Material	219	49.55	147	50.17
Relational	185	41.86	133	45.39
Sensory	2	0.45	1	0.34
Mental	3	0.68	0	0.00
TOTAL	442	100.00	293	100.00

Table 6.6 Linguistic analysis of the adjective count in the student text productions

	School 1		School 2	
	N	*%*	*N*	*%*
Attributive (gradual)	33	12.99	20	14.93
Attributive (qualifying)	154	60.63	62	46.27
Predicative (gradual)	0	0.00	8	5.97
Predicative (qualifying)	61	24.02	44	32.84
Perfective	6	2.36	0	0.00
TOTAL	254	100.00	134	100.00

Table 6.7 Descriptive analysis of the relationship between school and presentation order of information

| | | Text structure according to input order | | Total |
		No	Yes	
School 1	N	5	16	21
	%	23.8%	76.2%	100.0%
School 2	N	0	20	20
	%	0%	100.0%	100.0%
Total	N	5	36	41
	%	12.2%	87.8%	100.0%

performed and $p = 0.048$ ($p < 0.05$) was verified, proving that there is a relationship between the variables. Therefore, the fact that School 2 maintained a high percentage of the model provided (100% compared with 76.20% of School 1), is owing to School 2, as a group, having greater difficulties with the language of instruction, and also their being monitored more closely when preparing their documents.

With regard to discovering whether the students placed the text and images following the input model, no significant results were extracted between the groups in terms of Fisher's exact text ($p = 0.663$ and one-sided exact sig. $= 0.47$): the majority of the students, regardless of the school, followed the model provided by the teacher.

Regarding the visual language resources, significantly statistical differences were found. First, with regard to students separating the text into paragraphs, no statistical significance is observed in terms of the Fisher test ($p = 0.0107$ and one-sided exact sig. $= 0.059$) once dichotomous variables have been validated (school and placement of headings and paragraphs) using the chi-squared test, with the result of a minimum expected frequency of 2.44 (less than 3). This is because students from School 2 presented the information responding to each of the questions given in the initial filing card, creating a paragraph for each one, while students from School 1 developed their texts more independently.

Second, with regard to whether the students used paragraph headings, as can be seen in Table 6.8, the results are statistically significant in terms of Fisher's exact test ($p = 0.000$ and one-sided exact sig. $= 0.000$). Similarly, students from School 2 provided headings for each one of the paragraphs with questions given in the initial filing card, while School 1 students reformulated the source text creating their own text.

Third, with regard to the use of bullet points to separate paragraphs, the differences are statistically significant in terms of Fisher's exact test ($p = 0.000$ and one-sided exact sig. $= 0.000$). These results are owing to

Table 6.8 Descriptive analysis of the question 'Provide paragraph headings'

		Headings given to paragraphs?		Total
		No	Yes	
School 1	N	18	3	21
	School %	85.7%	14.3%	100.0%
School 2	N	0	20	20
	School %	0%	100.0%	100.0%
Total	N	18	23	41
	School %	43.9%	56.1%	100.0%

students from School 2 using the PowerPoint program's predetermined bullet text formats 95% of the time, while students from School 1 designed their texts based on the models of reference (Table 6.9).

Finally, regarding the visual highlighting of text elements, such as key words (italics, bold, underlined, colours and font size), there is no significant evidence in terms of the Fisher test ($p = 0.232$ and one-sided exact sig. = 0.125). Despite there being little or no presence of these graphics details in the sessions dedicated to producing these texts, 14.8% of students at School 1 highlighted key words using different formats: italics, bold and red (differentiating from the body text in black).

With regard to the last aspect of uniformity and organisation, giving unity and legibility to the text, we also found differences. Uniformity in the PowerPoint design, expressing unity in the text, shows statistically significant differences (p = 0.002 and one-sided exact sig. = 0.001) as seen in Table 6.10. From these results we can deduce that 81% of students from School 1 graphically and visually designed their slides so that the informative text was intelligible, clear and understandable for the rest of their classmates,

Table 6.9 Descriptive analysis of the question 'Paragraphs separated using bullet points'

		Bullet points used to separate paragraphs?		Total
		No	Yes	
School 1	N	14	7	21
	School %	66.7%	33.3%	100.0%
School 2	N	1	19	20
	School %	5.0%	95.0%	100.0%
Total	N	15	26	41
	School %	36.6%	63.4%	100.0%

Table 6.10 Descriptive statistics on the relationship between school and whether or not the product had a uniform design

		Uniform design of the PPT?		Total
		No	Yes	
School 1	N	4	17	21
	School %	19.0%	81.0%	100.0%
School 2	N	14	6	20
	School %	70.0%	30.0%	100.0%
Total	N	18	23	41
	School %	43.9%	56.1%	100.0%

outlining the information in a uniform and well-distributed manner, whereas 70% of School 2 students used multiple backgrounds, fonts, etc., in a haphazard manner, without considering the importance of uniformity and distribution in the design of their PowerPoints.

Even so, regarding the legibility of the information, in terms of being understandable to the rest of the class, tests provided no overall statistical significance. In both schools, there was a high percentage of students who got carried away using a combination of visual elements that ended up interfering with the legibility of the subject contents of the informative text.

Discussion and Conclusions

The results obtained from this study indicate, first, that the intergroup differences lie in the linguistic aspect. These differences are expected according to the characteristics of each group of students. However, the differences do not affect the competences of multimodal resource use in the same way. As we have seen, the children in each group showed knowledge of the basic visual keys to organising language and information in the texts. A possible explanation is the exposure that children currently have to videogames, internet access, use of computers, and other multimodal means of communication.

Second, we have established that School 1 showed better linguistic abilities with regard to the total occurrences of words than School 2. This proves that School 1 children have a better precision, quality, specification and conciseness in the language used in their texts. However, these differences do not affect text type, as both groups produced informative texts; nor do they affect the density of lexicon, verbs and adjectives. In contrast, School 1 tended to use a larger number of nouns in the text productions compared with School 2. This is clear from the diversity of the lexicon of nouns. From a more theoretical point of view, it makes sense to predict that an informative-type text will contain more nouns than verbs and adjectives; however, the lexical diversity is attributable to the student's knowledge and to the school's educational work. We can therefore conclude that students from School 1 generate a larger occurrence of nouns and reveal a much richer lexicon than School 2 students.

Third, despite not discovering overall differences referring to the criteria of multimodal resource use, aspects relating to visual language were handled differently by the two schools. These differences are related to the acquisition of the design model provided by the teacher, the use of paragraph headings and bullet points to separate paragraphs, and also the uniformity and organisation that gave unity and legibility to the text. The scores for School 2 were higher because at the time of production the teacher monitored the students more closely. The use of predetermined PowerPoint templates that directly organise the text in bullet point paragraphs is also a cause of the results for this aspect. From this it could be deduced that the use of visual elements, such as visually highlighted headings in the text, its separation into paragraphs and the use of different components that are part of the computer program and help to highlight the slides (backgrounds, font types, colours, italics, bold, etc.), is irrespective of the knowledge of the vehicular language.

The results found reveal different competences between the groups of students, a greater linguistic competence in native students and a lower competence in students from immigrant families. This is obviously an expected result; what is less predictable are the good results in multimodal resource competences. From this, an educational observation can be made with regard to the stimulation of using visual language resources in *input* texts and of working with multimodal resources that increased comprehension in both groups, but notably among immigrant students. Additionally, in terms of production, reliance on the use of these resources improves expression among the students with limited linguistic competences. Finally, it can be stated that the use of digital competences is not only useful for expression and communication but also for linguistic and curriculum content learning.

Acknowledgement

This research was funded by Spanish Ministry for Science and Innovation (project EDU2009-11409) and IEC, the Institute for Catalan Studies (Project IECSFCS2009-02ARN).

References

Allington, R., Johnson, P.H. and Day, P.J. (2002) Exemplary fourth-grade teachers: Good fourth-grade teaching is an expert activity that is not amenable to any one-size-fits-all plan for instruction. *Language Arts* 79 (6), 462–466.

Anthony, L. (2007) AntCon Software. http://www.antlab.sci.waseda.ac.jp/software.html

Blanche-Benveniste, C. (2008) Les unites de langue écrite et de langue parlée. In M. Bilger (Coord.) *Donnés orales. Les enjeux de la transcription* (pp. 192–216). Perpignan: Presses Universitaires de Perpignan.

Bransford, J.D., Brown, A.L. and Cocking, R.R. (eds) (2000) *How People Learn. Brain, Mind, Experience, and School* (expanded edition). Washington, DC: National Academy Press.

Buckingham, D. (2003) *Media Education: Literacy, Learning, and Contemporary Culture*. Oxford: Blackwell.

Carrasquillo, A. and Rodríguez, V. (2002). *Language Minority Students in the Mainstream Classroom* (2nd edn, pp. 131–147). Clevedon: Multilingual Matters.

Coelho, E. (2006) *Enseñar y aprender en escuelas multiculturales. Una aproximación integrada*. Barcelona: Horsori.

Duke, N.K. (1999) *The scarcity of informational texts in first grade*. Ann Arbor: Center for the Improvement of Early Reading Achievement (CIERA), University of Michigan. Retrieved from http://www.ciera.org/library/reports/inquiry-1/1-007/Report%201-007.html

Echevarria, J., Vogt, M.E. and Short, D. (2004) *Making Content Comprehensible for English Language Learners: The SIOP Model* (2nd edn). Boston: Allyn and Bacon.

Fisher, D. and Frey, N. (2008) Student and teacher perspectives on the usefulness of content literacy strategies. *Literacy Research and Instruction* 47 (4), 246–263.

Halliday, M.A.K. and Martin, J.R. (1993) *Writing Science: Literary and Discursive Power*. Pittsburgh: University of Pittsburgh Press.

Krashen, S. (1981) *Second Language Acquisition and Second Language Learning*. Oxford: Pergamon. Retrieved from http://www.sdkrashen.com/SL—-Acquisition—-and—-Learning/index.html

Manjarrez, J. (2007) *Infografía*. London: London University. Retrieved from http://www.astraph.com/udl/biblioteca/antologias/infografia.pdf

Nagy, W.E. and Scott, J.A. (2000) Vocabulary processes. In M.L. Kamil, P. Mosenthal, P.D. Pearson and R. Barr (eds) *Handbook of Reading Research* (Vol. 3) (pp. 269–284). Mahwah, NJ: Erlbaum.

Nation, I.S.P. (1990) *Teaching and Learning Vocabulary*. New York: Newbury House.

Ogle, D. and Blachowicz, C. (2002) Beyond literature circles: Helping students comprehend informational texts. In C. Block and M. Pressley (eds) *Comprehension Instruction: Research-Based Best Practices* (pp. 259–274). New York: Guilford Press.

Pappas, C.C., Varelas, M., Tucker-Raymond, E. and Keblawe-Shamah, N. (2006) *Enacting Integrated Science-Literacy Units in Primary Classrooms: Opportunities and Tensions*. Retrieved from http://www.esiponline.org/csl/christinepappas.html

Rose, D. (2005) *Learning to Read: Reading to Learn. Submission to the National Inquiry into the Teaching of Literacy*. Canberra: Department of Education, Science and Training.

Spencer, H. (1969) *The Visible Word*. London: Lund Humphries.

Stead, T. (2002) *Is That a Fact? Teaching Nonfiction Writing in K-3*. Portland, ME: Stenhouse.

Swain, M. (1985) Communicative competence: Some roles of comprehensible input and comprehensible output in its development. In S. Gass and C. Madden (eds) *Input in Second Language Acquisition* (pp. 235–253). Rowley, MA: Newbury House.

Swain, M. (1995) Three functions of output in second language learning. In G. Cook and B. Seidlhofer (eds) *Principle and Practice in Applied Linguistics: Studies in Honour of H.G. Widdowson* (pp. 125–144). Oxford: Oxford University Press.

Vogt, M. and Echevarria, J. (2008) *99 Ideas and Activities for Teaching English Learners with the SIOP® Model*. Boston: Pearson / Allyn and Bacon.

Walker, S. and Reynolds, L. (2000) Screen design for children's reading: Some key issues. *Journal of Research in Reading* 23 (2), 224–234.

7 Interlinguistic Reflection on Teaching and Learning Languages

Oriol Guasch Boyé

This chapter presents a project, shared by the areas of Catalan and English in a Catalan high school, for teaching and learning grammar reflection in secondary education. Certain aspects of student interactions are analysed together with interactions between students and their teachers, focusing on the metalinguistic interlinguistic activity that is created in its implementation, with conclusions being established about the potentialities of the experience itself.

Introduction

The education system in Catalonia stipulates the simultaneous teaching of three languages throughout compulsory schooling for all students: Catalan, Spanish and a foreign language, which is usually English (Arnau & Vila, this volume). One of the peculiarities of the classrooms where this project is carried out is the fact that there are students with a diverse range of first languages. In most cases the language is Catalan or Spanish, but there is also a small but significant percentage of Arabic, Berber, Chinese, Urdu and a long list of more than 300 languages. Achieving minimum efficiency in this linguistic training programme requires an educational plan working in two directions: the coordination of the linguistic areas (Catalan, Spanish and a foreign language) with the other curricular areas and coordination between the linguistic areas.

This chapter focuses on the second part of planning and presents the analysis and subsequent discussion of some relevant aspects related to interaction among students, and interaction between students and their teachers, in the development of a collaborative project between the Catalan and English languages areas. The experience takes place in a second-year classroom in compulsory secondary education (14-year-old students) and discusses the achievement of linguistic learning objectives through the development of metalinguistic reflection and also includes comparisons between languages in the curriculum (Catalan, the co-official and vehicular teaching language and English, a foreign language). The planning of this intervention and its implementation in the classroom was developed as part of a research project with the objective of deepening our knowledge of how students construct grammatical concepts.[1]

We will begin with a synthetic presentation of three of the aspects that the theoretical basis of the research is centred on, which are particularly relevant to our research. We will then continue with the description of the characteristics of the project that the students carried out. Third, we will specify the objectives of the analysis that forms the main part of this chapter, analyse the process of its explanation in detail and ultimately formulate conclusions.

Theoretical Frames of Reference

We will focus on three study areas chosen from the theoretical frames of reference we base the teaching proposal on and in accordance with the issues that will be the subject of our attention in analysing the development of the project. The first area refers to linking linguistic and metalinguistic knowledge of different languages in the minds of the learners; the second is the construction of grammatical concepts by the students; and the third is the acquisition of the concept of temporality.

The connections between linguistic knowledge of and about different languages

Many authors, both in the English-speaking world (Hawkins, 1974; James, 1996; Sharwood Smith, 1993) and in the French-speaking world (Dabène, 1992; De Pietro, 2003; Roulet 1980) have considered the importance of building a common space of reflection on languages as a tool for improving the teaching and learning of first languages and of other additional ones (those learned after the first). We consider the proposals from Bill VanPatten, Anne Trévise and Irit Kupferberg to be symbolic in this area.

VanPatten and Cadierno (1993) and VanPatten (2002) proposed the teacher's intervention in processing linguistic input that the learners receive as a way of teaching and learning to read in an additional language based on an instruction process that: (a) focuses on a certain linguistic structure; (b) provides information on a reading strategy that may lead to misinterpretation and; (c) to avoid this misinterpretation, provides the learner with the tools to self-regulate their reading processes and arrive at a correct construction of the meaning of this input. What VanPatten and Cadierno ultimately proposed is an implicitly reflexive activity on the language, which depends on the construction of the meaning of the formal characteristics of certain structures. What is more significant to us, however, is that the formal structures that these authors refer to are the more common reading errors, and part of these errors they consider to be extremely relevant stem from the interference of languages previously learned with the new language. This means that the comparison of differentiated structures of the learners' first language and an additional language constitutes the basis of points (b) and (c) of the recommended instruction process.

Trévise (1994, 1996) takes linguistic knowledge into consideration and understands it as an intuitive knowledge of linguistic uses that language users construct from a combination of several factors. She sees metalinguistic knowledge as a more or less conscious understanding that can be verbalised, largely thanks to schooling. She considers the balance and the distinct relationships between these two knowledge types in the first languages and in additional languages, and she joins in the beliefs regarding the interlinguistic linking of linguistic knowledge by multilingual people. However, unlike what was considered normal in the mid-1990s and still remains usual in present-day educational approaches, she also postulates the interlinguistic linking of metalinguistic knowledge, namely, the conscious knowledge of languages. Trévise carefully examined the students' grammatical knowledge of their first language and found it often consists of a mixture of wide-ranging knowledge, which can be projected onto the second language with positive learning effects in some cases and negative ones in others.

Kupferberg (1999), in agreement with Trévise and following in the footsteps of Sharwood Smith (1993) in his formulation of induced input salience (a procedure to facilitate the perception of certain differentiated linguistic phenomena between the first language and an additional language), proposes explicit teaching of contrastive metalinguistic input (the grammatical explanation of differing formal characteristics between certain languages) to provide more visibility and therefore facilitate the awareness of certain relation patterns between certain languages and as a result facilitate their learning. In short, what these authors do is postulate the propriety of metalinguistic interlinguistic reflection in teaching as an adjunctive factor in students' learning additional languages. Their assumption is based on the hypothesis of a connection between the linguistic knowledge of several languages in the multilingual mind.

The construction of grammatical concepts by the students

The coincidence between Myhill (2000) and Fisher (2004) is significant in their appreciation of the difficulties schoolchildren have in constructing precise and functional grammatical concepts. Myhill, in a study on teaching grammar in Great Britain, collected ethnographic data from 12-year-old students and future teachers, and observed three types of misconceptions in the learners' grammar concepts. Fisher, as part of a reflection on what happens in the French-speaking population, considers the distance between the knowledge taught and what the students grasp, and explains this distance as challenges the students must overcome to construct the new knowledge from their previous learning.

We can establish a correspondence between the misconceptions that Myhill discusses and the challenges put forward by Fisher as follows:

- The misconceptions that are acquired in academic life from grammar learned, which gives definitions that are simplified and not sufficiently answered later, leading to errors, and which is accompanied by fragmented approaches and activities that suggest the mechanical application of rules that must be memorised, as Myhill mentions, are a methodological challenge in terms of Fisher's perspective to constructing a coherent and functional knowledge of grammar.
- Myhill's study on the distances and inefficiencies of certain grammatical analyses (descriptive or normative) to account for some linguistic phenomena is consistent with Fisher's observations on the difficulties posed by the approach to certain problems, such as the articulation of sentence perspective, textual perspective and the expository perspective of school grammar, or the difficulties in establishing consistent formulations of interlinguistic variation in the simultaneous teaching of several languages. Here Fisher speaks of the epistemological challenges arising from the intrinsic complexity of teaching and learning.
- According to Myhill there are misconceptions that are attributable to the high demands of abstraction that metalinguistic activity requires: the conceptual difficulties deriving from the use of language to describe the language itself, or, for example, the difficulties in agreeing on prototypical grammatical concepts with linguistic variation. The obstacles that may depict the learners' cognitive deficiencies in these cases are considered by Fisher to be psychogenetic obstacles.

In conclusion, therefore, according to these authors, interventions for teaching grammatical reflection in classrooms should be established on the basis of careful and detailed attention to the methodology of the intervention itself, to the control of the intrinsic complexity of the grammatical phenomena that are dealt with and to the cognitive capacity of the students at different levels.

The acquisition of temporality

In keeping with emergentist research on the acquisition of languages (Bates, 2003), Starren (2003) refers to the significant influence of the comprehensive principles of discourse organisation in language acquisition and use at the sentence level: she states that the macro-organisation of texts has an extremely important impact on the use of linguistic tools at the level of micro-organisation of utterances (the semantic organisation defines the linguistic resources to be used in production). Citing Klein and von Stutterheim (1987), this author specifies a macro-organisation for the narrative that is formalised in a main structure by specifying a series of events and a set of secondary structures such as evaluations, descriptions and comments.

Comajoan (2005), based on Labov and Waletzky (1967), tells us that narrative fiction is characterised by its structure (introduction, orientation, complication of the action, evaluation, resolution and coda) and its texture. This latter term refers to the fact that the progression of the narrative in some situations or events is more relevant or more noticeable than in others. This perceptibility or relevance, which cannot be defined in a single way, allows us to distinguish, for example, the first level or foreground from the second level or background: the former corresponds with the level on which the narrative explains narrated events; and the latter describes the context in which the events are developed.

The structure and texture of the narrative are universal phenomena; however, the linguistic mechanisms that formalise them are not. Therefore, unlike what happens with Germanic languages, for Romanic languages, for example, the foreground and background of the narrative in the past tense have formal markers that distinguish them. This is because the verb paradigm of Romance languages has, in the indicative form, a past perfect tense (the past, e.g. *va sortir* in Catalan) and a past imperfect tense (the imperfect, e.g. *sortia* in Catalan). These two tenses conform respectively to temporal notions that are updated in the foreground and background. Therefore, we find ourselves before a linguistic phenomenon that establishes a clear connection between the discourse level (textures) and the morphosyntactic level (the verb paradigm) of the functioning of the language.

Both Starren and Comajoan refer to the research carried out by Bardovi-Harlig (2000) on the processes in the acquisition of temporality in second languages using narrative fiction. This author has synthesised two apparently contradictory assumptions: one that highlights the demands of verb morphology and the semantic value of verbs in sentence uses as a vehicle for acquiring the mechanisms to express temporality in a language and another that gives prominence to the discursive uses of this language.

The results of these studies lead us to conclude that lexical aspect and narrative structure conspire to shape the distribution of tense-aspect morphology in interlanguage. Whereas the basic semantic features of predicates attract verbal morphology with the same features, in actual production these inflected predicates are pressed into the service of communication and may take on features appropriate to the narrative structure, thus going beyond the most basic predicate-level pairing of verbal and morphological features. The understanding that interlanguage temporal systems are shaped by both the semantics of lexical aspect and the pragmatics of discourse provides a point of departure for future research. (Bardovi-Harlig, 2000: 317)

What Bardovi-Harlig points out in this paragraph has become a benchmark for designing contents and the procedures to address them and for establishing the goals of the project that we shall now present.

The Project

The project presented here stems, in the first instance, from the New School theories of Dewey (1910) and Kilpatrick (1918) who developed the proposal of 'project work'. This is a model that proposes teaching from work plans that structure a set of tasks for achieving an objective and give the students an active part in their learning.

Second, our project arises from the project work proposals for the teaching and learning of language uses, theorised, elaborated and implemented in classrooms from the specific perspective of teaching a first language in the 1980s in the French-speaking world (Halté, 1982; Jolibert, 1988; among many others). In this second case, the design of the project is greatly influenced by the orientation of Leontiev's activity theory, for studying cognitive psychology in the mental processes involved in linguistic uses, the postulates of social–cultural psychology on the social character of learning and the contributions of language sciences to text, pragmatics and discourse (Camps, 2003).

Our project is unique in that the main goal is not the learning of language uses, but rather the learning of grammar and grammar reflections. A work-type proposal for this kind of project is divided into three phases (Camps, 2006). The first phase defines the subject of the study, looks at the problem that must be resolved and defines the language-learning objectives. The second phase develops an itinerary of activities for researching information, analysing language uses, manipulating linguistic corpora, etc. This is designed by the teachers and carried out by alternating small-group work by students with occasional attention from the teacher and with teacher-led, whole-class work. In the third phase the results of the task are produced in a final report, the processes used to carry out the work are reviewed and evaluated, and verification is made as to whether the anticipated learning outcome has been achieved.

A first version of the project was designed by researchers and was then discussed with the Catalan and English language teachers. In the final design special emphasis was placed on:

- Explaining to the students the work they would do and the learning objectives to be achieved: the observation of how different languages can resolve the diverse ways of expressing similar grammar concepts, in this case verbal aspect and its functionality in fictional stories. While Catalan, as we have seen previously, requires the use of the *past tense (va cantar)* in the foreground and the *imperfect (cantava)* in the background, English does not distinguish the texture quite so clearly. This is because its verbal paradigm has a single form, the *past simple,* which expresses both a past perfect and a past imperfect. Thus, in narrations in English we find the *past simple* with the past perfect in the foreground; and the *past continuous* and the *past simple,* but here with an imperfect past sense (common action), in the background.
- Reviewing the differences between informal conversations and conversations to solve problems in academic contexts with the students (Mercer, 2004) in order to try and strengthen the epistemic value of their conversations.
- Designing activities that involve alternating self-regulated situations of interaction among peers in small groups and situations of interaction between the teachers and the whole class, to observe the impact of group conversations on whole-class discourse and how the students' independent reasoning and that guided by the teachers combine.
- Promoting metalinguistic interlinguistic reasoning as an instrument to explain the implicit knowledge about the relationships between languages as a possible learning instrument.
- Simultaneously paying attention to sentence-level and textual perspectives in analyses of linguistic productions as possible factors contributing to the learning of certain grammar concepts.
- Avoiding strictly formal approaches to linguistic and discourse phenomena, and adopting one's own perspectives of cognitive linguistics as a guarantee for constructing grammar concepts that suit the needs derived from use.

The project was carried out in two parts. The first (Table 7.1) consisted of two introductory group-work sessions related to problem-solving. The second (Table 7.2) involved five work sessions, the last three of which were jointly led by the Catalan language teacher (the vehicular language of teaching in the school) and the English language teacher (the students' first foreign language).

All the small-group work sessions in the class were audio recorded, and the whole-group sessions led by the Catalan and English language teachers

Table 7.1 Introductory sessions

Session	Activities	Learning objectives
A	– Presentation of the preparation activity for group work: explanation and analysis of the criteria to follow for effective interaction in group problem-solving. – In groups, working on an exercise in problem-solving with an observer to ensure compliance with the interaction rules. – Analysis of the functioning of the interaction based on the data provided by the observer.	Awareness of the difference between informal conversations and discussions among the members of the working groups, who interact to solve problems in teaching–learning activities.
B	– In groups, reading the transcription of selected passages of the interactions recorded in the previous session and analysis of the interaction and its level according to the proposed rules. – Sharing the analysis of each of the groups, led by the teacher.	

were recorded on video. The transcriptions of these recordings, the documents written by the students and the field notes taken by the researchers form the basis for the points we will now make.

Analysis of the interaction

The main objectives of our analysis of the interaction among the students and between the students and their teachers within the framework of the project are as follows: (a) to argue in favour of the functionality of project work as an educational tool for promoting reflective activity among students, which is essential for their progressive independence, both in solving problems related to language use and in tasks focused on the construction of knowledge about languages; (b) to show the validity of metalinguistic interlinguistic reflection as a tool in the construction of transversal and/or specific grammar concepts in each language.

Execution of the project's activities

We pay particular attention to how two groups of four students carried out the planned activities in the third session of the project and observe

Table 7.2 Work sessions

Session	Activities	Learning objectives
1	Presentation of the project and its objectives.	Difference between the textures: background, foreground, direct discourse.
	Reading a story in Catalan: identification of textures: (a) Modelling of the activity by the teacher. (b) Group analysis of the textures in a story: *El rei, la puça i el poll* (see Appendix 7.1). (c) Sharing: explanation of the results and group discussion with the teacher and the entire class.	
	Identification of the verbs in the story: (a) In groups, identifying verb tenses for each texture. (b) In groups, writing up conclusions on the relationship between the verb tenses and the textures. (c) Sharing the results of each group, led by the teacher.	Identification of the verb forms that appear in the different textures. Establishing conformity between textures and verb tenses.
2	Comparison of a well-constructed story with versions that have had verb-form alternations removed (one with all the verbs in the imperfect and another with all the verbs in the past): (a) In groups, indication of the differences between the initial story and one of the new versions, and discussion regarding whether or not the new version is well constructed.	Differentiating the semantic values (aspectual) of the imperfect and the past from the narrative's needs.
	(b) Sharing the observations of each group led by the teacher, and reaching conclusions on the temporal value of the imperfect and the past.	Concept of aspect.

Session	Activities	Learning objectives
3	Identification of textures and verb tenses in English: (a) In groups, reading the English translation of the same story and marking the textures. (b) In groups, classifying the verbs according to the textures and reaching conclusions on the relationship between the verb forms and the textures. (c) Sharing the observations of each group led by the teacher and reaching conclusions on the relationship between the textures and verb tenses in English.	
4	Contrast between Catalan and English: (a) In groups, comparison of the textures of the Catalan and English versions of the story and comparison of the relationship between verb forms and textures in Catalan and English. (b) Sharing the contributions of each group led by the teacher and reaching conclusions on the differences between the verbal systems in Catalan and English in narrative fiction in the past tense.	Differences in formalising the perfect/imperfect aspect in Catalan and English.
5	Recapping the conclusions from the previous session: (a) In groups, writing a short narrative in English. (b) In groups, observing the verb forms in the narrative. (c) Sharing the contributions of each group led by the teacher and reflecting on the verb forms in each language. (d) Reflecting on what has been done and learned throughout the group session.	

some significant peculiarities in the way they work. This session had two parts: the first consisted of defining the textures (the foreground, the background and direct speech in the English version of the same story for which the textures had been established in the first session); and the second, in classifying the verb forms that appear in each of the textures and forming conclusions on the relationship between the textures and verb tenses. This was, therefore, a session that paralleled the previous one, but with the added difficulty of it being centred around the English version of the story.

Synthesis of the activity carried out by Group 1

The members of this group began the work session by comparing the Catalan and English versions of the text (see Appendix 7.1) and considering that the marking of the textures in English would correspond with that of the Catalan text, defined in the previous session. They began the exercise by marking the passages that corresponded to direct speech and then continued by marking the foreground. They read the text in English, verbalising its meaning in Catalan. Subsequently, and depending on the meaning, they marked the passages corresponding to this foreground without any difficulty. One of the members of the group, Nano, took the initiative and clarified the meaning of many of the passages in the text for his peers, and they followed his lead. These two facts: (a) that of limiting themselves to establishing the textures based on what they had done in the previous session with the Catalan version and (b) the group's dependence on Nano's knowledge, explain why the exercise was done quickly and without too much difficulty.

The activity of classifying the verb forms according to the textures in which they appeared was carried out based on the same idea as in the previous activity: they worked according to the instructions; their dialogue developed paying special attention to the tenses of the verbs in the narrative, spelling and meaning in Catalan. It was always Nano who took the initiative, and the role of his classmates was minor in solving the small problems and questions that arose.

There were two very brief incidents when the English teacher interrupted the group's work. The first time, the teacher asked if the students had any questions, and Nano raised the question about the tense of 'there was' (in the first line of the text). The teacher responded, explaining the relationship between the textures and verb tenses. This did not seem appropriate, as the group members had not even considered this relationship until that moment, and their only concern was to follow the instructions of the task they had been given: categorising verb tenses. The second incident is related to the same problem, which remained unresolved from the previous incident. This time, after clarifying that 'was' is the *past simple*, the teacher proposed a reflection on the differences between the verb paradigm in Catalan and English that was far removed from the reflections generated by this group's activity.

At the end of this second part of the session, the exercise of reaching conclusions about the possible relationship between textures and verb forms in the English language did not take place.

From this synthesis we can conclude that: (a) it is not possible to say that there was collaborative group activity in this work session, as only one person in the group actually did the work. The other students simply copied what he suggested into their workbooks; (b) this lack of communication among the group members worked against the emergence of any reflective activity in carrying out the task; and (c) not doing the last exercise, probably the most demanding and most interesting one in the session, resulted in preventing this reflective activity from taking place.

Synthesis of the activity carried out by Group 3

The group members began by recalling the analysis they had made of the Catalan version of the story (apparently checking the text against this version). From their dialogue we can deduce that they thought the same would happen in the English text as in the Catalan text, that each texture would have its own verb form (imperfect in the background and the perfect in the foreground). This is probably one of the reasons why, when it came to carrying out the task, they did not follow the strategy proposed in the work instructions ((1) define the background, foreground and direct dialogue; (2) classify the verbs according to where they appear, (3) establish the tenses of the classified verbs; and (4) reach conclusions regarding the relationship between the verb forms and the textures) but another of their own. Another reason for departing from the strategy proposed by the teachers is that, based on the relationship between the verb forms and the textures in the Catalan version, they tried to use the verb tenses that appeared in the English text as clues to distinguish and mark the textures of this version.

The idea of a parallelism between the two languages led them to assume that Catalan and English shared the same concept of temporality, which was articulated in a parallel manner in both languages and was formalised in each of them in specific differentiating markers in the verb forms. For this reason they searched for a verb tense in the English version equivalent to the imperfect in Catalan (see Appendix 7.1, symbols used in the transcription):

28   **Sara:**   so, if we know the imperfect in English
29   **Eva:**   I think it's the past simple↓ no-
30   **Sara:**   I don't know if it's the past continuous-
31   **Pau:**   no↓ because here were the two↓ there was: ah no no↓

In the following passage (Table 7.3), from Sara's initiative and with the help of the rest of the group, an interesting reasoning is developed on this supposed concept shared by both languages.

Table 7.3 Comparing Catalan and English languages

Dialogue	Observation
50 Sara: look and: the imperfect is: when you were doing something at that moment no↑ no, let's see↑ it's what you did and is now done↓	(50) Sara explains a difference between the temporal values of the imperfect and the past in Catalan.
51 Pau: = yes↓=	(51, 52) Pau and Eva agree.
52 Eva: =yes↓=	
53 Sara: so this is the past continuous: and this is the past simple↓	(53) With the deictic 'this', we do not know for sure if Sara is pointing out in a text the verb tenses she is referring to.
54 Pau: hmm	
55 Sara: so- the past continuous is the background↓	(55) From what she has seen for Catalan, Sara associates a verb tense in English with a texture.
56 Eva: the past continuous is the imperfect, no↑	(56) Eva explains the similarity between the two verb tenses in Catalan and English, possibly based on their function in the textures expressed in (55)
57 Sara: yes↓ because the past continuous is what =was done=	
	(57) Sara confirms the similarity of the verb forms, but this time according to their temporal value.
58 Eva: =haa haa= and the past continuous is there was↑	From (58) to (63) two voices overlap: a) Sara, who continues with her statement associating the past simple with the action plane; b) Eva, who is looking for an example of the past continuous in the text.
59 Sara: =and the past simple:=	
60 Eva: =what is the past continuous↑=	
61 Sara: it's the:	
62 Eva: ok↓	
63 Sara: foreground	
64 Eva: but if we first mark-	From (64) to (70) it becomes apparent that despite the initial hypothesis about this passage, the group members have doubts about the examples of verb tenses or about categorising certain verb forms.
65 Pau: no↓ the past continuous is did- did you:	
66 Eva: not the past continuous	
67 Sara: so↑	
68 Pau: ah it's true↓	
69 Sara: the past simple is also did you↓	
70 Pau: ah yes, yes↓	

In short, the similarities between the aspectual temporal value of the imperfect in Catalan and the *past continuous* in English (both are imperfect) leads them to propose that the *past continuous* is the prototype verb form in the background and the *past simple* (which is compared with the past perfect, without any reasoning) in the foreground.

It is interesting to observe, from this point on, how these students dealt with the evidence that contradicted their initial hypothesis. We will do so by transcribing four passages from their conversation following the chronology of the work carried out in this session of the project.

A first indication of the faultiness of the hypothesis appears in the following passage in which Sara is correct in questioning the temporal value of 'had'; this probably stemmed from comparing the Catalan and English versions of the text (*un rei que tenia dos servents/a king who had two servants*):

85	**Pau:**	no↓ em: there was once a King that- em: (trying to translate from English)
86	**Eva:**	that had:
87	**Pau:**	that had two servants who took care of him↓
88	**Sara:**	so↓
89	**Pau:**	this doesn't explain anything↓
90	**Sara:**	had↓
91	**Pau:**	and↑
92	**Sara:**	it could be *tenia* or *va tenir*↑ how do you know that it's *tenia* and not *va tenir*↑
93	**Eva:**	because =here it says tenia↓=

In previous sessions they had been informed that the foreground is the order of actions and events that occur in the narrative and that the background is where the characteristics of the protagonists and setting are explained. This is why Pau says in line 89 'this doesn't explain anything'. With this expression he wishes to point out that the passage in the English version he has just interpreted, in his opinion, does not correspond to the background and therefore the presence of a past simple (had) is consistent with the theory the group has constructed. Sara, however, in line 92 asks about the temporal value of this past simple and its equivalence in Catalan. The question is closed without further discussion with Eva's response in line 93, in which she uses the Catalan version of the text as a proof of authority.

In short, in this passage, while Pau tries to save the group's hypothesis from an unjustified affirmation in line 89 regarding the texture in which the past simple (*had*) appears, Sara questions this hypothesis. Finally the contradiction is abandoned without resolving the issue.

The decision to establish the tenses of the verbs in the narrative as an indication for marking the textures leads the students to wonder about the verb forms of the past continuous and the past simple of the verb 'to be' and other verbs, and about their temporal value. In the following passage, in line 136, Pau confirms that 'had' is a past simple and, in lines 138 and 140, Sara explains that according to their hypothesis it is inconsistent for a verb tense typical of the foreground to appear in the background. In the followings lines (141–151) we see how, on the one hand, they relate the temporal value of the past continuous and their supposed equivalence with the Catalan imperfect, and, on the other, the formal characteristics typical of the past continuous, which allows them to distinguish this tense from the past simple.

134	**Pau:**	no, but the past continuous is followed by the verb in 'ing'
135	**Sara:**	and where do you see that here↑
136	**Pau:**	that's why↓ it isn't there↓ that's why it's past continuous, oh↑ past simple↓
137	**Eva:**	I, ah, I- I: can't =find the class sheet=
138	**Sara:**	=the past- the past simple= the past simple we said is the foreground↓
139	**Eva:**	no:↓
140	**Sara:**	then it's wrong↓
141	**Pau:**	no, no↓
142	**Eva:**	ok↓ ok↓
143	**Pau:**	let's see↓ past simple↑ how is: it:
144	**Sara:**	past↑ look↓ past simple is:
145	**Eva:**	it's:
146	**Sara:**	ok, one moment: of course, according to what- the: English teacher↓ said, the past continuous is when =you said past continuous thinking=
147	**Pau:**	=it's an action that hasn't finished= or that was an action that hasn't finished, right↑
148	**Eva:**	exactly:
149	**Sara:**	so it's like the imperfect↑
150	**Eva:**	yes↓
151	**Pau:**	and↑
152	**Sara:**	it's like the imperfect↓
153	**Pau:**	XXX
154	**Eva:**	yes, yes↓ I think it's right↓
155	**Sara:**	of course: because the imperfect is also what you were doing↓ you're thinking about what you were doing↓ and this is past simple but there's no 'ing' here↓

It is apparent in this passage, therefore, that one effect of the unresolved contradiction is the students' special attention to the formal characteristics of the verbs and their temporal values, which they compare with those of Catalan verb forms. It is true, on the one hand, that they do not manage to resolve the contradiction, and this could be assessed negatively; it is also true that their effort to reduce it provides them with an analytical activity on verb forms and their temporal values which we consider to be very valuable.

One of the characteristics of the reflective activity that emerged from the interaction needed among the students, and sometimes between the students and the teachers, to solve problems is the difficulty involved in constructing precise concepts and using specific terminology to refer to them. In this passage, the members of the group are reading and translating the sentence: *'The king was sitting on his royal throne'* to establish the verb tense and to decide which texture it corresponds to, and they did so with the English teacher's help.

187	**Pau:**	let's see↓ I have a question Marta [the English teacher]↓ if it's the past continuous it means it is the background↑
188	**Sara:**	past continuous is the background
189	**Marta:**	why↑
190	**Sara:**	the background↓
191	**Marta:**	what happened with the present continuous, it's also↑ used for:
192	**Eva:**	=to express events that happened↓=
193	**Sara:**	=XXX=
194	**Marta:**	ok↓
195	**Sara:**	why↑ why↑
196	**Pau:**	ah ok↓ to describe↓
197	**Sara:**	to describe:
198	**Marta:**	and what are we doing here↑
199	**Pau:**	we're describing↓
200	**Marta:**	one thing:
201	**Sara:**	that he was sitting↓
202	**Eva:**	oh-
203	**Sara:**	that- that was happening
204	**Marta:**	exactly↓
205	**Eva:**	ah::
206	**Sara:**	what- what do you think- when you think about it you think that he is still doing it↓

In 187, Pau asks a question in line with the hypothesis established by the group about the relationship between the textures and the verb forms, and in 191 the teacher asks for reasons that justify this affirmation. The answer to this question comes from Eva in line 192, but her answer is very vague. However, the teacher accepts it as being correct in line 194. How is this approval possible, if the answer is not clear to us? It is probably because the dialogue produced in a certain context allows one to accept students' intuition at a given moment, even though it may not be precise. It may be perceived as a tentative approximation to a valid answer.

In fact, in line 196, after Sara has shown (195) that she does not understand Eva, Pau gives a clarifying paraphrase of the possible meaning of what Eva said in 192. In line 198 when the teacher asks for affirmation of Pau's comment in line 196, Pau responds (199) as does Sara (201 and 203). This last comment (203) returns to Eva's initial assertion in 192. In this way, the three group members relate the characteristics of the background (basically the description of the context where the events occur), and in coherence with this content the prototype temporality is that of processes in progress.

From the point of view of discourse about language (and in this particular passage, discourse about discourse) we can see, on the one hand, that if you provide students with tools, as we did in this project, they are able to carry out a vehicular reflexive activity using a type of discourse that allows them to discuss how to solve the problems that are posed. On the other hand, however, we can also see that the limitations of this discourse, which is conceptually confusing, hinders mutual understanding and makes finding a solution to the problems they are faced with difficult.

To conclude with this group, the following is a passage from their conversation when they were drawing conclusions about the relationship between textures and the verb tenses that appeared in them, in which the English teacher also participated. Despite evidence to the contrary, the students still believe that, as in Catalan, English also regularly uses specific verb forms for each of the textures. Following this criteria, in line 435, Eva assumes that the verbs in the background are all past continuous, Sara tells her this is not right in line 436, and Pau confirms this in line 437.

435   **Eva:**   everything is past in the background:
436   **Sara:**   no, because 'had' isn't past continuous↓ it's past simple:
             but what happens is that as it's:
437   **Pau:**   here this 'had' is not past simple↓

Once again, in the next passage, they come up against something that contradicts their beliefs and is difficult for them to accept (444). In line 445 Pau links this past simple to the past continuous. We do not know if he states this based on the affirmation that given that this form appears in the background then it must have the same textual function as the past continuous (the verb form they believe is used in the background), or based on the idea that the temporal value of this past simple may in some cases be similar to the imperfect (the tense they compare with the past continuous in their initial hypothesis). In line 447, the teacher suggests the presence of other possible verb forms in the background. She does this however without intending to provide clues that would help the students to discover their initial mistake. She does not help them, maybe because she does not want to: because she thinks that she should not interfere in the students' reasoning and that she will intervene in the sharing session later with the entire class; or maybe because she can not: because when they formulated their inaccurate hypothesis she was not with them and is therefore unaware of it.

443	**Teacher:**	I know that it's the past simple↓
444	**Sara:**	so we put past simple and nothing else↑
445	**Pau:**	but it's like the past continuous because:
446	**Sara:**	because here it says↓ past simple:
447	**Teacher:**	ok, but when you describe something you do not say what you were doing the whole time↓
448	**Pau:**	then what do we put↑

The teacher subsequently adds to the students' confusion in the next passage when, in line 449, she asks them to translate 'Once upon a time there was a king who had two servants', because she implicitly reinforces an equivalence between the past simple and the imperfect, which creates even more confusion, as Sara shows in line 453. Finally, in 460 and 461 the teacher explains, and the students finally understand that their hypothesis is inaccurate and that in the background we can find verbs in the past simple and in the past continuous. In 468 the teacher promises to give them the key to understanding this puzzle.

449	**Teacher:**	what do you say apart from this↑ how would you translate this↑
450	**Sara:**	I made
451	**Pau:**	ah- *tenia: tenia*↓
452	**Teacher:**	exactly
453	**Sara:**	then do we put↑ had↑ in past continuous or past simple
454	**Teacher:**	just put what it is↓ that it's *had*↑
455	**Pau:**	=past simple=

....

| 460 | **Teacher:** | but the fact that- the fact that it's past simple doesn't mean that it doesn't have to be in this background |
| 461 | **Pau:** | but 'was' can be in both↑ |

....

| 468 | **Teacher:** | what happens is that after: when you have to compare you will realise something↓ you will see at a later stage why you had these difficulties now↓ |

In this incident the distance between the students' and the teacher's discourse is evident. Each is rooted in their own assumptions and, because of this, their development makes them think more in two parallel monologues rather than in one dialogue. The students' efforts to construct an explanation to a problem, in order to learn, do not connect with the teacher's effort to provide them with reference points, in order to teach.

Conclusions

The analyses made of the interactions that were under study have led us to establish four conclusions.

The first point we believe interesting to highlight is the potential of project work as constructions in which the teacher invites the students to follow an itinerary with two objectives: learning the curricular content and solving specific problems. In our case, we believe it is important to highlight two aspects of this possibility: (a) that the same itinerary can be followed in many different ways, as we have seen with the members of group 1 and group 3, depending on a wide range of variables, which correspond with the belief in the diversity of paths along which problems can be solved and knowledge built; and (b) that within this itinerary spaces are created that promote interaction among students and between students and teachers in order to meet project goals; from this interaction a reflective activity emerges, in our case a reflection on languages, which from our point of view is a decisive factor in constructing grammar concepts.

A second point that we consider important, and proven once again, is the fact that learners of different languages tend to simultaneously apply the knowledge of language use (linguistic knowledge) and linguistic system (metalinguistic knowledge) that they have developed with regard to the language(s) they know better or have learnt previously, to a language they know to a lesser degree or have learnt subsequently. However, what seems more relevant here is how naturally the students from our project resorted to comparisons between the languages and formed hypotheses about their possible similarities to explain and understand certain linguistic and metalinguistic phenomena.

Also relevant is a third matter, which presents itself in an apparently contradictory manner: on the one hand, the students' ability to produce discourse about the metalinguistic and linguistic problems they face if we provide some basic concepts and terminology for them to refer to and, on the other hand, the enormous difficulty posed by reflection on language uses with the aim of explaining and understanding certain phenomena. This difficulty arises from: (a) the intrinsic complexity of linguistic phenomena; (b) the intrinsic difficulty of heuristic processes; and (c) the students' cognitive limitations in the training process. This means that the value of their reflective processes is, in our case, more of a true understanding of the grammar concepts and categories established according to educational criteria, than a procedure for reaching their own conclusions.

And finally we believe that the difficulty is significant in reconciling the teachers' activity, teaching, with the students' activity, learning, which we have observed in some of the interactions between the teacher and the students. The transition from the traditional way of teaching, where the teacher gives a lesson about the contents and later the students do exercises, to teaching through projects, in which, as in our case, the teacher works alongside the students, does not in and of itself provide the fit between teaching and learning in the Vygotskian zone of proximal development. To unite these two endeavours, it is essential in project work that, beyond the shared space of the set of activities that make up a given project, teachers be able to develop a sharp eye attuned to the problem-solving processes and the construction of knowledge in which the students are engaged.

Note

(1) 'La actividad metalingüística en situaciones plurilingües' (SEJ2006-10417) Ministerio de Educación y Ciencia

References

Bardovi-Harlig, K. (2000) *Tense and Aspect in Second Language Acquisition: Form, Meaning, and Use*. Oxford: Blackwell.

Bates, E. (2003) *On the Nature and Nurture of Language*. 4 November 2011 http://crl.ucsd.edu/bates/papers/pdf/bates-inpress.pdf

Camps, A. (2003) Proyectos de lengua entre la teoría y la práctica. In A. Camps (comp.) *Secuencias didácticas para aprender a escribir* (pp. 33–46). Barcelona: Graó.

Camps, A. (2006) Secuencias didácticas para aprender gramática (SDG). In A. Camps and F. Zayas (coords.) *Secuencias didácticas para aprender gramática* (pp. 31–38). Barcelona: Graó.

Comajoan, L. (2005) The acquisition of perfective and imperfective morphology and the marking of discourse grounding in Catalan. In D. Ayoun and M.R. Salaberry (eds) *Tense and Aspect in Romance Languages* (pp. 34–77). Amsterdam: John Benjamin.

Dabène, L. (1992) Le développement de la conscience métalinguistique: Un objectif commun pour l'enseignement de la langue maternelle et des langues étrangères. *Repères* 6, 13–21.

De Pietro, J.F. (2003) La diversité au fondement des activités réflexives. *Repères* 28, 161–186.

Dewey, J. (1910, 1933) *How We Think*. Stilwell, KS: Digireads.com Publishing, 2007.

Fisher, C. (2004) La place des représentations des apprenants en didactique de la grammaire. In C. VARGAS *Langue et études de la langue. Approches linguistiques et didactiques* (pp. 383–393). Aix-en-Provence: Publications de l'Université de Provence.

Hawkins, E.W. (1974) Modern languages in the curriculum. In G. Perren (ed.) *The Space Between: English and Foreign Languages at School*. London: CILT.

Halté, J.F. (1982) Travailler en projet. *Pratiques* 32, 38–77.

James, C. (1996) A cross-linguistic approach to language awareness. *Language Awareness* 5 (3–4), 138–148.

Jolibert, J. (1988) *Former enfants producteurs de textes*. Paris: Hachette.

Kilpatrick, W.H. (1918) *The Project Method: The Use of the Purposeful Act in the Educative Process*. New York: Teachers College, Columbia University, 1929.

Klein, W. and von Stutterheim, C. (1987) Quaestio und referentielle Bewegung in Erzälungen. *Linguistische Berichte* 109, 163–183.

Kupferberg, I. (1999) The cognitive turn of contrastive analysis. *Language Awareness* 8 (3–4), 210–222.

Labov, W. and Waletzky, J. (1967) Narrative analysis: Oral version of personal experience. In J. Helm (ed.) *Essays on the Verbal and Visual Acts* (pp. 112–144). Seattle, WA: University of Washington Press.

Mercer, N. (2004) Sociocultural discourse analysis. *Journal of Applied Linguistics* 1 (2), 137–168.

Myhill, D. (2000) Misconceptions and difficulties in the acquisition of metalinguistic knowledge. *Language and Education* 14 (3), 151–163.

Roulet, E. (1980) *Langue maternelle et langues secondes: vers une pédagogie integrée*. Paris: Crédif/Hatier.

Sharwood Smith, M. (1993) Input enhancement in instructed SLA. *Studies in Second Language Acquisition* 15 (2), 165–179.

Starren, M. (2003) How temporal coherence pushes the development of grammatical aspect in French L2. *Marges linguistiques* 5, 56–76.

Trévise, A. (1994) Représentations métalinguistiques des apprenants, des enseignants et des linguistes: Un défi pour la didactique. *Bulletin Suisse de Linguistique Apliquée* 459, 171–190.

Trévise, A. (1996) Contrastive metalinguistic representations: The case of 'very French' learners of English. *Language Awareness* 5 (3–4), 188–195. *Approaches to Second Language Research* (pp. 135–156). Norwood, NJ: Ablex.

VanPatten, B. and Cadierno, T. (1993) Explicit instruction and input processing. *Studies in Second Language Acquisition* 15 (2), 225–243.

VanPatten, B. (2002) Processing instruction: An update. *Language Learning* 52 (4), 755–803.

Appendix 7.1

THE KING, THE FLEA AND THE LOUSE

Once upon a time there was a king who had two servants who took care of him. One day the king was sitting on his royal seat, a lot of barons and knights were present. One of the servants who was next to him could see a flea on the white robe that the king was wearing.

The servant asked the king: 'Sir, let me come closer to take the flea that is on your robe'. The king gave him permission and the servant picked the flea up.

The king wanted to see the flea. He showed it to his knights and said: 'It is amazing to see a little animal dare to approach the king'.

The king gave the servant one hundred golden coins.

The other servant was jealous of his partner. The next day he put a louse on the robe of the king and he spoke to him in the same way as the other servant did.

The servant gave the louse to the king and the king got very angry and said: 'You deserve to be killed because you are incapable of taking care of the king's dresses'. He punished the servant to receive one hundred smacks.

EL REI, LA PUÇA I EL POLL

Un rei tenia dos servents que cuidaven de la seva persona. Un dia seia al seu setial i davant seu tenia molts barons i cavallers. L'un d'aquells criats que era al seu costat va veure una puça en una vestidura de vellut blanc que el rei vestia.

Aquell servent va demanar al rei: 'Majestat deixeu-me acostar per prendre la puça que hi ha al vostre mantell.' El rei li va donar llicència i el servent va prendre la puça.

El rei va voler veure la puça. La va mostrar als seus cavallers i va dir: 'És molt gran meravella com una bèstia tan petita gosa acostar-se a un ésser tan gran com un rei'.

El rei va fer donar al servent cent monedes d'or.

L'altre servent tenia enveja del seu company, i l'endemà va posar un gran poll en el mantell del rei i va dir-li paraules semblants a les que el seu company havia dit.

El servent va donar el poll al rei, però aquest cop el rei es va enfadar molt i va dir-li: 'Ets digne de mort perquè ho has guardat de polls els meus vestits'. Dit això va fer donar cent assots a aquell servent

Transcription code

Word cut-off	-
Ascending tone sequence	↑
Descending tone sequence	↓
Overlapping speech	=text=
Incomprehensible text	XXX
Lengthened sound/syllable	:

8 Affording Students Opportunities for the Integrated Learning of Content and Language: A Contrastive Study on Classroom Interactional Strategies Deployed by Two CLIL Teachers

Cristina Escobar Urmeneta
and Natalia Evnitskaya[1]

This paper is concerned with content and language integrated learning (CLIL) in English as a foreign language in secondary education in Catalonia. Through the use of tools from conversation analysis and sociocultural discourse analysis, the study contrasts the way two different CLIL teachers organise and manage, respectively, an academic conversation. Its goal is to empirically identify components of classroom interactional competence (Walsh, 2006), present in the particular conditions of CLIL settings, by showing how the teachers' instructional choices in the form of conversational adjustments afford students more or fewer opportunities for the integrated learning of language and content. The study concludes that the different sets of conversational strategies deployed by each teacher determine the quality of each conversation and its outcomes in terms of affordances for the integrated learning of content and language.

Introduction

Content and language integrated learning (CLIL) has become a successful umbrella term that 'covers a wide range of educational practices and settings whose common denominator is that a non-L1 is used in classes other than those labelled as "language classes"' (Dalton-Puffer, 2007: 2). The acronym is used for programmes that go from kindergarten to tertiary education; and for programmes in a second language available in everyday interactions in the context where the learner lives (i.e. learning through English in Britain), or in a foreign language of international use (i.e. learning through English in Spain). Needless to say that CLIL programmes vary enormously depending on the specific settings and programme goals (Marsh *et al.*, 2001).

This chapter is concerned with CLIL in English as a foreign language in secondary education in Catalonia. It builds on Escobar Urmeneta and Evnitskaya's (2011) preliminary study and contrasts the way two different CLIL teachers organise and manage, respectively, an academic conversation. Its goal is to empirically identify components of classroom interactional competence (Walsh, 2006), present in the particular conditions of CLIL settings, by showing how the teachers' instructional choices in the form of conversational adjustments afford students more or fewer opportunities for the integrated learning of language and content.

The study is part of a larger research project that seeks to gain understanding of how the integrated acquisition of scientific and communicative competences in a foreign language is instantiated in CLIL classrooms, and its ultimate goal is to shed light on how the interactional spaces created by CLIL teachers allow students (or not) to become full participants in the co-construction of scientific knowledge in inclusive environments.

Catalonia, a complex sociolinguistic setting

Catalonia is a bilingual region from a legal and a sociological point of view, where both Catalan and Spanish are co-official languages. The Act on Linguistic Normalization (Generalitat de Catalunya, 1983), and its derivate Decree 75/1992, generalised the use of Catalan, the minority language, as the medium of instruction for content subjects in infant and compulsory education, where it had been banned for 40 years (Escobar Urmeneta & Unamuno, 2008). Catalan immersion programmes have received the support of independent national and European evaluations (Arnau, 1985, 2004; Arnau & Vila, this volume; Council of Europe, 2005; Organisation for Economic Cooperation and Development (OECD), 2001, 2010; for example) and a majority acceptance from the Catalan society.

In this complex sociolinguistic situation, yet one third language, English, is slowly but steadily gaining grounds as a language of instruction in Catalan schools, ratifying once more the Catalan aspiration of combining *'linguistic policies aiming at (apparently) opposing targets (...) promoting a vernacular language and adopting global policies which favour the free circulation of workers and goods across Europe'* (Escobar Urmeneta & Unamuno, 2008: 229). Contrary to Catalan, English is a truly foreign language for schoolchildren in Catalonia as, on general bases, it is only available to learners in institutionalised settings for an average of three English as a Foreign Language (EFL) lessons per week since the age of six[2] (Escobar Urmeneta & Nussbaum, 2010), which is considered one of the causes of the low results obtained by Catalan students in international EFL tests (see Arnau & Vila, this volume).

CLIL: Threats versus opportunities

In the last decade the CLIL approach has gained the interest of institutions and researchers in Europe as a privilege strategy to foreign language learning (see, for example, Cenoz, 2009; Cenoz & Genesee, 1998; Escobar Urmeneta, 2009, 2011; Escobar Urmeneta & Nussbaum, 2008; Escobar Urmeneta & Sánchez Sola, 2009; Evnitskaya & Aceros, 2008; Evnitskaya & Morton, 2011; Lasagabaster & Ruiz de Zarobe, 2010; Lorenzo *et al.*, 2011; Moore, submitted; Muñoz, 2007; Pérez-Vidal & Juan-Garau, 2011, for studies centred in the context of Spain: Coyle *et al.*, 2010; Dalton-Puffer, 2007; Dalton-Puffer *et al.*, 2010; Dalton-Puffer & Smit, 2007; Llinares i, in press; Nikula, 2005; Ruiz de Zarobe & Jiménez Catalán, 2009, for studies in other European countries).

The enthusiasm shown by administrators, teachers, families and researchers is overshadowed by the suspicion that some external factors may undermine the success of such programmes. Some of the most commonly alleged are:

- The risk of lowering in the 'academic standards' in the content subject owing to the students' low command of the foreign language (Escobar Urmeneta, 2011).
- The inadequate preparation of teachers to teach CLIL programmes usually attributed to linguistic deficits.[3]
- The specific difficulties that a number of students may experience under the assumption that only those students who meet certain conditions, such as (above the average) intellectual capacities, (solid) previous academic background or (intermediate or higher levels of) communicative competence in the foreign language, are able to successfully meet the communicative and cognitive demands imposed by a foreign language curriculum.
- The threat of interferences caused by the simultaneous acquisition of English and Catalan, or English and Spanish, respectively, by students from non-Catalan and/or non-Spanish speaking families.

The third and fourth asserts are, in our opinion, particularly perilous. Not only because available research does not support them, but also because admitting them would offer a rationale to justify that those students raised in less stimulating milieus, and/or with certain sociolinguistic backgrounds, and/or with fewer opportunities for foreign language practice outside school, would be denied of access to multilingual education, triggering in this fashion the undesired 'Matthew' effect[4].In other words, the risk is that the enduring tension between selective and comprehensive approaches to education, always present in the Spanish context, may find in CLIL a strong ally to support selection as the most adequate strategy to educational success (Escobar Urmeneta, 2011).

Democratising CLIL

The Spanish curriculum[5] is partly aware of the potential problem outlined above and has tried to prevent some of its effects by proscribing any kind of segregation in CLIL programmes owing to linguistic reasons. However it would be naive to believe that legal prohibitions suffice when educational practices are at stakes. It is clear that a definition of democratic CLIL is needed as a tool that may help identify those teaching practices that will ensure equal opportunities of access to students with different linguistic, academic or social backgrounds.

In this fashion we advocate that democratic:

Content and Language Integrated Learning or CLIL embraces those educational practices in which content subjects – excluding those labelled as 'language subjects' – are taught and learned through a language of instruction, second or foreign, in which a learner has a basic or advanced developing communicative competence, and which explicitly:

1. Promote the preservation and development of the learner's first language(s) and the consideration and misse en valeur of cultural forms attached to that (those) language(s);
2. Promote a truly integrated approach, with a dual focus of pedagogical attention, i.e. language and content;
3. Provide learners with all the assistance needed to comprehend, produce and negotiate academic messages in the target language adopted as the medium of instruction. (Escobar Urmeneta, 2011: 203–204)

The first requirement rejects subtractive approaches to plurilingualism and language substitution policies. In the Catalan context, this implies the coordinated planning of school language policies in order to guarantee adequate exit levels in at least the two co-official languages, and the third language of instruction: English in the vast majority of cases.[6] The second one calls attention to the often forgotten dual focus of pedagogical attention in compulsory education: unlike other contexts, such as tertiary studies, the adequate treatment of content here is as important as the adequate treatment of language. The third requirement departs from the undeniable fact that CLIL students face *extra-ordinary* challenges, which, in turn, call for specific interactional competences from teachers in order to assist learners in overcoming those challenges. The constructs of classroom interactional competence (CIC) and competence as situated practice become particularly useful to characterise quality interaction in this type of environments and will be presented in section *'Situated classroom interactional competence in CLIL settings'*.

Theoretical Framework

Sociocultural theory, zone of proximal development and CLIL

This study is framed within the paradigm of current sociocultural theory, which derives from the work of Vygotsky (1978, 1986). *'Sociocultural approaches emphasise the interdependence of social and individual processes in the co-construction of knowledge, overcoming the Cartesian dichotomy between the external and the internal'* (John-Steiner & Holbrook, 1996: 191). Under this paradigm, knowledge is not located in the individual mind, nor owned privately by each person in isolation. On the contrary, all learning is viewed as a social process embedded in social interaction between learners and more knowledgeable others.

Although the work of Vygotsky was devoted to analyse first language acquisition processes in informal settings, his statement that the psychological behaviour of human beings is mediated or facilitated by *signs, symbols, and languages* at individual and collective levels of experience (De Valenzuela *et al.*, 2000) has borne crucial implications for education in general, and for second language education in particular (Lantolf, 2000). Hence, the *'sociocultural perspective highlights the possibility that educational success and failure may be explained by the quality of educational dialogue, rather than simply in terms of the capability of individual students or the skill of their teachers'* (Mercer, 2000: 139).

Moving sociocultural postulates one step forward so as to apply them to CLIL settings, we suggest that in the CLIL classroom it is the job of the CLIL teacher to interpret and react to the learners' emerging utterances and project them into more advanced stages of development, whereas providing assistance to sustain the learners' actions throughout the conversation in an interactional space created and co-built *ad hoc* in each lesson. Only after a number of experiences of supported participation in interactional experiences in the 'Zone of Proximal Development' or ZPD (Vygotsky, 1978), will the CLIL student be able to carry out those actions on their own, independently from the CLIL instructor.

Situated CIC in CLIL settings

The construct of CIC (Walsh, 2006), initially developed to interpret foreign language classrooms, becomes particularly useful in CLIL settings as it tries to capture the interplay of the various factors that result in high quality interaction that is conductive to learning. According to Walsh:

> CIC is concerned to account for learning-oriented interaction by considering the interplay between complex phenomena that include roles of teachers and learners, their expectations and goals; the relationship between language use and teaching methodology; and the interplay between teacher and learner language. Although CIC is not the sole domain of teachers, it is still very much determined by them. (Walsh, 2006: 130)

CIC encompasses those characteristics of classroom interaction that result in high quality interaction and, thus, make the teaching–learning process more efficient. Understanding the nature of those conversational adjustments is paramount, as it might become the bases for teacher education programmes specifically addressed at CLIL teachers.

The following adaptation of Walsh's (2006) categorisation includes some of the teaching strategies so far identified by research.

- The use of *learner-convergent language*, which is both appropriate to teaching goals and adjusted in relation to the co-construction of meaning and the unfolding agenda of a lesson.
- The *facilitation of interactional space* so that learners are given the opportunity to contribute to the class conversation and to receive feedback on their contributions. Some teaching strategies that may contribute to afford students interactional space are:
  - effective eliciting strategies in the form of good questions;
  - refining, adjusting and clarifying those questions for learners;
  - allowing for increased wait-time;
  - promoting extended learner turns, i.e. asking 'why' questions;
  - creating opportunities for students to ask their own questions;
  - providing more freedom to self-select or remain silent.
- The *'shaping' of learner contributions* by seeking clarification, modelling, paraphrasing, reiterating or repairing the learners' productions. Through shaping the discourse, the teacher helps learners to say what they mean by using the most appropriate language to do so.

Mercer's (1995) classification of teaching strategies (Table 8.1), elaborated as a result of research in the domain of teaching different types of subjects in L1 settings, bears a great resemblance with that of Walsh's. The most outstanding difference among them is the importance attributed by Walsh to learner-convergent language.

The teaching strategies identified by both researchers represent different elements of *scaffolding* (Wood *et al.*, 1976), which, if successful, can help

Table 8.1 Some techniques that teachers use (Mercer, 1995: 34)

- To elicit knowledge from learners:
  - Direct elicitations
  - Cued elicitations
- To respond to what learners say:
  - Confirmations
  - Rejections
  - Repetitions
  - Elaborations
  - Reformulations
- To describe significant aspects of shared experiences:
  - 'We' statements
  - Literal recaps
  - Reconstructive recaps

learners to acquire the target language and the content. In this sense, CLIL settings have proved to be particularly rich in the use of scaffolding procedures and modelling (Escobar Urmeneta & Evnitskaya, in press) as well as in the use of multimodal resources and material objects to mediate the teaching–learning process (Evnitskaya, 2012; Evnitskaya & Morton, 2011), or a diversity of elicitation techniques (Simon Auerbach, in press).

However, it would be erroneous to describe CIC as an inventory of potentialities possessed by individual teachers, who deploy a catalogue of teaching strategies independently from macro-, meso- or micro-contexts. On the contrary – borrowing Mondada and Perakek Doehler's (2004) definition of communicative competence as situated practice – we envisage CIC *'as a plurality of capacities embedded and recognized in the context of particular activities'* (2004: 503).

To sum up, if CLIL is to become a democratic option made available to students within a wide range of linguistic, academic or social backgrounds, teachers need to be able to enact CIC in a context-sensitive way, in environments in which learners are expected to acquire academic concepts and scholastic skills through the use of a system of signs and symbols – the foreign language – in which they are also apprentices.

Method

Data and participants

The natural occurring data analysed here come from the CLIL-SI university-schools partnership project (Tsui *et al.*, 2009) corpus. More specifically, the study examines two extracts from two teacher-led lessons (one from each lesson) consisting in the checking of true/false exercises designed to review previously covered content. Lesson A revises basic concepts in the domain of biology and lesson B is devoted to renewable energies. The lessons were selected for analysis because of the apparent disparities observed in the way conversations were unfolded in each lesson, in spite of the noteworthy number of common traits that both lessons shared, which include: geographical context (Metropolitan Barcelona); sociolinguistic context (bilingual Catalan–Castilian students; English = L3); sociocultural context (middle class), compulsory subject (science); type of interaction (teacher-fronted lessons); type of activity (public correction of true/false revision exercise).

Two excerpts were selected for a detailed analysis basing on their representativeness of the type of conversation carried out throughout the activity. Other relevant contextual information about the lessons, the participants and the excerpts is provided in Table 8.2 to help the reader contextualise the conversations.

Although some of the circumstances outlined above may have surely influenced the quality of the interaction, the study is not concerned with establishing cause–result relationships among factors and outcomes, and does not provide enough data to do so.

It is essential to point out that every teacher had her own teaching and personal developmental goals when planning, implementing and assessing the lessons under analysis. Those goals were met to a large extent in both cases and, under this perspective, it can be concluded that both lessons were successful. In short, the goal of the paper is not to judge how well the teachers teach (we will not provide enough data to reach this type of conclusion),

Table 8.2 Relevant contextual information on both lessons

	Lesson A	*Lesson B*
Lesson on	Cells	Materials
Teacher's experience	Experienced	Novice
Teacher's level of English	B2 CEFR	C2 CEFR
Number of students	15	30
Age	13	17
Class	First lower secondary education (compulsory)	First higher secondary education (post-compulsory)
Students' average level of English	A2.1 CEFR	A2.2 CEFR
Sitting arrangement	Circle. The teacher forms part of it.	Rows and columns. The teacher stands at the front.
Excerpt content	Amoebas	Steel

but to make a small contribution to the understanding of the intricacies of teacher-led academic conversations in CLIL classrooms and the enacting of CIC in those settings.

Research questions

The interpretive analysis seeks to:

- Determine the way each teacher structures the conversation and makes it progress.
- Explore the conversational strategies and adjustments deployed by each teacher in order to afford students interactional space, and the use students make of these affordances.
- Identify the conversational moves used by each teacher in order to shape the learners' contributions and the outcomes of those moves in terms of the creation or consolidation of the learners' linguistic–discursive repertoire in the target language.
- Identify indicators of gains in the understanding of key aspects of the content addressed in the activity.

Methodological framework

The postulates enunciated by Vygotsky have given rise to a number of methodological frameworks that share fundamental tenets, but differ in focus and in the specificity of their respective analytical tools and methods. This interpretive study draws from two of these traditions: on the one hand, that of sociocultural discourse analysis or SDA (Mercer, 2004), a branch of discursive psychology (Edwards & Potter, 1992), used to study how people use language as a tool for thinking collectively, mainly in L1 settings. On the other hand, conversation analysis or CA (Markee, 2000; Seedhouse, 2004) and multimodal analysis (Pekarek Doehler, 2010; Moore & Nussbaum, 2011), extensively used in the micro-analysis of second-language learning sequences, mainly with the purposes of uncovering the fine-grained mechanisms of L2 talk, and documenting language acquisition processes. Whereas SDA allows *'to relate the content, quality and temporal nature of dialogue during joint activities to outcomes such as the success or failure in the task, or to specific learning gains'* (Mercer, 2004: 139), CA offers a privileged set of tools for the detailed analysis of sequential organisation, turn-taking or repair that may reveal how participants use language as a tool to jointly accomplish social actions.

Data treatment

Video recordings of the two excerpts were transcribed using *Transana* software (Woods & Fassnacht, 2007). Detailed transcripts of talk and other semiotic resources were made employing conversation analysis conventions proposed by Gail Jefferson (Atkinson & Heritage, 1984), which are provided in Appendix 8.1. Non-verbal actions were described using line-to-line narratives, while additional contextual information relevant for the analysis is provided with video screenshots.

Once the transcripts were obtained, SDA and a micro-analysis of multimodal data (Moore & Nussbaum, 2011; Pekarek Doehler, 2010) were used to explore multimodal conversational resources used by each teacher, to identify recurrent conversational patterns and to relate them to the differences in results observed in each lesson.

Analysis

Despite all these resemblances outlined above, the preliminary analysis of conversational data showed important differences in the way teachers led the conversation, responded to students and extended their demands, and, as a result, both conversational styles seemed to create two very different interactional spaces, which afforded students different types of opportunities for learning.

Lesson A: 'amoebas'

After a brief introduction to the activity (lesson A on *cells*), the teacher starts a public correction of the homework revision exercise (see a screenshot in Figure 8.1) by passing to Jaume the interactional floor and the responsibility to read aloud the first statement (excerpt 1, line 9).[7]

Figure 8.1 Public correction of a true/false exercise in lesson A (lines 26–27)

Excerpt 1

9	TEA:	<u>Jaume</u> (.) the first one‹
10	JAU:	((reads)) amoebas have a nucleus and a cytoplasm. e:::
11	**TEA:**	is it true or false‹
12	**RIC:**	true
13	**JAU:**	true
14	**ARN:**	<u>no</u> false
15	**QUI:**	no <u>false</u> <u>false</u>
16	**JOA:**	true
17	**JAU:**	a:: true
18	**RIC:**	true
19	**TEA:**	<u>why</u>‹ is true or why is false‹
20		you have to <u>tell</u> me why (it)-
21	**SS:**	it's [true
22	**JOA:**	[it's true
23	**MIQ:**	it's true
24	**TEA:**	why it's true‹ ((turns to RIC and JAU))
25	**JOA:**	becau::se
26	**JAU:**	I found i::t ((looks at TEA))
27		((raises shoulders and hands, slightly shakes head))
28	**JOA:**	they are::
29	**RIC:**	yes
30	**TEA:**	((laughs, shakes head)) no no
31	**JOA:**	they are::
32	**TEA:**	this is not a reason ((looks at JAU))
33	**JOA:**	<eukaryotic cells>
34	**TEA:**	very good ((nods))
35		amoebas are:: or have got eukaryotic cells.
36		so=
37	**ARN:**	it's-
38	**TEA:**	=they have got a nucleus and a cytoplasm.
39		it's true
40	**QUI:**	***molt bé***

Translation: QUI: very good

Jaume reads the statement but doubts in providing an answer (line 10). The teacher explicitly asks for the response (line 11) and it is another student, Ricard, who offers his opinion (line 12, 'true'). His contribution is followed by a series of divergent replies among Jaume, Arnau and Quim (lines 13–15), which are discursively marked by an emphasis on the words 'no' (line 14) and 'false' (line 15). The dispute ends with the mutual acceptance that the statement is true (lines 16–18).

During this brief but intense discussion of seven turns, the teacher has stayed out of the discussion and intervenes again only when it seems that the consensus among the students has been implicitly established. It is noteworthy that her intervention in lines 19–20 is not evaluative but, rather, aims at eliciting a more elaborated answer from the students, an answer that would include not only the verdict of whether the statement is true or not, but also a justification for such a verdict. Moreover, at this point she refrains from offering any clues about whether the provided answer is correct or not. On the contrary, she reopens the spectrum of possibilities by suggesting the rejected answer as a feasible one: 'why is true or why is false?' (line 19).

The difficulty experienced by the students to meet this new demand is reflected in their inconclusive statements in lines 21–23. Yet, the teacher seems not to be willing to exempt them from the challenge (both in relation to the scientific content under discussion and at the linguistic–discursive level) because she proposes it again while looking at Ricard and Jaume (line 24). From line 25 to 34 we can observe a complex interactive sequence in which students use an extremely limited range of resources (marked by their single word answers, hesitations and monosyllables) that they have at their disposal to meet the teacher's challenge. In this sequence, two of them, namely Jaume and Joan, suggest their arguments.

Hence, Jaume offers an explanation ('I found it', line 26), which is pragmatic and valid from his perspective of 'student' (additionally supported by his shoulders and hands raised and slight head shaking, line 27, see Figure 8.1) and grammatically correct (simple past, irregular verb, subject–verb–object). Jaume's answer is ratified by Ricard (line 29), but not by the teacher. The latter evaluates it negatively through a set of multimodal resources: a double negation ('no, no') is reinforced by a synchronous head shaking (line 30). At the same time, the teacher broadly smiles thus using a negative politeness strategy (Kasper, 2009) in order to smooth things over and avoid a potential face-threatening act. The sequence concludes with the teacher's justification of the unacceptability – from the content/academic point of view – of the argument provided by Jaume: 'this is not a reason' (line 32).

In parallel, another student, Joan, makes an effort to construct his own argument despite the difficulties he is faced with, reflected in sound stretching, repetitions and clearly slower speech rhythm along the lines 25, 28, 31 and 33. Apparently, the teacher pays no attention to him as at this moment she is oriented toward Jaume (both verbally and through her gaze, line 32). Nevertheless, Joan manages to construct a complete sentence in the target language: 'because they are eukaryotic cells'. The clause is correct from a linguistic point of view and bears a certain level of complexity (correct agreement between subject, copula and attribute, causal subordination; active use of relevant target vocabulary: 'eukaryotic cells').

Joan's statement also reveals his knowledge about the micro-organism in question (amoeba) and its elements, both facts being corroborated by the positive multimodal feedback from the teacher (verbal 'very good' and nodding, line 34). In the next line the teacher picks up Joan's contribution and reformulates it, thus confirming again its validity and utility for a more complex explanation that she constructs in line 35.

The linguistic and discursive adjustments introduced by the teacher in her more elaborated version of the student's answer include the replacement of the indefinite pronoun 'they' with the micro-organism's name and 'are' with 'have got'.

In line 36, Arnau tries to contribute to this process of joint construction and suggests the continuation of the unfinished utterance initiated by the teacher in line 35. Considering that what Arnau produces is the interactional pattern already used several times in the discussion ('it's'), we could interpret his intervention as an attempt to propose the verdict ('it's true') as the closing of the argument. However, the teacher ignores his attempt and moves the conversation forward by establishing a cause–effect link between Joan's contribution and the initial statement from the exercise ('so they have got a nucleus and a cytoplasm', lines 36 and 38). With the utterance in line 39 ('it's true') the teacher finally and explicitly acknowledges the students' previous interventions in which they claimed the veracity of the statement and closes the argumentative circle.

The result is an argument constructed by several voices: **'It's true because they are eukaryotic cells.** Amoebas are or have got eukaryotic cells. So they have got a nucleus and a cytoplasm' (lines 21–23, 25, 28, 31, 33, 35, 36 and 38, in bold the students' contribution). After this the sequence closes with the final (implicitly positive) evaluation of the teacher, 'it's true' (line 39), followed by a more explicit positive evaluation of one of the students (*'molt bé'*, line 40). It should be noted that though the teacher carries out most of the explanation, she is able to share the interactional floor with the students and obtain, as a result, their multiple and discursively rich interventions.

Lesson B: 'steel'

After a brief introduction into the topic of the lesson (*materials*), the teacher asked students to do a true/false exercise that reviewed previously covered content. The screenshot (Figure 8.2) and excerpt 2 below correspond to the public correction of one of the statements.

Excerpt 2

38	**TEA:**	((reads)) steel has become the most used (.) metal
39	**SS:**	tru[e
40	**SS:**	[false

41	**SS:**	[true false
42	**TEA:**	((nods))
43		[(0.7) ((TEA looks at students, smiles))
44	**SS:**	[true false false
45	**TEA:**	((turns to screen, coughs fakely)) what⸮
46		((points to column 'True' on screen)) what⸮
47	**SS:**	((keep repeating 'true' and 'false'))
48	**TEA:**	e:::: ((smiles, moves her body rhythmically))
49	**SS:**	((smile, keep repeating 'true' and 'false'))
50	**TEA:**	e::m
51	**SS:**	(it's true or false⸮)
52	**TEA:**	((smiles)) okey
53	**ORI:**	((to another student))
54		***por eso te preguntaba qué era*** (.) steel (.)

Translation: **ORI:** that's why I was asking you what was (.) steel (.)

| 55 | | ***no sé (.) creo que-*** |

Translation: **ORI:** I don't know (.) I think that-

56	**SS:**	xxxxxxxx
57	**TEA:**	((smiles, looks over class))
58	**SS:**	xxxxx false
59	**TEA:**	(1.9) ((looks at her notes))
60	**ORI:**	*és* <u>false</u>
61	**TEA:**	((looks at ORI))
62		((to students)) it's <u>TRUE</u>
63		((nods))
64	**SS:**	UU::: ((shouts of happiness))
65	**TEA:**	it's true, ok⸮
66		((looks at handout)) it's <u>true</u>
67		(3.8) ((students speak simultaneously))
68	**TEA:**	((continues the activity reading the next item))

Excerpt 2 starts with the teacher reading aloud the statement: 'steel has become the most used metal' (line 38). This is followed by the numerous contributions of the students (lines 39–41) whose authorship is difficult to recognise since many of them are produced almost simultaneously. There is no consensus among the students on whether the statement is true or false and, although the teacher nods confirming the correct answer (line 42), it is still unclear which one is this answer. Therefore, for the next 0.7 second the students continue trying to guess it like in a guessing game (line 44) while the teacher looks at them smiling (line 43).

It seems that finally the teacher decides to give a more explicit clue about which answer is correct and which one is wrong. To do this, she uses a variety of multimodal resources: first to gain the students' attention, she slightly turns to the blackboard with the screen over it on which an empty activity

Figure 8.2 Public correction of a true-false exercise in lesson B (line 46)

sheet is projected (see Figure 8.2) and pretends to cough several times, after which she produces an overtly faked clarification request ('what¿') (line 45). With a minimal pause in between, she finally provides the clue to the students by pointing to the column 'True' on the screen and repeating the request (line 46). However, the teacher's attempt seems to have brought no results as the class continues repeating alternatively both options without reaching any agreement (line 47).

The teacher's actions in lines 48 and 50 suggest that she wants the class to finally state their verdict. However, the way she does it – by employing paralinguistic and non-linguistic resources, such as stretching the sounds, smiling and moving her body rhythmically – shows that she tries to keep a friendly and positive atmosphere that seems to have been established between her and the students. This is confirmed by the fact that the students also smile while they keep saying the two answers (line 49). Finally, some (unidentified) students ask again for a final verdict (line 51).

At this moment, one of the students, Oriol, addresses his peer in a private turn (line 53) in order to express his doubt about the term 'steel' (*'that's why I was asking you what was (.) steel (.) I don't know (.) I think that-'*, lines 54–55), the key term in the statement in question. Being clearly audible, it is however ignored by the teacher who continues her agenda. Meanwhile, in the *official* conversation, among the general noise created by the simultaneously speaking students (line 56), we can distinguish some of them saying that (probably) the statement is false (line 58). The teacher who, smiling, was looking around the class, takes some time to check her notes (line 59). At this moment, Oriol, who has not been attended by the teacher in his private turn, publicly states that the answer is 'false', highlighting it emphatically (line 60). This time his intervention is heard by the teacher (perhaps because he produced it aloud or because she was standing nearby when checking her notes), who reacts by looking at him (line 61). Then she addresses the whole class with the correct answer 'it's true' which she repeats three times (lines 62, 65 and 66) and accompanies with a set of multimodal resources: an emphasis on and an increased volume of the word 'true' and several nods in lines 62–63 and a comprehension check 'ok?' in line 65. This officially closes the sequence even though the students continue speaking for approximately four seconds until the same teacher reads aloud the following item, thus continuing the same teaching and conversational pattern.

Discussion

The analysis carried out in the previous section shows that both in lesson A and B the teachers' use of learner-convergent language in conducting the public correction of a true/false exercise made possible that all participants – teachers as well as students – used English exclusively or almost exclusively as the language of instruction.

In both classrooms the atmosphere was inviting and the teachers' proposals were well received by the students. The predominance of self-selection also contributed to the building up of a low-stress milieu in both settings, which made possible a large number of voluntary contributions on the part of different students. This was a particularly important outcome in the case of lesson B, as previous ethnographic data portrayed the group as a low responsive one. Additionally, both teachers showed a tight control of the pedagogic conversation and managed it quite successfully to enforce their respective instructional agendas through the use of Initiation-Response-Feedback (IRF) sequences (Sinclair & Coulthard, 1975), typical of pedagogic discourse in general (Mercer, 1995) and particularly ubiquitous in CLIL classrooms (Dalton-Puffer, 2007). However, the analysis also reveals that these agendas were interactively constructed in very different ways and, as a result, the degree of complexity in the interactional organisation achieved in both lessons differs to a great extent.

Hence, in lesson B students' participation was achieved thanks to the enthusiastic and friendly attitude of the teacher, observable in her smile (lines 43, 48, 52 and 57), her dynamism (rhythmic movements, line 48) and her complicity with the students (fake cough, line 45). Her contagious liveliness was evidenced in the way she elicited the students' answers using a range of multimodal resources. She also employed a wide variety of strategies to guide the students towards the correct answer, opting for those that simultaneously functioned as a reward for the mere fact that the students had made a contribution. The effects of this strategic approach are clear: the students felt comfortable enough to follow the lesson path set by the teacher and respond chorally and enthusiastically to her demands. Table 8.3 summarises the guiding strategies observed in lesson B:

Table 8.3 Guiding strategies in lesson B

When the students' contribution is correct:	*When the students' contribution is wrong:*
A nod (lines 42, 63).	A faked cough (line 45).
	An overtly faked clarification request (*'what?'*) (line 45) repeated almost immediately (line 46).
	A gesture pointing to the column 'True' on the screen (line 46).

On the other hand, we do not observe instances in which the students were required to clarify, develop or justify the declared veracity or falsehood of the statement under discussion, since the teacher exclusively oriented the students' attention towards the guessing of the answer. In the same vein, she opted for not elaborating on the answers provided.

The result was, on the one hand, a way of managing classroom conversation that was highly successful in capturing and maintaining the students' attention, which, additionally, produced a great sense of achievement among all the participants, the students and the teacher. On the other hand, the conversation afforded students few opportunities to develop their linguistic and discursive repertoire beyond the mere comprehension of the messages produced by the teacher. It also provided little interactional space for students to state their questions and doubts, to make more elaborated contributions or to receive more adjusted and appropriate feedback on them.

Additionally, the teacher overlooked the clarification request that emerged in Oriol's private turn (line 54), even though it was quite audible and closely related to the target content. This inattention may be interpreted as a result of a combination of factors, such as a certain degree of her unawareness of the difficulties experienced by the students; and/or difficulties to cope with all the simultaneous demands that doing teaching posed on her; and/or an attachment to her lesson plan that prioritised plan completion over any other instructional facets, all phenomena being commonly observed in the teaching practice of novice teachers (Escobar Urmeneta, in press).

Conversely, the conversation in lesson A evolved in very dissimilar ways. In relation to the facilitation of interactional space the following moves have been identified:

- To start with, the teacher offered the students the opportunity to read out the statements, an option which announces that students may later occupy a relevant role in the unfolding conversation.
- The students in turns took the floor in an orderly way with few overlappings or choral answers. The fact that this is achieved without using the

hand-raising procedure suggests that the class has developed so far a common culture on how to run academic discussions based on the contributions of self-designated individuals. The teacher's gaze and body orientation to individuals, as well as to the group, seemed to favour the efficiency of this procedure in this context.

- The teacher remained silent for seven turns (lines 12–19) thus allowing students to discuss independently until they reached a verdict. Only then did she demand a more elaborate answer in the form of a 'why' question.
- She refrained from providing hints toward the 'guessing' of the true/false answer. On the contrary, she reintroduced uncertainty as a strategy to push students to supply an acceptable justification of their verdict.
- As a result she obtained from one of the students a valid token of science knowledge that she used as a starting point to build up her explanation.

The teacher also shaped the learners' discourse in efficient ways:

- She rejected the information provided by Jaume (line 32), which might be true but was certainly unacceptable from the academic viewpoint, to insist on the type of argument needed at this point.
- By collecting Joan's contribution (line 35) and returning it to the rest of the class in a more accurate, elaborated and acceptable way – from the point of view of the subject matter – the teacher incorporated it into the collective argument that was being interactively co-constructed in the classroom. In such a way she was helping her students to express their ideas and opinions in a more appropriate L2 academic language (Mercer, 1995; Walsh, 2006).

In lesson A, the limited set of linguistic resources that the students exhibited when they had to construct the required justification was not considered an obstacle by the teacher. She managed to help the students succeed, enacting a complex scaffolding process that was the result of the multifaceted articulation of all the moves identified within the reach of the students' ZPD. And, in doing so, she managed to bring to fruition her agenda for the lesson in adaptive ways (Duffy, 1998).

From a linguistic point of view, one of the observable consequences of such a teaching approach is that the teacher obtained from the students a diverse set of discursive forms ('true', 'false', 'it's true'; 'because'; 'I found it'; 'they are'; 'yes'; 'eukaryotic cells'), which reveal an enormous effort of attention and cooperation in the joint construction of academic discourse that students carried out under her guidance.

Table 8.4 summarises the main differences identified in the study.

Table 8.4 Main conversational features and outcomes identified in lessons A and B

	Lesson A	Lesson B
Teacher's orientation.	Toward individuals through direct nomination, gaze and body (allocating turns and providing feedback), as well as toward the group.	Toward the group.
Students' contributions.	*Individual* contributions predominate and are taken into account. Individual students are given the floor to read statements aloud.	Choral contributions predominate. Teacher reads sentences aloud.
Students' private turns.	No data available in the excerpt.[8]	Relevant private turns do not have public implications.
Wait-time.	Wait time which allows for discussion among students.	No wait-time.
Teacher's feedback.	Feedback is withheld and uncertainty is exploited to favour discussion among students.	Immediate (verbal and non-verbal) feedback on right or wrong answer.
Clues provision.	Provided clues lead to students' *argumentation* of the correct answer.	Provided clues lead to students *guessing* the correct answer.
Students' speech.	A variety of discourse forms is elicited.	Two monosyllabic utterances ('true' and 'false') are elicited.
(School) science discourse produced by students.	One token of science argumentation, plus two tokens signalling comprehension and approval.	Not observable.

To Conclude

Foreign language CLIL is currently seen as an advantaged educational strategy for the democratisation of active plurilingualism, in line with the European language policy. Simultaneously, CLIL runs the risk of becoming one more pretext for the segregation of the least favoured students on the basis of their lack of ability to participate successfully in the development of the lessons. To preserve CLIL's foundational democratic character, it is crucial to organise classwork in such a way that all students are offered access to active participation in the academic conversations. To achieve that goal, CLIL teachers need to provide learners with tailor-made assistance that will help them comprehend, produce and negotiate academic messages in the target language adopted as the medium of instruction. Success in this undertaking depends to a great extent on the quality of the conversations generated and, therefore on the teacher's classroom interactional competence.

By contrasting two different lessons, this study has contributed to the ongoing research in the field by empirically identifying the set of classroom conversational strategies deployed by each teacher. Or, in other words, the teachers' CIC profile enacted by them. Second, it has shown how those strategies relate to the students' participation and turn-taking patterns, on the one hand, and to the variety of discourse forms displayed by learners, on the other. Third, although the students' production of (school) science discourse is small in lesson A and inexistent in lesson B, the degree of conceptual problematisation achieved in the former is very high if compared with that observed in the latter.[9] For all these reasons, it can be concluded that lesson A provides students with more interactional space situated in their ZPD, and therefore affords them more opportunities for the integrated learning of content and language than lesson B, fulfilling in this way requirements two and three in the definition of democratic CLIL proposed in section 'Democratising CLIL'.

The analysis also hints toward the importance of the use of gaze and body language as semiotic resources to control learners' behaviour and signal turn allocation. Clearly, more work needs to be done in this area.

Content teachers' linguistic deficits are often presented as an obstacle for the implementation of CLIL programmes in some Catalan schools. Undoubtedly, a certain level of communicative competence in the target language on the part of the teachers is a pre-requisite for any CLIL programme to come into existence. However, the data analysed show that CIC is somewhat more complex than general communicative competence and, to some extent, independent from it,[10] as it is the teacher with a lower certification who is the one who achieves higher levels of complexity in the conversation.[11] The development of a sophisticated set of interactional skills that compose CIC – some of which have been identified in the study – requires something more than just offering teachers English for Specific Purposes (ESP) courses; or unspecific pedagogical training, one may add.[12] CLIL quality teaching requires specific teacher-education programmes addressed at the development of CIC in CLIL settings in particular contexts.

Finally, it is hoped that the study may contribute to help policy makers and course developers to make informed decisions in relation to the design of pre-service or in-service teacher-development programmes.

Acknowledgements

This study has been carried out thanks to the R + D + i EDU2010-15783 project 'Academic Discourse in a Foreign Language: Learning and Assessment of Science Content in the Multilingual CLIL Classroom' (DALE-APECS), funded by the MICINN.

Special thanks go to Dr Espinet for her feedback on an earlier version of this paper and her trained eye on all aspects referring to the teaching–learning of science. And to M. Jiménez for her useful comments on the readability of the paper.

Notes

(1)   C. Escobar Urmeneta and N. Evnitskaya are members of the GREIP (http://greip. uab.cat) research group and the CLIL-SI collaborative team (http://grupsderecerca. uab.cat/clilsi).

(2)   Although a significant number of middle class families invest considerable amounts of money in providing their children with extra tuition or language stays in English-speaking countries.

(3)   In response to such needs, the Catalan Education Act (LEC) requires a CEFR B2 level in a foreign language from all teachers in whatever speciality in order to access the teaching profession. LLEI 12/2009, del 10 de juliol, d'educació. (LEC) DOGC núm. 5422 - 16/07/2009. http://www.gencat.cat/diari/5422/09190005. htm.

(4)   The Matthew effect is a term used in sociology which origins in a citation from the Gospel of Matthew (Matthew 25:29). In the field of education it is used to refer to the fact that the more educated an individual is, the more possibilities s/he has to access further education.

(5)   Ministerio de Educación y Ciencia (2006) *Decreto de enseñanzas mínimas de ESO*. http://www.boe.es/boe/dias/2007/01/05/pdfs/A00677-00773.pdf; Departament d'Educació (2007) *Decret d'ordenació dels ensenyaments de l'educació secundaria obligatòria*. DOGC 4915. https://www.gencat.cat/diari/4915/07176092.htm.

(6)   See, for example, Guasch Boyé (this volume) who reports on a collaborative teaching project between the Catalan and English linguistic areas; and Ramírez and Serra (this volume) who present a successful model of integrating the three languages – Catalan, Spanish and English – in a plurilingual school.

(7)   Screenshots have been manipulated and pseudonyms have been used throughout the paper so as to protect participants' identities.

(8)   Escobar Urmeneta and Evnitskaya (in press) argue that students' private turns can help them become ready to publicly state their questions, clarification or repetition requests, demands for help, etc., which eventually leads to their increased participation in classroom interaction.

(9)   Still, it is not to be understood that we imply that true/false exercises are, *per se*, exemplary in the teaching of science. On the contrary, Dr Espinet, expert on the field, let us know that this is not the case.

(10)   At least for teachers with a CEFR B2 level or higher.

(11)   To falsify a given hypothesis, a single case will suffice (Popper, 1963).

(12)   Arnau and Vila-i-Moreno (this volume) and Arnau et al. (this volume) argue for the need of specific pedagogical training for EFL teachers and language-awareness training for L1 content teachers. We argue that these two components are indispensable in the case of CLIL quality teaching but not sufficient, as the ability to conduct

academic conversations leading to the integrated learning of content and language outreaches the above mentioned skills.

References

Arnau, J. (1985) Educación en la segunda lengua y rendimiento escolar: una revisión de la problemática general. In M. Siguan (coord.) *Enseñanza en dos lenguas y resultados escolares* (pp. 7–20). Barcelona: ICE-Publicacions de la Universitat de Barcelona.

Arnau, J. (2004) Sobre competències en català i castellà dels escolars de Catalunya. *Llengua, Societat i Comunicació* 1, 1–7.

Atkinson, J.M. and Heritage, J. (1984) *Structures of Social Action: Studies in Conversation Analysis*. Cambridge: Cambridge University Press.

Cenoz, J. (2009) *Towards Multilingual Education: Basque Educational Research from an International Perspective*. Bristol: Multilingual Matters.

Cenoz, J. and Genesee, F. (eds) (1998) *Beyond Bilingualism: Multilingualism and Multilingual Education*. Clevedon: Multilingual Matters.

Council of Europe (2005) *Monitoring the implementation of the European Charter for Regional or Minority Languages*. Reports and Recommendations: Application of the Charter in Spain. Online at: http://www.coe.int/.

Coyle, D., Hood, P. and Marsh, D. (2010) *CLIL*. Cambridge: Cambridge University Press.

Dalton-Puffer, C. (2007) *Discourse in Content and Language Integrated Learning*. Amsterdam: John Benjamins.

Dalton-Puffer, C., Nikula, T. and Smit, U. (2010) *Language Use and Language Learning in CLIL Classrooms*. Amsterdam: John Benjamins.

Dalton-Puffer, C. and Smit, U. (eds) (2007) *Empirical Perspectives on CLIL Classroom Discourse*. Franktfurt, Vienna: Peter Lang.

De Valenzuela, J.S., Connery, M.C. and Musanti, S.I. (2000) The theoretical foundations of professional development in special education: is sociocultural theory enough? *Remedial and Special Education* 21 (2), 111–120.

Duffy, G. (1998) Teaching and the balancing of round stones. *Phi Delta Kappan* 79 (10), 777–780.

Edwards, D. and Potter, J. (1992) *Discursive Psychology*. London: SAGE.

Escobar Urmeneta, C. (2009) Cuando la lengua de la escuela es diferente de la lengua familiar. In Monograph *Aprender en ingles. Cuadernos de Pedagogía* 395, 46–51.

Escobar Urmeneta, C. (2011) Colaboración interdisciplinar, Partenariado y Centros de Formación Docente: Tres ejes para sustentar la formación del profesorado AICLE. In C. Escobar Urmeneta and L. Nussbaum (coords) *Aprendre en una altra llengua/Learning through another language/Aprender en otra lengua* (pp. 203–230). Bellaterra: Servei de Publicacions de la Universitat Autònoma de Barcelona.

Escobar Urmeneta, C. (in press) Learning to Become a CLIL Teacher: Teaching, Reflection and Professional Development.

Escobar Urmeneta, C. and Evnitskaya, N. (2011) La corrección de ejercicios es una buena ocasión para aprender ciencias e inglés. True or false? Conversaciones de clase exitosas en contextos 'AICLE'. In M.P. Núñez Delgado and J. Rienda (coords) *La investigación en didáctica de la lengua y la literatura: Situación actual y perspectivas de futuro*. In Proceedings of the *XII SEDLL International Conference* (31 November–2 December, 2011). Granada: SEDLL. CD-Rom. ISBN: 978-84-96677-54-8.

Escobar Urmeneta, C. and Evnitskaya, N. (in press) 'Do you know Actimel?' The adaptive nature of science explanations in the CLIL classroom.

Escobar Urmeneta, C. and Nussbaum, L. (2008) Tareas de intercambio de información y procesos de aprendizaje en el aula AICLE. In A. Camps and M. Milian (coords)

Miradas y voces. Investigaciones sobre la educación lingüística y literaria en entornos plurilingües (pp. 159–178). Barcelona: Graó.

Escobar Urmeneta, C. and Nussbaum, L. (2010) Politiques, pratiques et perspectives de l'éducation linguistique en Espagne. In U. Ammon, J. Darquennes and S. Wright (eds) *Fremdsprachen an den Schulen der Europäischen Union/Foreign languages in the schools of the European Union/Langues étrangères dans les écoles de l'Union européenne* (pp. 120–133). Sociolinguistica book series 24. Berlin, NY: Walter de Gruyter.

Escobar Urmeneta, C. and Sánchez Sola, A. (2009) Language learning through tasks in a CLIL science classroom. *Porta Linguarum* 11, 65–83.

Escobar Urmeneta, C. and Unamuno, V. (2008) Languages and language learning in catalan schools: from the bilingual to the multilingual challenge. In C. Hélot and A-M. de Mejía (eds) *Forging Multilingual Spaces. Integrated Perspectives on Majority and Minority Bilingual Education* (pp. 228–255). Clevedon: Multilingual Matters.

Evnitskaya, N. (2012) Talking science in a second language: The interactional co-construction of dialogic explanations in the CLIL science classroom. Unpublished Doctoral Dissertation. Universitat Autònoma de Barcelona.

Evnitskaya, N. and Aceros, J.C. (2008) 'We are a good team': el contrato didáctico en parejas de aprendices de lengua extranjera. *Revista Española de Lingüística Aplicada* 21, 45–70.

Evnitskaya, N. and Morton, T. (2011) Knowledge construction, meaning-making and interaction in CLIL science classroom communities of practice. *Language and Education* 25 (2), 109–127.

Generalitat de Catalunya (1983) *Act on Linguistic Normalization* 7/1983, 18 April 1983. DOGC No. 322 of 22/04/1983.

John-Steiner, V. and Holbrook, M. (1996) Sociocultural approaches to learning and development: A Vygotskian framework. *Educational Psychologist* 31 (3–4), 191–206.

Kasper, G. (2009) Politeness. In S. D'hondt, J-O. Östman and J. Verschueren (eds) *The Pragmatics of Interaction* (pp. 156–173). Amsterdam: John Benjamins.

Lantolf, J.P. (2000) *Sociocultural Theory and Second Language Learning*. Oxford: Oxford University Press.

Lasagabaster, D. and Ruiz de Zarobe, Y. (2010) *CLIL in Spain: Implementation, Results and Teacher Training*. Newcastle: Cambridge Scholars Publishing.

Llinares, A., Morton, T. and Whittaker, R. (in press) *The Role of Language in CLIL*. Cambridge: Cambridge University Press.

Lorenzo, F., Trujillo, F. and Vez, J.M. (2011) *Educación Bilingüe: Integración de contenidos y segundas lenguas*. Madrid: Síntesis.

Markee, N. (2000) *Conversation Analysis*. Mahwah, NJ: Lawrence Erlbaum.

Marsh, D., Maljers, A. and Hartiala, A-K. (2001) *Profiling European CLIL classrooms. Languages Open Doors*. Jyväskylä: University of Jyväskylä.

Mercer, N. (1995) *The Guided Construction of Knowledge: Talk Amongst Teachers and Learners*. Clevedon: Multilingual Matters.

Mercer, N. (2000) *Words and Minds: How we Use Language to Think Together*. London: Routledge.

Mercer, N. (2004) Sociocultural discourse analysis: analysing classroom talk as a social mode of thinking. *Journal of Applied Linguistics* 1 (2), 137–168.

Mondada, L. and Pekarek Doehler, S. (2004) Second language acquisition as situated practice: task accomplishment in the French second language classroom. *The Modern Language Journal* 88 (4), 501–518.

Moore, E. (submitted) Content and language learning in teamwork tasks in academic lingua franca.

Moore, E. and Nussbaum, L. (2011) Què aporta l'anàlisi conversacional a la comprensió de les situacions d'AICLE? In C. Escobar Urmeneta and L. Nussbaum (eds) *Aprendre en una altra llengua/Learning through another language/Aprender en otra lengua* (pp. 91–115). Bellaterra: Servei de Publicacions de la Universitat Autònoma de Barcelona.

Muñoz, C. (ed.) (2007) Models and practice in CLIL practice. *Revista Española de Lingüística Aplicada* Special Issue 1.

Nikula, T. (2005) English as an object and tool of study in classrooms: Interactional effects and pragmatic implications. *Linguistics and Education* 16, 27–58.

Organisation for Economic Cooperation and Development [OECD] (2001) *Programme for International Student Assessment* (PISA 2001).

Organisation for Economic Cooperation and Development [OECD] (2010) *PISA 2009 Results*.

Pekarek Doehler, S. (2010) Conceptual changes and methodological challenges: On language and learning from a conversation analytic perspective on SLA. In P. Seedhouse, S. Walsh and C.J. Jenks (eds) *Conceptualising 'Learning' in Applied Linguistics* (pp. 105–126). London: Palgrave MacMillan.

Pérez-Vidal, C. and Juan-Garau, M. (2011) Trilingual primary education in Catalonia. In I. Bangma, C. van der Meer and A. Riemersma (eds) *Trilingual Primary Education in Europe: Some Developments with Regard to the Provisions of Trilingual Primary Education in Minority Language Communities of the European Union* (pp. 68–92). Leeuwarden: Mercator European Research Centre on Multilingualism and Language Learning.

Popper, K. (1963) *Conjectures and Refutations: The Growth of Scientific Knowledge*. London: Routledge.

Ruiz de Zarobe, Y. and Jiménez Catalán, R.M. (2009) *Content and Language Integrated Learning: Evidence from Research in Europe*. Bristol: Multilingual Matters.

Seedhouse, P. (2004) *The Interactional Architecture of the Language Classroom: a Conversation Analysis Perspective*. Malden, MA: Blackwell.

Simon Auerbach, J. (in press) Energy resources: A teacher–student image based interaction experience in a CLIL classroom. In the Proceedings of the *XXX AELSA International Conference: Applied Linguistics in the Age of Globalization*. Lleida: University of Lleida.

Sinclair, J. McH. and Coulthard, R.M. (1975) *Towards an Analysis of Discourse: The English Used by Teachers and Pupils*. Oxford: Oxford University Press.

Tsui, A.B.M., Edwards, G. and Lopez-Real, F. (2009) *Learning in School-University Partnership. Sociocultural Perspectives*. New York. Routledge.

Vygotsky, L.S. (1978) *Mind in society: The Development of Higher Psychological Processes*. Cambridge, MA: Harvard University Press.

Vygotsky, L.S. (1986) *Thought and Language*. Cambridge, MA: MIT Press.

Walsh, S. (2006) *Investigating Classroom Discourse*. London: Routledge.

Wood, D., Bruner J.S. and Ross, G. (1976) The role of tutoring in problem solving. *Journal of Child Psychology and Psychiatry* 17 (2), 89–100.

Woods, D. and Fassnacht, C. (2007) *Transana, rel. 2.20*. Wisconsin Centre for Education Research: University of Wisconsin-Madison.

Appendix 8.1

Transcription conventions

JAU:	Initials followed by a colon correspond to the speaker's pseudonym.
(.)	A dot in parentheses indicates an unmeasured (micro-)pause of less than two-tenths of a second.
(1.5)	Numbers in parentheses indicate measured pauses in tenths of seconds.
=	An equal sign indicates 'latching' (no gap) between utterances produced by the same speaker or different speakers.
over[lap [overlap	Square brackets indicate start of concurrent speech.
<u>word</u>	Underlining indicates speaker's emphasis.
CAPITALS	Talk is louder than that surrounding it.
.	Falling intonation.
,	Low-rising intonation, suggesting continuation.
?	Rising intonation, not necessarily a question.
cu-	A single dash indicates a sharp cut-off.
:	Colon indicates that the speaker stretched the preceding sound, more colons more stretching.
<fast> <slow>	'Greater than' and 'less than' signs indicate that the talk was produced noticeably quicker or slower than the surrounding talk.
xxx	'xxx' indicate an unintelligible fragment with one 'x' equal to one syllable.
word	Bold italics indicate utterances produced in any other language that is not English.
((laughs))	Description of speaker's non-verbal actions.

9 Integrated Languages Project

Rosa Maria Ramírez and Teresa Serra

This chapter describes the integrated education project in Catalan, Spanish and English at the Vila Olímpica School, a primary education centre, located in the city of Barcelona. This is a middle-class school, where 70% of the students are Catalan speakers, 20% are Spanish speakers and 10% speak other languages. The project is based on three basic ideas: open-mindedness to all languages and cultures, languages as a means of communication for all subjects, and the importance of the use of oral and written language. Catalan is the school's preferred language. Beginning with students who are four years of age (preschool), Spanish and English are gradually introduced. From year three in primary school, social sciences and maths are taught in the centre's three languages. The teaching methods for the languages are defined, as are the criteria for distributing contents, organisational aspects and the teamwork for the teachers. The assessments periodically carried out by the educational administration indicate that the students obtain optimum results in the three languages and in maths.

Introduction

The Integrated Languages Project (PILL – *Projecte Integrat de Llengües*) has been implemented in a public preschool and primary school (3–11 years), founded in 1996–1997, and it gives the school and the team of teachers their identity. The school is located in Barcelona, in a neighbourhood created in 1992 owing to the Olympic Games that were held in the city that year. The sociocultural level of the majority of the families is middle-class. The school is committed to inclusion and therefore, 2% of the children have serious or permanent learning difficulties and 5% of the children have special learning needs. With regard to the linguistic composition of the centre, 70% of the students speak Catalan with one or the other of their parents, the remaining 20% only speak Spanish at home and 10% speak other languages. When starting school (Preschool P3, at three years of age) all the children have more or less knowledge of the two languages spoken in Catalonia (Catalan and Spanish) although their level in each one differs. These are two languages that are very similar and with which they live on a daily basis.

Bases of the Project

The following is an explanation of the bases on which the PILL project is established. This will serve to explain with more precision the project's concretion with regard to language as a cross-curricular theme, the methodology followed by the school and how the different languages (Catalan, Spanish and English) are dealt with. Finally, the essential role, that of the teamwork by the teachers, and also the evaluation of the project, will be highlighted.

Some considerations regarding languages and cultures

The school is the first meeting place of cultures after the family environment. The children bring the culture of their homes to school and share it with the other children. The school provides them with its culture and at the same time accepts that which the children bring. The cultures are transmitted through the language and languages present in our society. If the school is open to different cultures and different languages, and if the families are in agreement with the project, this facilitates the children's open-mindedness to this diversity.

These ideas are the basis of our project, which involves the presence of Catalan, Spanish and English from preschool; the acceptance of and open-mindedness towards all languages and cultures, and cross-curricular language work through the different areas of the curriculum. This approach favours the development of linguistic, multilingual and intercultural competence, as it helps the children to transfer their knowledge of one language to another and to use it in new learning contexts. The development of a good level of competence in English is a fundamental objective of the project in a context like that of Catalonia, in which, for reasons already commented on, results in this area are not optimum (see Arnau & Vila, this volume).

Language as the central theme in the learning process

Language is considered to be a central tool for learning in all curricular areas. Language acts as a mediator for communication and interaction among the children, as well as between the students and teachers, at all times during the educational activity. When studying literature, art, maths, social and natural sciences or any other area, we always use language to learn, because languages are necessary for explaining what we know, for obtaining new knowledge, for explaining it to others, etc.

We could therefore say that, as we teach and as we learn the different contents of each area, whether conceptual, procedural or referring to values, the language that supports it is taught and learned. As the children put words to the knowledge they learn, these become clear and connect with other knowledge, and, vice versa, as they are taught and learn language, they absorb the contents of the different curricular areas. This is precisely why language is considered a central work theme for each and every one of the areas in the school curriculum.

The importance of spoken language: Expression, understanding and interaction

To be able to advance with the project specifications and analysis, we needed a theoretical model to establish a base language shared by all the teachers in the school. We decided on an analysis model from the perspective of language use in different educational activities, and this enabled us to differentiate the uses of the language and group them together in accordance with the categories related to different teaching/learning strategies. This model is based on the proposal by Tough (1987, 1989) and includes different functional categories: self-assertion, addressing our actions and those of other people, relating, reasoning, predicting, imagining, designing and planning.

It is a model that helps us to understand and analyse the different uses of spoken language by teachers and students irrespective of the teaching–learning activity being carried out. It forces us to ask ourselves which questions are necessary to guide a conversation and how to plan different activities to reflect on and develop language within different curricular areas. One of our reasons for choosing this model was based on the fact that Tough's proposal is precisely focused on spoken language. This is a fundamental condition in our case, as spoken language in preschool and primary school courses forms the basis for all the work done in the school.

Agreeing on this common language allowed the teaching staff to analyse activities in small and large groups, and propose different tasks to be completed depending on the areas and subjects they are working on. Children can tell a story and afterwards talk about different aspects of the story or imagine a new situation and how they would feel if they experienced it. Students can poetically describe a landscape or feeling. This can also help in predicting and anticipating situations, and also mathematical or scientific processes, which can later be checked for accuracy. Students can verbally manage the steps required to solve problems and afterwards listen to their classmates propose other steps. All of this is done through speaking and discussing.

Speaking about a topic, organising it and reaching conclusions helps considerably when it comes to writing about it later on. When teachers are teaching mathematics for example, they teach how to speak, write and read mathematics. To talk and discuss mathematics means that students learn language in addition to the mathematical content. This is also true for social sciences or any other subject. However, teachers need to work as a team to ensure that all the proposals are reflected in the school's curriculum and in the classroom planning and organisation.

Written language

Written language (reading and writing) is closely connected to the spoken language, which is the starting point for all learning. The nature of the central theme of speaking and writing is greatly determined by the different texts used in the curriculum and shapes the knowledge that is accrued (Adam, 1985, 1987; Casas et al., 2007; Cassany, 1993; Jorba et al., 1998; Noguerol, 1995, 2003; Ramírez & Serra, 2008).

As of the first years of school, great importance is given to storytelling and narratives so that the children gradually begin to read and write more complex stories, which in turn leads them to understand both real events and fiction. More functional texts are studied, in contexts relevant to the children, such as letters, notes and news articles; descriptive texts that help with understanding the reality of science or the subjectivity of poetry; explanations and justifications are also worked on, mainly when the students have to read or write about social or natural sciences, or when they have to explain mathematical processes.

In conclusion, the aim is to make sure that the pupils are faced with different types of texts that share the same common characteristics in all three languages.

Methodology

The PILL understands that the teacher is the person who guides and organises the learning and gives a voice to the students so they can interact in the classroom. Moreover, it considers that what is learned is a result of this interaction, and of reflection that leads to thinking, speaking, re-thinking and speaking again. With this in mind, we propose open topics and ask questions to encourage the students to think and reason, and this requires them to look for the answers by observing, taking action and experimenting. Different work projects are proposed, covering a wide range of topics. The children work individually and in large and small groups, and each form of organising the work requires different ways of dealing with learning and makes the students use different strategies.

Three Languages in the School: Catalan, Spanish and English

This distribution of hours takes into account, among other aspects, the environmental weight of the languages in our context and has a great influence on knowledge of them. The children who speak Catalan when they start school already understand Spanish and some speak it, as it is a socially and environmentally important language in Catalonia. Those who speak Spanish or another language have a limited level of Catalan, depending on what they have had the opportunity to hear, sometimes limited to TV3 (Catalan TV) or another Catalan TV channel, although some have had the chance to learn Catalan in nursery school (0–3 years of age). This situation means that in our school, and in others, children are in nursery school and preschool for five or six years. When they start primary school these children already understand and speak Catalan to a greater or lesser extent, according to their abilities. Those who have not gone to preschool usually have problems, and it is at school where they are immersed in the language. When it comes to English, this is a new language for all the students, a language that they do not know or speak, a language they are not familiar with, and because of this the learning of it is academic.

For these reasons the pace and grading of the teaching and learning of the three languages in the school must be different for each one (Table 9.1).

Catalan

The preferred language in the school is Catalan: 17 of the 25 teaching hours are conducted and carried out in Catalan. Preschool P3 (three-year-olds)

Table 9.1 Distribution of the timetable for the three languages at the school, in hours per week

	Catalan	Spanish	English
Preschool			
3 years	17		
4 years	17	2	2
5 years	17	2	3
Primary education			
1	17	2	4
2	17	2	5
3	17	2	5
4	17	2	5
5	17	2	5
6	17	2	5

is the first course in the school, and all the teaching is done in Catalan. Spanish and English are gradually introduced when the children are four-years-old.

When children arrive at the school at the age of three, they are greeted in Catalan by the teacher and the other people working at the school regardless of whether they are Catalan speakers or not, although the majority are. The boys and girls feel welcome in a positive emotional environmental, they communicate and learn the language and in no time at all are speaking it naturally. At first the teacher speaks in Catalan but with easily understood messages for the non-Catalan speakers, who in turn respond in Spanish, another language, or with gestures. Bit by bit, and in a very natural way, they express themselves in an interlanguage and gradually move towards standard Catalan. By the end of the first year (3–4-years-old), all of the children speak Catalan and it becomes their natural language at school, apart from when they are being taught in Spanish or English.

Catalan is taught and learned in all areas of the curriculum: science, mathematics, literature and other subjects. Gradually, as we will see later, these areas are divided between Catalan, Spanish and English. Catalan is the language used for learning to read and write, and the children become familiar with the written language from the time they start school. This is always related to spoken language in order to elaborate on meaning and is central to all areas and all situations in the classroom. The methodology uses conversation as a starting point. The children ask different questions and this helps them to think, to contextualise, and to say what they know and what they want to know. These questions trigger their use of the different areas of the language that we spoke about earlier. Being able to write after learning to speak, observe, listen to others and develop knowledge: all of this helps to structure and be able to explain things.

Just as we consider the importance of the first year of preschool (three year olds) to be fundamental in adapting to the school, when the children are four-years-old we believe it to be equally important that they become aware of the fact that more than one language is spoken in the school. From this time on, the three languages are gradually introduced and taught.

Spanish

In preschool P4 (four-year-olds) the school dedicates two hours a week to activities in Spanish. A different teacher comes to the class for these activities. The PILL method is based on the presumption that people are multilingual and therefore the teachers must be too. It is important that the pupils become aware of this, and although we change the teacher for Spanish, this teacher will speak Catalan to the children in other situations. The pupils are happy to accept the change in languages when the teacher also changes and are very relaxed about it.

In preschool the activities carried out in Spanish are the same type as those in Catalan. The students tell stories, study animals, do simple arithmetic, solve problems, suggest artistic activities, etc. In all of these activities, as the knowledge of the language increases, linguistic and cognitive skills are developed, such as reasoning, reciting, planning and self-assertion, in short, important skills for all the languages the children speak.

The Catalan speakers who already understand Spanish, and some who speak it, gradually become more fluent and sure of the language. Science and mathematics are taught in Spanish in the first and second years of primary school and the students read stories or poems or do small performances. As they become more confident with Spanish, the students try to write their first text or read stories in the language. In the second year of primary school (seven-year-olds) the students have to write short texts related to different areas of the curriculum. Environmental knowledge and mathematics content are divided between Catalan and Spanish at these levels, but Catalan is always more prevalent. For example, if the students are working on the theme of 'aquatic life' they learn about the beach, the sea, living creatures, the different types of fish, the sand and aquatic plants in Catalan, whereas in Spanish, they learn about the morphology and dissection of fish (Table 9.2). In mathematics they work more in blocks of content, for example, geometry is taught in Spanish and all other mathematical areas are studied in Catalan in the second year.

At intermediate and upper primary school levels (from 8–11-years-old), the students continue working along these lines and English is introduced in mathematics and environmental knowledge classes. Literary aspects, such as stories, plays and poetry, are also carried out in the three languages.

English

English is a foreign language with limited presence, and as such the starting point for teaching and learning it is different from those of Catalan and

Table 9.2 An example of the distribution of contents in the two languages in natural science (second year of primary school)

Catalan	Spanish
Aquatic life:	Aquatic life:
The beach. Living elements: animals and plants. Lifeless elements: sand, water.	Study of fish: Internal and external morphology.
Observation, description and classification of animal and plant remains.	Relation between different organs and their functions.
Observation of lifeless elements. Observation and description of the sand: a mixture.	Vital functions: feeding, respiration, reproduction.
Observation and description of seawater: a solution.	Habitat.

Spanish. Our educational proposal is one that is firmly based on the idea of immersion. As previously explained, the aim is for the children to learn the languages by using them in the contents found in the different curricular areas. In any proposal of this type it is extremely important that the children be comfortable with their own language and know the teachers understand them, which makes them feel comfortable at an emotional level. A good relationship between teachers and students holds great weight when it comes to learning languages.

For this reason English is always spoken during the assigned hours from the very beginning (preschool P4, four year olds). To make it easier, there are two teachers in the classroom who speak English to each other; they create and design activities in front of the children and offer more personalised attention. The children know that when they speak in Catalan the teachers understand them, but they are encouraged to speak in English and show great interest when they understand it.

They know that the teachers are multilingual and speak more than one language and that they move between them depending on the class they are teaching. They know the teachers are trilingual and they will be, too.

All teachers in Catalonia are competent in Catalan and Spanish, but this structure in three languages means a large part of the teaching staff are also proficient in English.

When teaching English, just as with other languages, we must always take into account the linguistic abilities we wish the students to develop. To do this, we help the children predict situations, narrate, imagine and create projects in order to develop the necessary linguistic and cognitive abilities to communicate and learn. We propose functional and meaningful situations for them to be able to carry them out.

We always begin with the spoken language, which is the basis for communicating and learning. Written language follows spoken language and the children become familiar with it. By the second year of primary school (eight-year-olds) the children can read and write in Catalan and Spanish, and they also have a command of certain vocabulary and grammatical structures in English. This allows them to speak a little, have acceptable listening skills and begin to read and write in English. Spoken language continues to play an important role after the third year and is progressively complemented with written language.

Integrating English in Preschool and During the First Two Years of Primary School

The first five school years (preschool P4 and P5, four and five-year-olds, and the first two years of primary school) are based on tales or stories that provide the children with interesting facts and help them learn vocabulary and required structures and materials. The stories and tales make them understand the narrative of events, as there are always characters that perform, and there are also a number of elements and objects from daily life that help the children to relate what is happening in the story with the reality surrounding them. Songs and rhymes are also very interesting in this respect and help with memorising structures, while explanatory drawings and pictures from the texts help with the understanding and development of specific vocabulary and sentences. Theatrical performances that the children act out from stories they have learned are also very valuable activities.

Artistic expression, such as drawing, painting or other techniques, is closely connected with the activities the children do in Catalan and Spanish. A basic vocabulary is repeated during these processes and little by little the children understand and use it independently.

In the first and second years of primary school the pupils study activities related to mathematics or environmental knowledge. For example, they learn about wolves after being told the story of Little Red Riding Hood, or comment on a specific plant because they are interested in it and have already studied and seen things related to plants in Catalan and Spanish.

The Integration of Languages in Intermediate and Upper Primary School

In the third, fourth, fifth and sixth years of primary school (intermediate and upper), all contents related to social, natural and cultural environments and mathematics are taught in the three languages. The criteria for distributing contents differ depending on the nature of the areas and the methodology used. There is also an adjustment in the methodological approach in the third and fourth years; more work is done in larger groups (25 children), but the children receive more personal attention when they have to write. In the fifth and sixth years, the groups are smaller and we focus on problem solving; this means the children have to speak with each other to find the answers in the language of communication.

In environmental knowledge, the proposal is that the same general theme of the social environment, for example the city, is divided into different subtopics and each is taught in one of the three languages: Barcelona, historical developments (Catalan), the Olympic Games (Spanish) and an explanation of the services and places in the city for tourists (English). This is the same proposal we use for the natural environment: general topic; plants and vegetables; reproduction and the life cycle of plants (Catalan); fruit and vegetable recipes (Spanish); observation and classification of fruit and aromatic plants (English).

Each course has specific environmental topics and mathematics areas that are taught in Catalan, while others are taught in Spanish or English.

The theme in each of the languages is different in each course and the content is organised in a cyclical pattern.

With the PILL model we consider it best to start more complex learning in Catalan or Spanish and then later in English. This is because we take into account the complexity of the subject and the language the children need to access it and learn it (Table 9.3).

In mathematics, content is divided between the three languages according to the different blocks of curricular contents: numbers and operations, size and measurement, geometry and statistics (Table 9.4).

At the end of this stage all the students have had the opportunity to learn the contents of all the blocks in all three languages.

Mathematics is taught and learned in the three languages every week. Three sessions are done in Catalan, one in English and in Spanish on average half a session.

Teaching mathematics in English is gradually introduced (Serra, 2011). In the third year the children do mental arithmetic activities in English one hour each week. During these sessions the methodology used is always the same, short and guided activities are done with the whole group and each student must solve them individually. The teacher always follows the same routine in each session: first the activity is read out; the teacher gives an example if the activity is difficult to understand; and the children then solve the problem. When correcting the activity, the teacher asks the students for the answer and whenever possible asks them to explain the mathematical process used to reach the answer. This last step is important as the children have to use the language to explain the process. At first they always need help from the teacher but ultimately they are able to explain it themselves after having acquired the necessary vocabulary and grammatical structures. This routine helps the children to improve both their linguistic and mathematical abilities, and then in the fourth year they do mental arithmetic and problem solving.

Understanding these activities presents no difficulties for the students at a linguistic or mathematical level; the teacher always provides a model as an example when introducing an activity with new vocabulary or grammatical structures, and the children are familiar with these types of activities as they have worked with the same methodology in Catalan and Spanish in previous years. The level of the mathematical activities chosen corresponds to a level at the end of the first cycle of primary school to encourage understanding.

Geometry and measurements are taught during the third cycle, in the fifth and sixth years. Normally the children are given a problem to solve in small groups, and they have to find the answer and subsequently explain to the other groups the process they used to arrive at their answer, often producing, showing and explaining how they did so. By this time in their schooling the children are already using written language in their explanations.

Table 9.3 Examples of content distribution in the three languages for social and natural environment knowledge

Natural, social and cultural environments content distribution for the three languages: Catalan, Spanish and English

Third year, primary school

Social science	*Catalan*	*Spanish*	*English*
Discover the locality	Barcelona city. Historical evolution: the first settlers. The Iberians. The Roman city. The city's services.	The Olympic Games. Olympic logos. Popular games. Explanation of popular games. The rules of the game.	Explaining services to a tourist.
Natural science	*Catalan*	*Spanish*	*English*
Plants and vegetables	Using plants to feed people. Wheat and flour. The process of making bread. The main characteristics of certain plants and their life cycles. Description of plant organs. Study of the reproduction of certain plants in their environment.	Different salad recipes. Recipes for cooking vegetables according to culinary styles and cultures.	Fruits and jams on the Sant Ponç feast day. The process of making jam. Observation and classification of fruits and aromatic plants.

Sixth year, primary school

Social science	*Catalan*	*Spanish*	*English*
Health education: Earth, a planet to discover	Tourism in Catalonia. Tourism, a form of recreation in the 20th century. Features of tourist places. Location: El Delta de l'Ebre. Infrastructure and transport.	Exploring the world: commercial, military and religious expeditions throughout history. Scientific expeditions.	Tourist itineraries. Creating an information leaflet.
Natural science	*Catalan*	*Spanish*	*English*
Movements	Concept: reference point, relativity, trajectory and measurement.	Movement and rotation of the Earth. Days and nights, the seasons depending on the position of the Earth relative to the Sun.	The Solar System: planets, satellites, asteroids and comets.

Table 9.4 Distribution of the mathematics content blocks in the three languages

Course	Catalan	Spanish	English
Third	Numbers and operations. Geometry. Statistics.	Size and measurement.	Mental arithmetic. Statistics.
Fourth	Numbers and operations. Geometry. Size and measurement.	Geometry.	Mental arithmetic.
Fifth	Numbers and operations. Geometry.	Numbers and operations. Statistics.	Size and measurement.
Sixth	Numbers and operations. Statistics.	Size and measurement.	Geometry.

Teacher Teamwork

Teamwork is a fundamental aspect of the school's project and is necessary on a daily basis. For this reason, different work areas are proposed for organising the activities of the school calendar and also for creating spaces for reflection on the teaching practice carried out. This means we make progress individually and as a team in methodological and curricular aspects.

The teachers' time outside class is organised around monthly work plans that include specific goals for each period, as well as goals for the groups and the specific coordination of the Catalan, Spanish and English languages and the areas covered in these languages.

Each year the teaching staff organise a work group and carry out an in-depth examination of the development of certain aspects of the curriculum related to using language as the cross-curricular theme. This work of reflecting on practical issues has enabled us make substantial progress in our project and increase our knowledge and focus on the points that appear weaker. In some courses we work on the transition from spoken to written activities in the different languages, and in others we focus more on how to encourage the children to write descriptive and explanatory texts in areas related to science. Another course looks at what conversation needs to be established in mathematics classes in order to delve more deeply into both mathematics and the language. In others, we decide on how to work on the literary aspects of the language in all the languages we teach at the school from preschool to the end of primary school. This method of reflecting as a group has helped make the PILL method more solid and an experience shared by all those working with it. The pupils at the school also benefit, as has been shown in the various external and internal assessments of the educational results over the years.

The organisation of support time for teachers in the classroom is decided on by considering the general lines of the project and more specifically is based on the following criteria:

- Doubling the number of teachers in the classroom when teaching English. All classes up to the second year and two hours a week from third year onwards.
- Doubling the number of teachers in the classroom when working in small groups and on different proposals (corners) for mathematics, languages, science or art. This work is done in Catalan and allows us to address the different learning paces within the classroom and facilitates learning to work in small groups. The students will then do this at other times when there is only one teacher in the classroom.
- Doubling the number of psychomotor skills classes in preschool.
- Doubling reading and writing time for the first three years in primary school.

Evaluation

At the school we believe that when a project is carried out it must be evaluated to see just exactly what has been achieved. Therefore, in each school year, proposals are made and carried out in the classrooms and the workgroup; these are reviewed at the end of the year and reports are written up; self-evaluation reports are performed to assess the improvements and difficulties encountered and to see where we need to continue researching and making progress.

We are also interested in learning from our students and seeing which processes help them learn and what results they obtain. The evaluation helps us to see where they are and what we should do to help them understand better and improve in all aspects. Therefore, activities are studied so that the children assess what they know and do not know and realise they need to learn in order to increasingly move forward.

The educational administration carries out an evaluation each year at the school and this is also important. A work plan is presented at the start of the school year and there is also an end-of-year report. The administration performs the monitoring and evaluation process through a school inspection. The children's families are also asked to complete a survey and give us their opinion.

Each year the students have to pass external assessment tests, in the sixth year of primary education, and the tests are validated by the Department of Education of the Generalitat of Catalonia (*Consell Superior d'Avaluació del Sistema Educatiu, 2010*). These tests assess the students' competence in Catalan, Spanish (written ability) and English (spoken and written competence) and also evaluate mathematical competence.

In these evaluations of the different languages, the sixth-year students at the school have an above-average level compared with others in Catalonia, regardless of whether we consider the results for boys and girls at the same sociocultural level or those from a higher level. They are also above average if we compare the level of public schools, such as ours, with private and semi-private schools in Catalonia.

The results in mathematics are also very good. These results allow us to see that learning mathematics in three languages does not hinder the children's learning, but actually has quite the opposite effect.

It is very important for the school to contrast the different evaluations, as they provide us with different points of view, enabling us to make greater progress.

Conclusions

The Vila Olímpica School in Barcelona is a trilingual school with a teaching programme in Catalan, Spanish and English based on curricular contents. The project is based on three ideas: open-mindedness to all languages and cultures, languages as a means of communication for all subjects, and the importance of using the spoken and written language, according to the theoretical model proposed by Tough (1989).

The pace and grading of the teaching and learning in the three languages is different depending on the environmental weight each one has. Catalan is the preferred language and is used in all areas of the curriculum (17 hours a week). Spanish is used for two hours every week in Preschool (four year olds) and for some content taught in the first year of primary education. The number of teaching hours in English gradually increases from two hours per week in preschool up to five hours a week beginning with the second year of primary school.

From the third year of primary education on, social science and mathematics contents are taught using the three languages. A given theme is divided into sub-themes and each of them is assigned a language. By the time the schooling has finished, all the students have had the opportunity to learn contents from all the subjects in the three languages, and this is something we consider extremely important for optimum language acquisition.

Assessments demonstrate that the students' results in the three languages are above the levels of other students with the same sociocultural level in Catalonia and also those with a higher sociocultural level.

The Integrated Language Project is possible because the teachers work in teams and reflect upon their teaching practice. Teamwork and reflection, and the evaluation of the work done, improve both individual and group work.

Listening to and speaking with other bodies in the educational community provides us with a broader vision of what is happening in the school and helps us all to improve.

References

Adam, J.M. (1985) Quels types de textes. *Le français dans le monde* 192, 39–43.

Adam, J.M. (1987) Textualité et sequentialité. L'exemple de la description. *Langue française* 74, 51–72.

Casas, M., Bosch, D., Márquez, C., Noguerol, A., Ramírez, R.M., Serra, M.T. and Valls, C. (2007) *Competències bàsiques per parlar i escriure ciència a l'educació primària.* Barcelona: Associació de Mestres Rosa Sensat.

Cassany, D. (1993) *Reparar la escritura. Didáctica de la corrección de lo escrito.* Barcelona: Graó.

Consell Superior d'Avaluació del Sistema Educatiu (2010) *L'avaluació de sisè d'educació primària 2010 i de la inserció laboral dels graduats en FPR* (Quaderns d'avaluació, 18). Barcelona: Generalitat de Catalunya Departament d'Educació.

Jorba, J., Gómez, I. and Prat, A. (1998) *Parlar i escriure per aprendre.* Barcelona: ICE UAB.

Noguerol, A. (1995) *Bases psicolingüístiques i lingüístiques per a l'ensenyament i aprenentatge de la Llengua a Catalunya.* Barcelona: UAB (unpublished doctoral thesis).

Noguerol, A. (2003) Leer para pensar, pensar para leer: La lectura como instrumento para el aprendizaje en el siglo XXI. *Lenguaje* 31, 36–58.

Ramírez, R. and Serra T. (2008) Llegir per parlar, parlar per llegir a l'etapa primària, *Articles* 46, 115–125.

Serra, T. (2011) *Parlant de matemàtiques per aprendre'n.* Barcelona: Associació de Mestres Rosa Sensat.

Tough, J. (1987) *Lenguaje oral en la escuela. Una guía de observación y actuación para el maestro.* Madrid: Visor/Aprendizaje.

Tough, J. (1989) *Lenguaje, conversación y educación. El uso curricular del habla en la escuela desde los siete años.* Madrid: Visor/Aprendizaje.